The Rise of Bardolatry in the Restoration

Enrico Scaravelli

The Rise of Bardolatry in the Restoration

Paratexts of Shakespearean Adaptations and other Texts 1660-1737

PETER LANG
Bern · Berlin · Bruxelles · Frankfurt am Main · New York · Oxford · Wien

Bibliographic information published by die Deutsche Nationalbibliothek
Die Deutsche Nationalbibliothek lists this publication in the Deutsche Nationalbibliografie; detailed bibliographic data is available on the Internet at ‹http://dnb.d-nb.de›.

British Library Cataloguing-in-Publication Data: A catalogue record for this book is available from The British Library, Great Britain.

Library of Congress Control Number: 2015959254

Cover illustration: George Romney, The infant Shakespeare attended by Nature and the Passions, c. 1791–1792.

ISBN 978-3-0343-2030-6 pb. ISBN 978-3-0351-0913-9 eBook

This publication has been peer reviewed.

Hochfeldstrasse 32, CH-3012 Bern, Switzerland
info@peterlang.com, www.peterlang.com

Printed in Switzerland

Contents

Acknowledgments

I want to express my deepest and sincerest gratitude to Fernando Cioni (University of Florence) for his steady support and the invaluable help he has always offered me throughout my postdoctoral years, and to Alessandro Serpieri (also from the University of Florence) whose early lesson will always be relevant. I am also indebted to the staff of the Biblioteca Nazionale Centrale, the Biblioteca Marucelliana, and the various libraries of Humanities of the University of Florence.

I wish to thank Ann Thompson (King's College London) for a splendid seminar on the afterlife of *Hamlet*, and Sonia Massai (also from the King's College London) for the insightful observations she offered me when this study was still in its infancy. I am also indebted to the staff of the British Library, the King's College Library, and the Senate House Library.

I would like to thank Kent Cartwright (University of Maryland) for the insightful suggestions he so kindly gave me some time ago, Virgina Vaughan (Clark University) for her observations on *The Tempest*, and Walter Cannon for his information on John Milton. I am also indebted to the staff of the Folger Shakespeare Library, and the Library of Congress.

Finally, I thank with all my heart all those who, during my postdoctoral years, were close to me personally and professionally. This book is the fruit of those hard years, and is dedicated to them.

Preface

This study is an examination of bardolatry in the "preliminaries" of the Shakespearean texts, placing particular emphasis on the adaptations of the Bard's plays from the Restoration period. By preliminaries, I am referring to what Genette calls *paratext* – the sum of the peritext and epitext.[1] In the analysis of the many voices that have contributed on bardolatry (some from before 1660), I have deemed it useful to refer to studies that were not exclusively literary: for example, I have used concepts such as those articulated by Mary Douglas in her anthropological studies from the second half of the twentieth century.[2]

The first chapter provides the theoretical framework for the key concepts of the book, such as bardolatry, paratext, and adaptation. The second chapter is the analysis of the paratexts of the Shakespearean adaptations themselves, while the third chapter completes the general picture with the discussion of texts that were relevant for the cultural milieu of the period. Finally, the appendix is a catalogue of the Shakespearean adaptations that I have analyzed previously, mainly in their paratextual aspect. In it, I have recorded the main information regarding staging, printed editions, and plot (for which I provide a detailed act-by-act account).

It is always necessary to apply certain limits to the material under consideration, in order to have a field of study that is as homogenous as

1 This is Genette's definition of paratext, outlining its constituent parts and function: "a title, a subtitle, intertitles; prefaces, postfaces, notices, forewords, etc.; marginal, infrapaginal, terminal notes; epigraphs; illustrations; blurbs, book covers, dust jackets, and many other kinds of secondary signals, whether allographic or autographic. These provide the text with a (variable) setting and sometimes a commentary, official or not, which even the purists among readers, those least inclined to external erudition, cannot always disregard as easily as they would like and as they claim to do." Gérard Genette, *Palimpsests: Literature in the Second Degree*, trans. Channa Newman and Claude Doubinsky (Lincoln: University of Nebraska Press, 1997). Originally published as *Palimpsestes. La littérature au second degré*. (Paris: Éditions du Seuil, 1982), 3.

2 Mary Douglas, *Purity and Danger: An Analysis of Concepts of Pollution and Taboo* (London: Routledge, 1966 [2006]).

possible. The material examined in the present study does not include farces, drolls, or other brief compositions taken from Shakespeare's plays, especially if they were originally composed in the age preceding the Restoration and published after 1660. Nor have I included closet drama, as its public impact is obviously very small.

Finally, a remark concerning chronological restrictions, as these are necessarily arbitrary and must be justified. The period examined here is from 1660 to 1737, although in some cases earlier events and texts are mentioned. The start date can be easily recognized, as it represents the Restoration of Charles II and the reopening of theaters, but the end date does not correspond with any similarly important historical and cultural event. The year chosen is that of the Stage Licensing Act, commissioned by Robert Walpole, which imposed strict censorship on drama and therefore heavily influenced theatrical life.

1 The Theoretical Background

1.1 Bardolatry

1.1.1 George Bernard Shaw and the coinage of the term

In 2015, according to the online edition of the *Oxford English Dictionary* (*OED*), bardolatry is the "Worship of the 'Bard of Avon', i.e. Shakespeare." A combination of the words "bard" and "idolatry," it is the term used to define the worship of William Shakespeare, who, at least since the nineteenth century, has been called the "Bard of Avon." Curiously enough, the word was born in a paratext where the author blames Shakespeare: it was, in fact, George Bernard Shaw who coined the term in 1901, when he used it in the preface to his *Three Plays for Puritans*.[3] Here, Shaw employed the term in a negative sense ("So much for Bardolatry!")[4] to criticize Shakespeare for creating works that, unlike his, did not deal properly with social themes. Likewise for adaptation, the use that will be made here of the word Bard is neutral, bearing neither the negative meaning applied by Shaw, nor the positive one attached by bardolators.

1.1.2 Early Attestations, Dryden, 1769 Shakespeare Jubilee

Although the term was coined at the very beginning of the twentieth century, the mental attitude defined as bardolatry began to develop a few years after Shakespeare's death, if not earlier, as Francis Meres attests as early as 1598. Since 1610, when the newly founded Bodleian Library "entered into an agreement which entitled it to a copy of every book registered with the Stationers' Company, … the intervening 200 years

3 George Bernard Shaw, *Three Plays for Puritans* (London: Grant Richards, 1901).
4 Ibid., xxxi.

mark a steady but incomplete evolution of Shakespeare's reputation towards the preeminence we now take for granted."[5] In fact, Samuel Holt Monk's opening statement of his essay on "Dryden and the Beginnings of Shakespeare Criticism in the Augustan Age"[6] is probably true: the main line, or rather lines, of critical thought about Shakespeare had been formulated before 1660.

In the middle of the first half of the seventeenth century Shakespeare's supremacy had not yet been consolidated. According to Graham Holderness, Beaumont, who died a month and a half before the Bard, was thought to deserve a place in Westminster; Jonson, who died in 1637, had crowds following his corpse to the Abbey; on the other hand, "Shakespeare had been laid to rest in 1616 in a relatively little, obscure grave in the chancel of Stratford church."[7]

Despite this, soon after the Bard's death, the tide had started to change. In the paratext of the 1623 *First Folio*, in the poem in memory of Shakespeare, Ben Jonson writes "He was not of an age, but for all time!"[8] paving the way for those in the seventeenth and eighteenth centuries (and beyond) to praise the eternity of the Elizabethan playwright. He also fosters the link between the Bard and nature, thus beginning to qualify his genius as natural and eternal; finally he also raises the vexed question of Shakespeare's learning, another crucial point that scholars have much debated. Leaving aside Milton, and Dryden's ambivalence towards Shakespeare, which did not prevent him from conveying the idea that the Bard was a universal and foundational figure in the English culture, the ratification of bardolatry is set at the end of the second decade of the second half of the eighteenth century with David Garrick's 1769 Shakespeare Jubilee, during whose celebrations he composed an ode to commemorate the great playwright, proclaiming him "the god of

5 Claude Rawson, ed., *Great Shakespeareans*, vol. 1 (London: Continuum, 2010), 1.

6 In Herbert M. Schueller, ed., *The Persistence of Shakespeare Idolatry* (Detroit: Wayne State University Press, 1964), 49.

7 Graham Holderness, "Bardolatry: or, The Cultural Materialist's Guide to Stratford-upon-Avon," in Graham Holderness (ed.), *The Shakespeare Myth* (Manchester: Manchester University Press, 1988), 3.

8 Ben Jonson, "To the memory of my beloued, The author Mr. William Shakespeare: and what he hath left us," in William Shakespeare, *Shakespeare's Comedies, Histories, and Tragedies. Published according to the True Originall Copies* (London, 1623).

our idolatry."[9] The year 1769 is the great formal inauguration of bardolatry as a national religion, which "marks the point at which Shakespeare stopped being regarded as an increasingly popular and admirable dramatist, and became a god."[10] And before the end of the century, another critical landmark was set by Samuel Johnson's pronouncement that Shakespeare is a "mighty genius"[11] and that "his works may be considered a map of life."[12]

Before reaching these peaks of adoration, during the course of the eighteenth century, the Bard's reputation had steadily improved, mainly due to Dryden's influence as critics "were to see Shakespeare pretty much as [he] had taught them to do."[13] In fact, "although still attacked occasionally, Shakespeare's work was [now] used as a standard of excellence by … critics":[14] Joseph Addison in the *Spectator*, and Richard Steele in the *Tatler* quite frequently praised and recommended the Bard to their readers, which had a direct and positive effect on the popularity of, and the attendance at, theaters, as Colley Cibber remarks in his *Apology* (1740).

Before Garrick's Jubilee, however, there was another relevant step in the path of bardolatry. It happened in 1709, when Nicholas Rowe published the first critical edition of the works of Shakespeare. This was the first seed of three centuries of Shakespeare studies, still ongoing. Graham Holderness observes that, in the Restoration, "both the unassailable Shakespearean reputation, and the stable Shakespearean text, were yet to be consolidated (the first edition of Shakespeare's works – other than simple reprints of the 1623 Folio – that of Nicholas Rowe, was not published until 1709)."[15] As decades passed, "with the consolidation

9 Michael Dobson, *The Making of the National Poet* (Oxford: Clarendon Press, 1992), 6.

10 Christian Deelman, *The Great Shakespeare Jubilee* (London: Michael Joseph, 1964), 7.

11 Samuel Johnson, "To the Right Hon. John Earl of Orrery," in *The Works of Samuel Johnson*, vol. 14 (London, 1788), 479. No editor for this book.

12 Ibid., 480.

13 Samuel Holt Monk, "Dryden and the Beginnings of Shakespeare Criticism in the Augustan Age," in Herbert M. Schueller (ed.), *The Persistence of Shakespeare Idolatry*, 66.

14 Louis Marder, *His Exits and His Entrances* (Philadelphia, Lippincott, 1963), 53.

15 Graham Holderness, *Textual Shakespeare* (Hatfield: University of Hertfordshire Press, 2003), p. 125.

of Shakespeare's prominence as Britain's national dramatist, the Shakespearean text became accepted as the only fictionalized version of the 'Lear' story to retain any enduring artistic value";[16] what happened to the story of King Lear, also happened to many other stories adapted by Shakespeare from previous sources.

When dealing with Shakespearean adaptations there is a point that is often underestimated, if not forgotten: Shakespeare himself was an adaptor. He adapted both within the same literary genre (drama to drama) and from one genre to another (prose or poetry to drama), as the numerous and detailed studies on his sources have shown. He drew from the Classics, from the Italians, from the English: Ovid, Bandello, Holinshed, and many more. With the rise of bardolatry, his plots, his versions of the stories, have eclipsed all other plots, all other versions to become a master narrative; but it has not always been so. In the early decades of the Restoration, when Shakespeare had not yet achieved the status of National Poet, his works had not yet become detached from the continuity of the tradition, so others still drew upon this material with relative freedom. Today, when we judge the adaptations inferior to the "original" we are looking at them under the influence of bardolatry; it is very easy to do so, as the cult of Shakespeare is a strong cultural process that started centuries ago.

1.1.3 Victorian Age, Twentieth Century, and Beyond

As Robert Sawyer has recently argued,[17] in the Victorian Age the excitement surrounding the Bard reached a point where his work was put in close connection with the Bible. Mary Cowden Clark and Henry Morley, churchmen like William Rolfe and Dean Frederic Farrar, and atheists like Robert Ingersoll, all united in praising the Bard. Many writers spoke of the work of Shakespeare as a secular equivalent of the Bible; but the such worship was obviously the fruit of seeds planted in previous centuries. One of these seeds produced buds in 1841 when, in *On Heroes, Hero-Worship, and the Heroic in History*, Thomas Carlyle

16 Ibid.

17 Robert Sawyer, *Victorian Appropriations of Shakespeare* (Madison NJ: Farleigh Dickinson University Press, 2003), 113.

posed a rhetorical question, "This King Shakspeare, does not he shine, in crowned sovereignty, over us all, as the noblest, gentlest, yet strongest of rallying-signs; indestructible …?"[18] before fearlessly plunging into adulation of the Bard:

> Of this Shakspeare of ours, perhaps the opinion one sometimes hears a little idolatrously expressed is, in fact, the right one; I think the best judgment not of this country only, but of Europe at large, is slowly pointing to the conclusion, that Shakspeare is the chief of all Poets hitherto; the greatest intellect who, in our recorded world, has left record of himself in the way of Literature. On the whole, I know not such a power of vision, such a faculty of thought, if we take all the characters of it, in any other man. Such a calmness of depth; placid joyous strength; all things imaged in that great soul of his so true and clear, as in a tranquil unfathomable sea![19]

One of the defining points of bardolatry is that Shakespeare is presented not only as the greatest author, but also as the absolute genius, the supreme intellect, the finest psychologist, and as the one who describes the human condition most faithfully. In other words, bardolatry views Shakespeare as the master of all human experience and of its intellectual inquiry. It also embraces the concept of realism of the characters of the Bard, pushing it as far as to regard them as "real people," for they have changed the consciousness and ways of perceiving human nature on a large scale in Western culture.

An authoritative mouthpiece of the above idea is Harold Bloom, whose bardolatry finds its highest expression in the paratext of his *Shakespeare: The Invention of the Human* (1998), which analyzes thirty-five plays by the Bard. In the preface addressed to the reader, Bloom's cult of Shakespeare impels him to assert, "He wrote the best poetry and the best prose in English, or perhaps in any Western language."[20]

The characters of the plays are also the subject of praise. In 1725 Alexander Pope asserted that Shakespeare had "look'd thro human nature at one glance,"[21] and from this had created the characters of his plays: "every single character in Shakespear is as much an individual,

18 Thomas Carlyle, *On Heroes, Hero-Worship, and the Heroic in History* (London: J. M. Dent & Co., 1900), 125.

19 Ibid.

20 Harold Bloom, *Shakespeare: The Invention of the Human* (New York: Riverhead Books, 1998), xviii.

21 Alexander Pope, preface to *The Works of Shakespear*, (London, 1725), iv.

as those in life itself."[22] Bloom occupies a position that loudly echoes Pope, despite the passage of more than two-and-a-half centuries: in his view the greatest characters of the Bard's plays are not simple but rather human modes of consciousness and awareness *tout-court*:

> The dominant Shakesperean characters – Falstaff, Hamlet, Rosalind, Iago, Lear, Macbeth, Cleopatra among them – are extraordinary instances not only of how meaning gets started, rather than repeated, but also of how new modes of consciousness come into being.[23]

In line with one of the tenets of the cult of Shakespeare that proclaim his proximity to the divine, the sacrum, and religion, Bloom states that bardolatry "ought to be even more a secular religion than it already is."[24] Sheer religious worship blends with the worship of the character through a common mode of transmission: the written text.

> A substantial number of Americans who believe they worship God actually worship three major literary characters: the Yahweh of the J writer …, the Jesus of the Gospel of Mark, and Allah of the Koran. I do not suggest that we substitute the worship of Hamlet, but Hamlet is the only secular rival to his greatest precursors in personality. Like them, he seems not to be just a literary or dramatic character. His total effect upon the world's culture is incalculable. After Jesus, Hamlet is the most cited figure in Western consciousness; no one prays to him, but no one evades him for long either.[25]

The book's closing essay titled "Coda: The Shakesperean Difference" (again, a paratext, like the opening essay), is the place for bardolatry without compromise. The praise for Shakespeare is absolute: he is "the best and central writer in English, already is the only universal author, staged and read everywhere."[26] Shakespeare's influence surpasses that of Homer or Plato, investing the very life of mankind, and is likely to rival the sacred scriptures:

> Shakespeare's influence, overwhelming on literature, has been even larger on life, and thus has become incalculable, and seems recently only to be growing.

22 Ibid., iii.
23 Harold Bloom, *Shakespeare: The Invention of the Human*, xviii.
24 Ibid., xvii.
25 Ibid., xviii–xix.
26 Ibid., 718.

> It surpasses the effect of Homer and of Plato, and challenges the scriptures of the West and East alike in the modification of human character and personality. Scholars who wish to confine Shakespeare to his context – historical, social, political, economic, rational, theatrical – may illuminate particular aspects of the plays, but are unable to explain the Shakesperean influence on us, which is unique, and which cannot be reduced to Shakespeare's own situation, in his time and place.[27]

In the above citation, just as in others that will follow, the work of the Bard is regarded as something sacred and is placed in the realm of the absolute, of eternity, of timelessness. They contrast with those recent historicist and relativist criticisms that consider the preeminence of Shakespeare as an exclusive product of the sociocultural context of Elizabethan England. According to these views, the above praises are strictly the result of an English nationalism that also exerts its influence on literature and literary criticism.

One may think that Bloom is the peak of bardolatry, but he somehow restricted the immense influence of Shakespeare to the Western world. In the early 1960s, in the wild blooming of life and culture of the decade, Louis Marder pushed even further. The conclusion of *His Exits and His Entrances* set the scale on planetary level:

> Certainly the existence of this book and the history it contains is evidence enough that the universal admiration and reverence for the works of Shakespeare are among the few emotional and intellectual responses around which all the literate people of the world can unite.[28]

Then, in the very last paragraph of the book, he jumps into interstellar space, with the works of Shakespeare and the Bible as the highest expression of human culture, the first two books that would best testify our civilization to another life form in the universe:

> On this planet the reputation of Shakespeare is secure. When life is discovered elsewhere in the universe and some interplanetary traveler brings to this new world the fruits of our terrestrial culture, who can imagine anything but that among the first books carried to the curious strangers will be a Bible and the works of William Shakespeare.[29]

---

27 Ibid., 717.

28 Louis Marder, *His Exits and His Entrances*, p. 361.

29 Ibid., p. 362.

Some contributions from the twenty-first century by other eminent Shakespeare scholars should also be noted for the various perspectives adopted to elevate the Bard at the highest peak of British culture such as Stanley Wells' *Shakespeare for all Times*;[30] Marjorie Garber's *Shakespeare After All*;[31] and Jonathan Bate's *Soul of the Age: The Life, Mind and World of William Shakespeare*.[32]

1.2 Paratext

1.2.1 Origin and Relevance of the Term

The word "paratext," a merging of the Greek *para* (near, similar, but also opposing), and the Latin *textus* (material, textile from the verb *texere*, which means to spin, to weave), is associated with the French literary critic Gérard Genette. The term arises from his reflections in *Palimpsestes: la littérature au second degré*[33] and from his work up to *Seuils*.[34]

Its significance is evidenced by Genette's statement that "a text without a paratext does not exist and never has existed" and that "paradoxically, paratexts without texts do exist, if only by accident: there are certainly works – lost or aborted – about which we know nothing except their titles."[35] In the field of Shakespeare studies, suffice it to remember *Love Labour's Won* and *Cardenio*.

30 Stanley Wells, *Shakespeare: For All Time* (London: Macmillan, 2002).

31 Marjorie Garber, *Shakespeare After All* (New York: Pantheon Books, 2004).

32 Jonathan Bate, *Soul of the Age: The Life, Mind and World of William Shakespeare* (London: Viking, 2008).

33 Genette, *Palimpsests: Literature in the Second Degree*.

34 Gerard Genette, *Paratexts: Thresholds of Interpretation*, trans. Jane E. Lewin (Cambridge: Cambridge University Press, 1997). Originally published as *Seuils* (Paris: Éditions du Seuil, 1987).

35 Genette, *Paratexts*, 3–4.

1.2.2 Definition

The text "is rarely presented in an unadorned state,"[36] that is, without the paratext, the second of the five subcategories of transtextuality[37] identified by Genette in *Palimpsests*. Here, he outlines most of the constituent parts the paratext and their influence:

> a title, a subtitle, intertitles; prefaces, postfaces, notices, forewords, etc.; marginal, infrapaginal, terminal notes; epigraphs; illustrations; blurbs, book covers, dust jackets, and many other kinds of secondary signals, whether allographic or authographic. These provide the text with a (variable) setting and sometimes a commentary, official or not, which even the purists among readers, those least inclined to external erudition, cannot always disregard as easily as they would like and as they claim to do.[38]

It also specifies that the paratext is "one of the privileged fields of operation of the pragmatic dimension of the work – i.e., of its impact upon the reader."[39] Five years later, in *Paratexts*, Genette reiterates this fundamental dimension of the paratext insofar as it is

> a zone not only of transition but also of transaction: a privileged place of a pragmatics and a strategy, of an influence on the public, an influence that – whether well or poorly understood and achieved – is at the service of a better reception for the text and a more pertinent reading of it (more pertinent, of course, in the eyes of the author and his allies).[40]

Since his first theoretical formulation, therefore, the paratext is seen as a powerful yet subtle element that guides and directs the use of the text with a force of intervention that is greater when the reader is least suspecting of it. Genette, indeed, notably concludes *Paratexts* with an observation that is very explicit about this action:

> the effect of the paratext lies very often in the realm of influence – indeed, manipulation – experienced subconsciously. This mode of operation is doubtless in the author's interest, though not always in the reader's.[41]

---

36 Ibid., 1.

37 That is, intertextuality, paratextuality, metatextuality, hypertextuality, and architextuality.

38 Genette, *Palimpsests*, 3.

39 Ibid.

40 Genette, *Paratexts*, 2.

41 Ibid., 409.

From a materialistic standpoint, Genette's second type of transtextuality is the set of a series of distinct textual and graphic elements that outline a text and extend it in time and space. This peripheral position, which does not always have defined limits, is strictly connected with an ontological dimension: the paratext is primarily added to the text "to *present* it, in the usual sense of this verb but also in the strongest sense: to *make present*, to ensure the text's presence in the world."[42] After the paratext has highlighted the existence of the text, the paratexts strictly connect the text with the distribution, the "reception and consumption in the form (nowadays at least) of a book."[43]

The elements of the paratext necessarily occupy a spatial physical location, and, thus, can be classified on a positional basis: if they are near the text, they are peritext; if they are further from it, they are epitext. Peritext and epitext are mainly detectable in written texts.

Paratextuality, therefore, establishes a relationship between the text and those "accessory signals" that can be considered as belonging to the text as either autographs or allographs, which provide the text with a (protean) outline and, at times, with a formal or informal commentary. This relationship has a strong impact on the recipient, be it on a reader of written texts, a listener of oral texts, or a spectator of dramatic texts.

Genette's second type of intertextuality is an element that is generally ignored by the public, which is often subjected to it without knowledge, and overlooked by specialists who usually avoid considering particulars that are seemingly marginal. The paratext is not an element that is always strictly connected to the text, nor does it have a function that is merely auxiliary. Indeed, it anticipates the text, ensuring its reception, functions as a *threshold*, a vestibule, "it is an undefined zone between the inside and the outside, a zone without any hard and fast boundary."[44] It becomes a sort of suggestion for the way the text is to be read and establishes an initial agreement with the addressee, inviting him or her to assume a determined interpretative attitude. From the paratext, the addressee gathers information pertaining to the literary genre, begins to form a range of expectations, assesses the type of communicative act suggested by the text and, at the same

42 Ibid., 1.
43 Ibid.
44 Ibid., 2.

time, identifies previously similar textual experiences that the reader is invited to engage with before proceeding with the interpretation of the same text.

Philippe Lejeune states that this *peripheral component* of the text actually directs and drives the reading and understanding of the same whole work.[45] As we have seen, it constitutes "a zone not only of transition but also of transaction: a privileged place of a pragmatics and a strategy, of an influence on the public,"[46] that is, of the authorial instance. It is here that the author, directly or indirectly, manifests his or her "authority" towards the text and its interpretation whose aim is a "better reception for the text and a more pertinent reading of it (more pertinent, of course, in the eyes of the author and his allies)."[47]

Genette summarizes by stating that

> The paratext, then, is empirically made up of a heterogeneous group of practices and discourses of all kinds and dating from all periods which I federate under the term "paratext" in the name of a common interest, or a convergence of effects, that seems to me more important than their diversity of aspects.[48]

A comprehensive study of Genette's second type of the transtextuality that investigates both its two constituent elements is hoped for by the same author given that so far literary criticism has chiefly concentrated on the epitext at the expense of the peritext:

> whereas on many occasions we have noted the relative neglect accorded to the peritext by the literary world (including specialists), the situation of the epitext is obviously very different. Critics and literary historians have long made extensive use of the epitext in commenting on works.[49]

The final sentence of *Paratexts* envisions the paratext as a metaphorical threshold, and "a threshold exists to be crossed."[50] With Genette's

45 Philippe Lejeune, *On Autobiography* trans. Katherine Leary (Minneapolis: University of Minnesota Press, 1988). Originally published as *Le pacte autobiographique* (Paris: Seuil, 1975).

46 Genette, *Paratexts* 2.

47 Ibid.

48 Ibid.

49 Genette, *Paratexts*, 346.

50 Ibid., 404.

theoretical contribution, this threshold can be studied with the due critical awareness. A little earlier, the paratexts is assimilated to another image, which is equally significant: the lock, be it for water of for air, sluice, or clearing house. The second kind of transtextuality,

> the paratext provides a kind of canal lock between the ideal and relatively immutable identity of the text and the empirical (sociohistorical) reality of the text's public … the lock permitting the two to remain "level." Or if you prefer, the paratext provides an airlock that helps the reader pass without too much respiratory difficulty from one world to the other, a sometimes delicate operation, especially when the second world is a fictional one.[51]

In Genette's vision, the text is unchanging "being immutable, text in itself is incapable of adapting to changes in its public in space and over time."[52] What is changing is the paratext. The paratext is, thus, a lock, a sort of membrane that turns such granitic textual harshness into something less rigid for the addressee: "the paratext – more flexible, more versatile, always transitory because transitive – is, as it were, an instrument of adaptation."[53] It seems therefore appropriate to use this category as a tool to reveal how Shakespeare was adapted to the culture of the succeeding centuries, and understand how over time he was not forgotten but remembered, and then praised, until he became the supreme literate.

Genette's second category of transtextuality of an *alteration* of a Shakespearean play will thus be an adaptation of an adaptation, an adaptation "in the second degree"; the paratext, an instrument of adaptation, of an adaptation of Shakespeare, can therefore be an instrument to study Shakespeare and his cult, bardolatry.

1.2.3 Parts of the Paratext: Peritext and Epitext

The main criterion to categorize the paratext is spatial. Genette defines the paratext with a mathematical formula: "for those who are keen on formulae, paratext = peritext + epitext";[54] it is an almost geometrical

51 Ibid., 407–8.
52 Ibid., 402.
53 Ibid., 408.
54 Ibid., 5.

continuum, a space without gaps: “peritext and epitext completely and entirely share the spatial field of the paratext.”[55]

The first spatial category is *peritext*, “the more typical one,”[56] the area that mostly characterizes the paratext. It is the area in which the paratextual elements that are closest to the text are gathered, either around the text or in the parts of the entire work, with a function that is almost exclusively one of presentation, address, and commentary on the text. It is the main and hard core of the paratext;[57] it possesses a form and its elements usually occupy fixed, nearly canonical positions: at the beginning of the text (e.g., title page, title, dedication, epigraph, preface, etc.), in the margins (e.g., notes, glosses, etc.), and following the text (e.g., afterword, tables, appendix, etc.). Finally, the format of the work, its graphic arrangement, and similar elements, are also part of the peritext.[58]

Genette calls *epitext* the more “distanced elements … that, at least originally, are located outside the book”:[59]

> the epitext is any paratextual element not materially appended to the text within the same volume but circulating, as it were, freely, in a virtually limitless physical and social space. The location of the epitext is therefore anywhere outside the book – but of course nothing precludes its later admission to the peritext.[60]

The epitext, which can also precede the text in its temporal function,[61] does not have a precise paratextual function. With the epitext, the commentary of the work expands indefinitely into a biographical discourse,

55 Ibid.

56 Ibid.

57 In *Paratexts* Genette devotes 11 chapters to the elements of peritext, 2 to the elements of epitext.

58 The categories identified by Genette are the publisher’s peritext, the name of the author, titles, the please-insert, dedications and inscriptions, epigraphs, prefaces (various types), intertitles, and notes.

59 Genette, *Paratexts* 7.

60 Ibid., 344.

61 “For example, prospectuses, announcements of forthcoming publications, or elements that are connected to prepublication in a newspaper or magazine and will sometimes disappear with publication in book form, like the famous Homeric chapter-titles of *Ulysses*, whose official existence proved to be (if I may put it this way) entirely prenatal.” Genette, *Paratexts*, 5.

critical or other, in which the connection with the work is often indirect and, at the very least, indistinguishable. The epitext is a vast and changing category that Genette subdivides into the public[62] and private[63], each of which is further subdivided.

1.2.4 Key Peritextual Categories

As Genette does not apply his theory to drama, I have adapted his categories to make them fit it. I have created a figure composed by three categories (two from Genette, plus a new one) whose center is the dramatic text.

Outside the circles, the space surrounding Fig. 1 is the epitext. For the most distant elements of the figure within the circles, I have adopted Genette's terminology of the publisher's peritext, which is conceived as

> The whole zone of the peritext that is the direct and principal (but not exclusive) responsibility of the publisher (or perhaps, to be more abstract but also more exact, of the publishing house) …[64]

This area, constituting the most peripheral peritext, consists of the cover, title page, and their appendages.[65] For pragmatic reasons, I have also included here the title of the work, which Genette does not do, but he makes it feasible insofar as "the title page did not appear until the years 1475–80, and for a long time – until the invention of the printed cover – the title page remained the only location of a title often loaded down, as we have seen, with various items of information that for us are appendages."[66]

Nearing the dramatic text, we encounter the second category, the prefatorial peritext, on the heels of Genette's vast definition of preface as "every type of introductory (preludial or postludial) text, authorial

62 In the chapter titled "The public epitext" Genette subdivides it into publisher's epitext, semiofficial allographic, and public authorial. The latter is further divided into auto reviews, public responses, mediations, and delayed autocommentaries. *Paratexts*, 344–70.

63 In the chapter titled "The private epitext" Genette subdivides it into correspondence, oral confidences, diaries, pre-texts (*Paratexts*, 371–403).

64 Genette, *Paratexts* 16.

65 Ibid.

66 Ibid., 64.

or allographic, consisting of a discourse produced on the subject of the text that follows or precedes it."[67] I have considered this area, which is an intermediary peritext, as consisting of dedicatory letters, prefaces, reader advisories, and theoretical essays.

Lastly, there is a new area, that I call dramatic peritext. This area is specific to the dramatic work, and it is the closest to the dramatic text. It actually frames it, and I consider it as consisting of prologues and epilogues.

Of the three categories, the intermediate one consists of the most varied elements. In fact, in the dramatic works of the Restoration, the elements that I have referred to as the prefatorial peritext can proliferate until they reach a rather wide-ranging variety, making it possible for the dedicatory letter to the patron, preface, reader advisory, and theoretical essay on dramatic art to coexist in this area. The three subdivisions, therefore, despite identifying one large group of peritexts, are generally intended with the obvious finality of an easier discussion on the single elements.

Nevertheless, a clear division is not always possible. For instance, Diana Solomon notes that

> Within such a schema, prologues and epilogues reveal their versatility; they function as both peritexts, performed and published alongside their plays, and epitexts, printed separately as broadsides that circulated to advertise the performance and collectively in eighteenth-century anthologies.[68]

This is confirmed by the research carried out by another scholar

> [Before going to theater] in the Restoration, one method of preparation consisted of reading broadside publications of prologues and epilogues. Autrey Nell Wiley has compiled a helpful list of the sixty prologues and forty-five epilogues still extant that were published individually between 1642 and 1872, showing the frequency and endurance of this practice.[69]

The target of the groups is obviously different. The epitext plus the first two groups of the peritext mainly address a reading public of private houses, coffee houses, and other social spaces where culture is exchanged; the

67 Ibid., 161.

68 Diana Solomon, *Prologues and Epilogues of Restoration Theatre* (Newark: University of Delaware Press, 2013), 7.

69 Ibid., 23.

third group of peritexts mainly addresses the viewing and hearing theatergoing public.

Depending on the circumstances under which the play is first encountered, one can experience different kinds of peritext, one after another; the public can belong to two different worlds, the page and the stage, or both, as often happens. Playwrights were well aware of this, and wanted to talk to both groups of people: the large variety of peritexts are a unique opportunity to communicate different messages to different sections of the public, hence the great proliferation of such texts.

Figure 1 provides a graphic representation of such areas of the peritext.

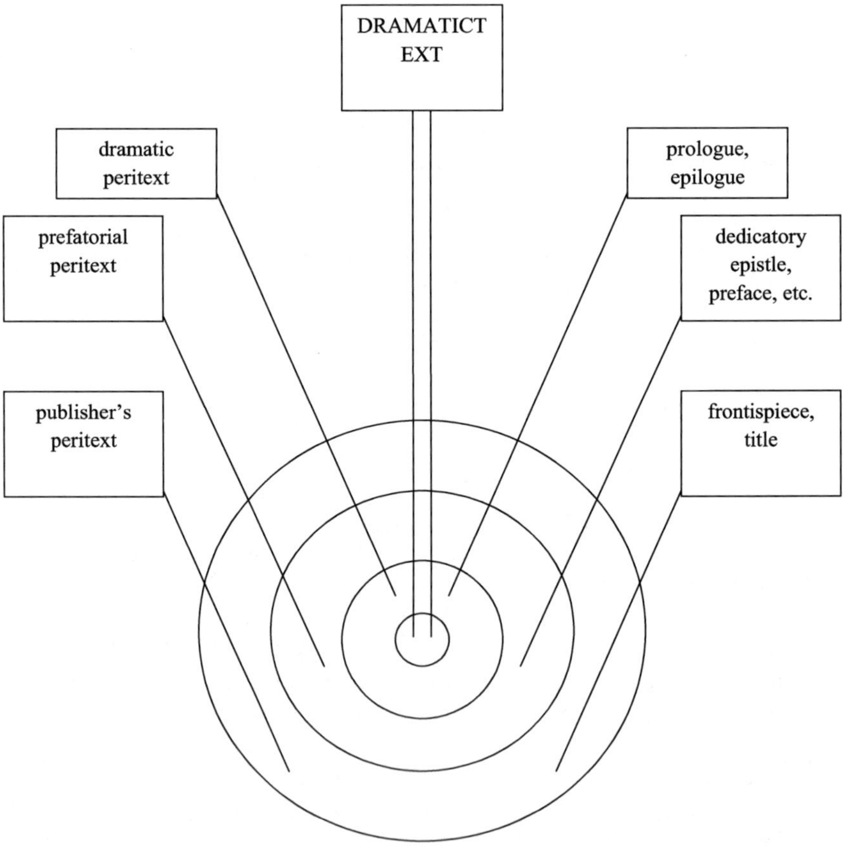

Fig. 1: Areas of peritext.

1.2.5 Prologues, Epilogues, Curtain Raisers, and Afterpieces

Genette is not the only one to draw attention to the paratext, especially the peritext. In the theatrical field a similar plea was made more recently in a study on the English theater of the seventeenth and eighteenth century edited by Daniel J. Ennis and Judith Bailey Slagle, whose aim is to draw attention to the performative paratexts in existence at the time.

Prologues, Epilogues, Curtain Raisers, and Afterpieces[70] has a primarily theatrical and performative focus. It is a collection of essays by scholars who maintain that these elements "were essential to the texture and form of British dramatic entertainment for over a century"[71] and "it is in these very elements – once dismissed as ephemera – that [we] can see the eighteenth-century London stage at its most responsive to the political, social, and cultural forces that were so responsible for the tenor of the drama in that age."[72]

The five-act tragedy or the three-act comedy is what they call the mainpiece, which represented the central part of the whole theatrical show; central, only in the sense that it was in the middle of a series of different and variegated performances. What preceded and followed the mainpiece are the small pieces, "parts that are difficult to study because they were ephemeral, tertiary, and irregular even in the eighteenth-century,"[73] which include opening music, curtain raisers, pantomime, dancing, afterpiece plus prologue and epilogue, and the entr'acte, performed in the middle of the mainpiece. In this situation it is easy to understand how "the play is never the thing; it is only part of many things."[74]

In a way, the purpose of the volume is similar to Linda Hutcheon's approach to adaptation, which needed to be freed from its enslaving relationship towards the "original." In this case the yoke comes from the mainpiece, usually a privileged element of the scholarship, which

70 Daniel J. Ennis and Judith Bailey Slagle, eds., *Prologues, Epilogues, Curtain-Raisers, and Afterpieces* (Newark: University of Delaware Press, 2007).

71 Daniel J. Ennis and Judith Bailey Slagle, introduction to Daniel J. Ennis and Judith Bailey Slagle, eds., *Prologues, Epilogues, Curtain-Raisers, and Afterpieces*, p. 13.

72 Ibid.

73 Ibid., 19.

74 Ibid., 15.

casts a shadow over the "aesthetic importance of the tertiary forms of eighteenth-century drama."[75]

From the Restoration onwards, the rise in importance of the side-pieces is testified by the fact that "by the turn of the nineteenth-century, afterpieces were routinely holding the stage longer than mainpieces"[76] creating a situation in which "eventually, the mainpiece becomes secondary."[77] The necessary conclusion is that the sidepieces "are not all that tertiary and, in fact, are in some ways the most important and enduring remains we have of the eighteenth-century London stage."[78]

Special attention is given to two elements whose relevance is paramount among the sidepieces: prologues and epilogues, which are strongly rooted in the social, "historical, and cultural contexts of their composition."[79] These two types of sidepieces can prove to be the best vehicle for the most diverse statements, be they social, aesthetic, or political. If studied carefully, they reveal themselves as a system, a network in which more participants are involved: they represent "a kind of conversation, a dialogue between playwrights and between playwright and audience,"[80] a conversation that could range "from topical minutia, to dramaturgy to metacommentary,"[81] always occupying two rhetorically strong positions – the beginning and the end of a particular play.

Robert Sawyer brings to our attention a controversial case study: Dryden's critical thought on Shakespeare, analyzed from the perspective of his prologues and epilogues, which predictably intersects with bardolatry. Sawyer's essay rereads Shakespeare "in the light of the Restoration criticism attached to his plays via prologues and epilogues."[82]

"Prologues and Epilogues: Performing Shakespearean Criticism in the Restoration"[83] discusses Dryden's conflicted response to Shakespeare,

75 Ibid., 17.

76 Ibid., 24–25.

77 Ibid., 25.

78 Ibid.

79 Ibid., 20.

80 Ibid.

81 Ibid.

82 Ibid., 22.

83 Robert Sawyer, "Prologues and Epilogues: Performing Shakespearean Criticism in the Restoration," in Daniel J. Ennis and Judith Bailey Slagle, eds., *Prologues, Epilogues, Curtain-Raisers, and Afterpieces*, 135–54.

analyzing the paratexts attached to his plays. Employing the Bakhtinian theory of conversation and authoritative discourse, Sawyer justifies Dryden's ambivalence towards Shakespeare by placing Dryden in a netherworld between French civility and English barbarism, where he had to find a compromise among three critical schools: the ancient Greek dramatists, the French neoclassical theory, and the English forefathers of the stage. The way Dryden delivered his criticism is also remarkable: "what is unique about [him], however, is that the debate was held onstage, and, … Dryden may have modified his criticism even as it was being performed."[84]

Sawyer does not deny "this startling duality"[85] of Dryden towards Shakespeare, but elaborates a middle way between Lennart A. Bjork and Samuel Holt Monk: the former is among those who find that it is futile to attempt "to prove any consistent, critical credo in Dryden's Shakespearean criticism";[86] the latter is among those who indeed praise Dryden, seeing "virtue [because his] criticism never hardened into a rigid system."[87]

He maintains that "Dryden's critical allegiance seems more akin to a skeptical supporter than a faithful follower of bardolatry"[88] and his position seem to place Dryden as an able cultural mediator between the court and the rising middle class, practicing a criticism deeply and quickly dialogical, i.e. responsive of the feedback returning from the counterpart. Sawyer's final conclusion is that "Dryden was no simple worshipper of the Bard, as Jonathan Bate has argued"[89] and "by resisting the powerful pull of the influence of Shakespeare, Dryden stand stands as an important, and early, responder to and rewriter of the Bard."[90]

---

84 Ibid., 148.

85 Ibid., 135.

86 Lennart A. Bjork, "The 'Inconsistencies' of Dryden's Criticism of Shakespeare," *Anglia* 91 (1973): 219–40 (225).

87 Samuel Holt Monk, "Dryden and the Beginnings of Shakespeare Criticism in the Augustan Age," in *The Persistence of Shakespeare Idolatry: Essays in Honor of Robert W. Babcock*, ed. Herbert M. Schueller (Detroit, Wayne State University Press, 1964), 27–75 (55).

88 Robert Sawyer, "Prologues and Epilogues: Performing Shakespearean Criticism in the Restoration," 136.

89 Ibid.

90 Ibid., 149.

1.2.6 Prologues and Epilogues of Restoration Theater

Six years after the volume edited by Ennis and Slagle, a book appeared by Diana Solomon called *Prologues and Epilogues of Restoration Theater.*[91] It is a study that approaches a variety of issues such as gender and comedy, performance and print, which are all united under a feminist perspective. Her investigation springs from the assumption that "we cannot underestimate the importance of paratexts to the period's drama";[92] by taking into account more than 1,500 paratexts written between 1660 and 1714, accurately classified into a taxonomy, it takes a relevant step into this relatively neglected area of study.

Against Bruster and Weimann,[93] she argues that Genette's theory is flexible enough to be applied to drama. This is also my point of view. She writes:

> The authors of *Prologues to Shakespeare's Theatre*, Douglas Bruster and Robert Weimann, for example, cite three reasons for rejecting Genette: he only considers a text circulating within a literate world; he acknowledges but does not explore paratexts produced by other besides the author; and he focuses on the novel. While these are legitimate criticisms, I wish to argue that there is enough flexibility and applicability in Genette's theory …[94]

Together with Ennis and Slagle,[95] when discussing the role of the audience, she stresses the variety and articulation of the whole theatrical show, which is much broader than the mainpiece:

> Restoration theater audiences could visit the theater for the two curtain-tunes and the prologue, then depart with a full refund; many patrons considered these three short performances worth the effort. Audiences similarly could pay "after-money" (normally one-half the price of a full ticket) to attend acts 4 and 5, the epilogue, and

91 Solomon, *Prologues and Epilogues of Restoration Theatre.*

92 Ibid., 187.

93 Douglas Bruster and Robert Weimann, *Prologues to Shakespeare's Theatre: Performance and Liminality in Early Modern Drama* (London: Routledge, 2004).

94 Solomon, *Prologues and Epilogues of Restoration Theatre*, 9.

95 Daniel J. Ennis and Judith Bailey Slagle, eds, *Prologues, Epilogues, Curtain-Raisers, and Afterpieces: The Rest of the Eighteenth-Century London Stage* (Newark: University of Delaware Press, 2007).

> any subsequent performance such as afterpieces. And scholarship has expanded Restoration audiences well beyond the upper classes; Judith Milhous, for example, has pointed out that Christoper Rich admitted servants of upper-class attendees to the upper gallery for free. In short, various audiences attended the theater in various ways, some of which did not prioritize watching an intact narrative. In considering Restoration theater in performance, it therefore may be appropriate to think of the theatrical evening as featuring not only narratives but also a series of momentary performances. Such an approach prioritize the prologue or epilogue.[96]

The case study of the epilogue of John Dryden's *Tyrannick Love* was meant to illuminate an area of study that, despite its size, has been overshadowed by Shakespeare, whose tiny production of dramatic paratexts has nevertheless attracted more attention than any other playwright, such as for instance Dryden, who wrote about ten times more prologues and epilogues than the Bard:

> To find such a rich text [the epilogue of *Tyrannick Love*, by John Dryden] lacking sustained analysis is unusual in literary criticism; such is the case, however, with nearly *every* Restoration prologue and epilogue. And there are many. Dramatic prologues and epilogues – poetic bids for the audience's favor – first appeared in ancient Greek and Roman theater, and developed through the medieval and early modern English stage until reaching their apotheosis in the Restoration. There are 1,570 extant prologues and epilogues written between the years under discussion here, 1660 to the death of Anne on 1 August 1714. Overall numbers are much lower for Renaissance plays, with fewer than half containing a prologue or epilogue, yet scholars routinely consider Shakespeare's two inductions, five prologues, and seven epilogues alongside his plays, and have also treated prologues *qua* prologues. Dryden wrote over eight time as many prologues and epilogues as Shakespeare (fifty-nine prologues and forty-four epilogues) yet even within Dryden scholarship these rarely receive more than a mention. When cited, prologues and epilogues are usually treated as factual references – used, for example, to document a royal's presence at the theater that night – but they remain largely bereft of critical analysis. While their utility as documentation is valuable, their political and social commentary, elucidation of theater practices and conditions, and customization for celebrated players are just three reasons that prologues and epilogues are vital to understanding Restoration theater and culture.[97]

96 Ibid., 17–18.

97 Ibid., 2–3.

The broad and ambitious goal of Solomon's book to treat prologues and epilogues "systematically, analytically, culturally, and theoretically as documents that shaped the viewing and reading of plays for audiences"[98] partially overlaps with our purpose, which is to investigate the paratexts of the Shakespearean adaptations in the light of their contribution to the cultural construction of bardolatry.

1.3 Adaptation

1.3.1 Alteration and Adaptation: OED and Patrice Pavis

The term *adaptation* is a relatively recent coinage by the critics with reference to the rewritings of Shakespeare, whereas in the Restoration and the eighteenth century the most commonly used term was *alteration*. For the purposes of this study, I will use both interchangeably; *adaptation*, is intended without the negative legacy that is often attributed to the term as a result of the opinions expressed by some scholars who praise Shakespeare and criticize his adaptors (for example, F. W. Kilbourne in *Alterations and Adaptations of Shakespeare* and H. Spencer in *Shakespeare Improved*). Indeed, I am inclined to give a positive connotation to the term, starting from the 2015 online *OED* seven definitions of adaptation, belonging to different areas of knowledge. For briefness' sake, I will only list those that are helpful to my line of reasoning, without mentioning the others; I will keep the original entry numbers:

> [#2.]
> a. The action or process of adapting one thing to fit with another, or suit specified conditions, esp. a new or changed environment, etc…
>
> [#3.]
> a. The quality or state of being adapted or suitable for a particular use, purpose, or function, or to a particular environment; adaptedness …

98 Ibid., 3.

[#4.]
An altered or amended version of a text, musical composition, etc., (now *esp.*) one adapted for filming, broadcasting, or production on the stage from a novel or similar literary source.

[#5.]
The action or process of altering, amending, or modifying something, esp. something that has been created for a particular purpose, so that it suitable for a new use.

[#6.]
A result of a process of adapting or being adapted; an adapted or modified version or form; a modification.

[#7.]
a. *Biol.* A process of change or modification by which an organism or species becomes better suited to its environment or ecological niche, or a part of an organism to its biological function, either through phenotypic change in an individual or (esp.) through an evolutionary process effecting change through successive generations.
b. An instance of this; an adaptive feature; a phenotypic or (esp.) evolutionary modification.

If the focus is on the literary field, the fourth definition has actually expanded so much that Patrice Pavis in his *Dictionnaire du Theatre* (1980)[99] offers three distinct definitions for *adaptation*, the *OED* being only one of them. According to Pavis, adaptation, in its first meaning, is a *transcodification*, "the re-casting of a work in one genre to another (adaptation of a novel for the stage, for instance)";[100] in its third, it is a *translation*: "the term 'adaptation' is often used in the sense of translation"[101] from one language to another.

The present study is concerned primarily with the second definition, which is worth extensive citation:

The concept of adaptation also refers to dramaturgical work based on the text to be staged. All imaginable textual manoeuvres are permissible: cuts, rearrangement of the narration, stylistic polishing, the use of fewer characters or locations, a dramatic focus on certain strong points …, the addition of external texts, montage and collage

99 Patrice Pavis, *Dictionary of the Theatre. Terms, Concepts, and Analysis*, trans. Christine Shantz (Toronto: University of Toronto P, 1998). Originally published as *Dictionnaire du theatre* (Paris: Editions Sociales, 1980).

100 Ibid., 14.

101 Ibid.

> of foreign elements, different endings and changes in the fabula as required by the staging. Adaptation, unlike translation or contemporization, can be very free; it does not hesitate to change or even invent the meaning of the original play … To adapt is to entirely rewrite the text, using it as raw material.[102]

The above definition fits the Shakesperean adaptations for more than one reason. It refers to a "dramaturgical work" that exists within a single literary genre, drama; and within a single tongue, English. Both the source text and the adapted text in the *alterations* of the Restoration occur in drama, so do not shift from one literary genre to another; likewise, the tongue is and remains English – both source language and target language are the same, which is not the case with translations.

The cases that will be discussed below are also covered by Pavis' second definition because Shakespeare's adaptors really make use of "all imaginable textual manoeuvres" in their *alterations* in the period between 1660 and 1737. The consequences of such operations, which are sometimes radical, are apparent even from a simple reading of the plots, available in the appendix of the present study.

The fourth *OED* definition, with Pavis' refinements, is therefore most fitting for our purposes, but the seventh and last is the most inspiring as it is suggestive of an exchange between biology and literary criticism. If "organism" and "species" are replaced by "text" and "literary genre" it would run as follows: "a process of change or modification by which a text or literary genre becomes better suited to its [cultural] environment," and this is something that happens quite often.

Aside from its scientific technical language, the original fourth *OED* definition recalls some key concepts that have appeared in a scattered way in the other definitions and are now more evident. It is impossible not to grasp the evolutionary-Darwinian orientation and its chronological-historical implications. A staunch endorsement of the former would proclaim the *alterations* superior to their source text, which is not the aim of this book; whereas the chronological-historical implications are much more reasonable and assist in placing these Restoration texts in their proper place, independent and free from a cumbersome, lumbering shadow cast by a more-or-less explicit comparison to their Elizabethan paragons.

---

102 Ibid.

1.3.2 Martha Tuck Rozett

Martha Tuck Rozett reports that "a number of critics have devised terms for the kinds of texts Shakespeare's plays have inspired":[103] Jonathan Bate proposes the term "afterlife," Ruby Cohn "offshoot," Michael Scott "feed off," while Charles Marowitz has his "quantum leap approach to Shakespeare." The list of possibilities is really very wide. The author herself prefers the term "transformation:"

> transformations are thus a form of interpretation, but interpretation of a particular kind; their main objective is not so much to explain or elucidate as it is to stretch the texts in new directions, testing the resiliency of their characters and structures, and trying out alternative scenarios[104]

Rozett's perspective is the end of the process of adaptation, where the analyzed texts are "in varying ways, acts of rebellion against the texts that have been elevated above all others in the conservative literary canon"[105] and "thus become ways of turning the establishment's most sacred cultural icons against themselves."[106] The Restoration, on the other hand, is towards the opposite side of this, as it sees the beginning of the process of adaptation, the creation of the literary canon, and its cultural icons.

1.3.3 Ruby Cohn

The first sentence of Ruby Cohn's book is a value judgment of the modern rewritings of Shakespeare, not all of which are superior to their source text: "It is easy to predict a conclusion to this book. Shakespeare offshoots are not Shakespeare. Or, a little less tersely, no modern Shakespeare offshoot has improved upon the original."[107] This is nothing but a blatant, politically correct declaration of the inferiority of the adaptations

103 Martha Tuck Rozett, *Talking Back to Shakespeare* (Newark: University of Delaware Press, 1994), 7.

104 Ibid., 7.

105 Ibid., 6.

106 Ibid.

107 Ruby Cohn, *Modern Shakespeare Offshoots* (Princeton, NJ: Princeton University Press, 1976), vii.

with terse references to bardolatry and the idea that the original text is the best. Some decades have passed since Kilbourne and H. Spencer, but their negative vision is still at work in 1976, when *Modern Shakespeare Offshoots* was published after five years of research.

Cohn's analysis focuses on drama, but strays into fiction, essay, and theater; for our theoretical purposes we will note her coinage of the "looser and more neutral word" *offshoot* to refer to the rewritings of Shakespeare, which are known by a very wide array of names, "adaptation" being probably the most overused term.[108] She identifies three groups of "offshoots," according to the proximity to the source text: reductions/emendations, adaptations, and transformations. The first group bears minor changes and is "properly considered as theater history rather than literary alteration";[109] the second group is mainly characterized by additions – "at least one and usually several important (or scene-length) additions."[110] The third group's basis is invention, mainly connected to characters: "Shakespearean characters are often simplified or trundled through new events, with the Shakespearean ending scrapped."[111]

As with every taxonomy, it is highly subjective, and problems arise when a play presents either the substantial presence of a feature that results in a radical modification of the source text, or coexistence of more features of modification, or both. This, along with Cohn's confidence in identifying an offshoot and placing it into a group was questioned by Mary Jane Kidnie more than thirty years later, as we shall see below.

1.3.4 Linda Hutcheon

In 2012, six years after the first edition, Linda Hutcheon returns to deal with adaptations with the second edition of *A Theory of Adaptation*, showing it to be a lively field of study. Hutcheon addresses the phenomenon of adaptation in its most wide-ranging sense, not being limited by boundaries of literary genre, medium, or language. In fact her aim is to trace the enormous proliferation of adaptations that cross these

108 Ibid., 3.
109 Ibid.
110 Ibid.
111 Ibid., 4. [ruby cohn, etc.]

boundaries, going beyond the current standard mode of fiction-to-film, with special attention to the new Internet, social and interactive media peculiar to the twenty-first century. The first sentence of the preface outlines this type of approach by proclaiming "if you think adaptation can be understood by using novels and films alone, you're wrong."[112]

There are two main goals. The second is "to consider the ever-widening range of forms of adaptations, well beyond the fiction-to-film discussions that dominated the field in its early years."[113] The first goal, which I fully endorse, is "to tackle head-on the subtle and not so subtle denigration of adaptation in our … culture that still tends to value the 'original', despite the ubiquity and longevity of adaptation."[114] In fact, despite the various brilliant ideas suggested and developed by Kristeva, Derrida, and Foucault, each of whom has his or her particular focus, but all tend to converge on the idea that "to be second is not to be secondary or inferior; likewise, to be first is not to be originary or authoritative,"[115] negative mindsets remain: "disparaging opinions on adaptation … persist."[116] This is even truer in the Shakespeare studies, especially with regard to the highly critical conceptual tenets on the idea of adaptation formulated many decades ago by Kilbourne and H. Spencer, which appear to be still at work nowadays. Hutcheon's reference to the field of biology (also suggested by the *OED*) moves on in the direction of re-evaluation of the adaptation "just as biology does not evaluate the merit of organisms relative to their ancestors – for all have equal biological validity – so too may all cultural adaptations one day be seen to have equal cultural validity."[117]

This is a very fruitful hint because it challenges an old, cumbersome negative legacy, suggesting at the same time a different horizon of interpretation based on *successful replication* and *change*: "this is how biology thinks about adaptation: in terms of successful replication and change. Perhaps cultural adaptation can be seen to work in similar

112 Linda Hutcheon. *A Theory of Adaptation*. (London: Routledge, 2006 [2012]), xiii.
113 Ibid. xx.
114 Ibid.
115 Ibid. xv.
116 Ibid.
117 Ibid. xxviii.

ways."[118] It is an invitation that I really hope can be accepted and developed by literary scholarship.

Hutcheon's idea that adaptation is an "ubiquitous phenomenon"[119] seems to find its peak in the nineteenth century as "the Victorians had a habit of adapting just about everything – and in just about every possible direction"; but it turns out that this practice was not peculiar to only one age since "we postmoderns have clearly inherited this same habit," and the action of adaptation was also present more or less in all past centuries. Then, if we recall Pavis when maintaining that "all imaginable textual manoeuvres are permissible," the possibility that all literature can be included in the concept of adaptation is feasible.

1.3.5 Daniel Fischlin and Mark Fortier

A similar risk is run in *Adaptations of Shakespeare* edited by Daniel Fischlin and Mark Fortier, whose definition of adaptation is wide and inclusive, as it incorporates not only rewritings, and performative modifications, but also the activity of editing:

> Adaptation as a material, performance practice can involve both radical rewritings, and a range of directorial and theatrical practices … One of the other ways in which Shakespeare is made fit is through criticism, itself a form of adaptive undertaking by virtue of its intertextual dependence on a source text. A related area that concerns adaptive practice has to do with how editorial practices that seek to stabilize or destabilize texts literally adapt Shakespeare, making him conform to a particular editorial vision.[120]

1.3.6 Margaret Jane Kidnie

Until today adaptation has been perceived as problematic. For instance, *Shakespeare and the Problem of Adaptation* by Margaret Jane Kidnie (2009) reveals, in its title, an intrinsic difficulty in dealing critically with

118 Ibid. xxvi.

119 P. xviii.

120 Daniel Fischlin and Mark Fortier, eds., *Adaptations of Shakespeare* (New York: Routledge, 2000), 17.

the process of adapting. The study discusses different kinds of Shakespearean adaptation at the turn of the last century ranging from theater, to television, to the new technologies of the digital hypertext, with a main focus on theatrical production and staging.

Kidnie opens by stating that "the issue of what should 'count' as adaptation is often taken for granted,"[121] immediately questioning the preceding assessments of the concept of adaptation. In fact, she rejects three positions that we have seen above: she criticizes Cohn in as much as "her position, in other words, seems to be that we all know an adaptation of Shakespeare when we encounter it";[122] Cohn, together with Hutcheon, "tend[s] to assume that there exists a relatively stable distinction between work and adaptation,"[123] an assumption that she rejects. In her view, the idea of adaptation as formulated by Fischlin and Fortier is also not satisfying because is too wide: "by finding adaptation potentially everywhere, Fischlin and Fortier are in danger of emptying the term of meaning."[124]

The starting point is that drama "is generically situated at the intersection of text and performance"[125] and that "the dramatic work, whether encountered as text or performance, is a dynamic process."[126] From these premises she develops an approach that is much more oriented towards production and reception, and which deals with adaptation "as a necessarily provisional category of study."[127] Her main argument is that "adaptation as an evolving category is closely tied to how the work modifies over time and from one reception space to another,"[128] but this leaves the door open for a great variety of changings according to the opportunities offered by performance and staging. The theoretical uncertainty that Kidnie found characterizing the definitions of adaptation mentioned above seems, therefore, in some way, transferred to the theatrical activity of production. In other words, the problem is not solved, because, as

121 Margaret Jane Kidnie, *Shakespeare and the Problem of Adaptation* (New York: Routledge, 2009), 2.

122 Ibid., 3.

123 Ibid., 4.

124 Ibid., 5.

125 Ibid., 7.

126 Ibid., 32.

127 Ibid., 5.

128 Ibid.

Holderness observes, "when dealing with theatre and film, we are in the somewhat different environment of performance interpretation, where it is not always easy to draw hard and fast distinctions between a radical and innovative production of the play, a free adaptation or systematic revision, and a spinoff."[129]

1.4 Linguistics and Anthropology: Mikhail Bakhtin and Mary Douglas

1.4.1 Introduction

The Commonwealth can be considered a period that marks a passage from the aesthetics and culture of the Renaissance and post-Renaissance to the aesthetics and culture of the neoclassic and pre-Enlightenment. English society during the Restoration period perceived itself as being much more distant from the Jacobean-Carolingian age than eleven years of republican experience (1649–60) would lead one to believe. Under the reign of Charles II, theater immediately returned to being a cultural focal point. Due to the rise in literacy, plays gradually gained a readership beyond that of theatergoers.

Like David Cressy,[130] Gary Taylor believes that between 1660 and 1700 there was a clear increase in literacy:

> Not everyone could read. In England in 1660 only about 30 percent of men and 20 percent of women could sign their names. Those who could were very unevenly distributed: literacy was high among the clergy, professions, and gentry; low among husbandmen servants, and laborers. Yeomen, tradesmen, and craftsmen fell in the middle, in terms of status and literacy; but by 1700 the commercial classes in London were almost entirely literate.[131]

---

129 Graham Holderness, *Textual Shakespeare* (Hatfield, University of Hertfordshire Press, 2003), 178.

130 David Cressey, *Literacy and the Social Order: Reading and Writing in Tudor and Stuart England* (Cambridge: Cambridge UP, 1980) 176–7.

131 Gary Taylor, *Reinventing Shakespeare* (Oxford: Oxford University Press, 1989), 32.

Literacy grows together with print. In the first decades of the Restoration, the number of printed texts grew more slowly than in subsequent decades,[132] but in the following century its rise was remarkable. As Jean Marsden argues, the new buyers of texts opened a new market; as a consequence, the number of printers grew steadily from the second part of the seventeenth century onwards: "The growth of the print industry can be charted through the number of London publishing houses: 60 at the time of the Restoration; 75 by 1724; 150–200 by 1757."[133]

Between 1660 and 1737, the printed texts of adaptations assumed a variety of forms in order to accommodate different readerships. They did so in an attempt to cater for both the old and new groups of readers. In fact, the author often added a dedicatory letter to the text, for the patron to whom the work was dedicated, thus following a tradition going back centuries. At the same time, many paratexts addressed a new group of unknown readers, whose individual financial weight was minimal compared to the patron, but whose growing number made their impact more and more difficult to ignore. Marsden's observation on the changed role of the critic is probably also true for other figures working in a literary context, such as poets and playwrights:

> In the first decades of the eighteenth century … the patronage system that had supported earlier critics such as Dryden and Howard decayed, making critics dependent on an expanded literary marketplace rather than on a single aristocratic patron.[134]

Regarding Shakespearean adaptations, the paratext is of the utmost importance in the process of bardolatrizing Shakespeare – that is, in the creation of the Bard as a cultural hero and in his elevation to icon. This procedure takes the form of a eulogy that refers to the creator and his work and has a manner and tone – albeit within the rhetorical and stylistic conventions of the encomium – reminiscent of religious and sacred rituals. Within the paratexts of Shakespearean adaptations, it is indeed possible to detect a semantic dissemination that, with its complex network of

132 Jean I. Marsden, *The Re-Imagined Text* (Lexington: Kentucky University Press, 1995), 5.

133 Ibid., 20 (note 159).

134 Ibid., 103.

echoes and crossreferences, creates an ideological system of a religious sort with its god, Shakespeare, at the top.

In my analysis of paratexts characterizing the bardolatry of the Restoration, I deemed it both useful and stimulating to apply conceptual tools that are not purely linguistic and literary. It is for this reason that, to investigate this universe of discourse, alongside the ideas of the philosopher and semiotician Mikhail Bakhtin, I found it very fruitful to present the line of thought articulated by anthropologist Mary Douglas.

1.4.2 Mikhail Bakhtin: "The Discourse in the Novel"

Like Genette, as a literary critic, Bakhtin's main area of interest was prose, and especially the novel. Since he was rediscovered in the 1960s, Bakhtin's ideas inspired many scholars working in diverse disciplines, including the renowned Italian scholar Alessandro Serpieri, who has shown the relevance and applicability of concepts like polyphony and dialogism to the analysis of drama, and especially Shakespeare.[135] Among the many brilliant ideas of the Russian semiotician, the concept of "authority" is the one that can be most useful for the present study.

The Restoration saw the beginning of the process of fashioning Shakespeare as an authoritative literary figure and as father of the English language; but in the second half of the seventeenth century the bardolatry, or rather the two elements that constitute it – Shakespeare himself and his language – were still in a fluid state: the Bard was praised, but his language was sometimes despised. For this reason, some of the characteristics identified by Bakhtin as specific to authority and the authoritative word, may sometimes appear to be only roughly outlined in this period, where bardolatry is at an early stage.

Among the many varieties of the authoritative word, Bakhtin identifies religious dogma, whose rhetorical system is a discursive typology identifiable in the paratexts of Shakespearean adaptations, and whose primarily aim is to elevate the Bard to the status of cultural icon, up until conferring him a sacred status. In the case of the Bard, it reached its full expression when not only Shakespeare himself but also his language had become objects of veneration, and this was something that developed over

135 Alessandro Serpieri, *Polifonia Shakespeariana* (Roma: Bulzoni, 2002).

time and became clearly evident in the first half of the twentieth century, when, as seen above, some scholars were indignant about the unbecoming (in their view) treatment that adaptors used on the Shakespearean texts.[136] Only after Shakespeare has achieved a sacred status, it can become the subject of profanity,

The authoritative word, "the word of the fathers,"[137] is characterized as follows:

> Authoritative discourse may organize around itself great masses of other types of discourses (which interpret it, praise it, apply it in various ways), but the authoritative discourse itself does not merge with these (by means of, say, gradual transitions); it remains sharply demarcated, compact and inert; it demands, so to speak, not only quotation marks but a demarcation even more magisterial, a special script, for instance.[138]

Let us now see how this can apply to Restoration adaptations of Shakespeare. In the first phase, the second half of the seventeenth century, the authority of the Bard begin to attract "great masses of other types of discourses" in the form of the *alterations*. Through the paratextual apparatus of these *alterations* the authoritative word of Shakespeare also began to be interpreted and praised in various ways. In this early phase there were still instances of merging, fusion and change of the original word, whereas from the eighteenth century onwards it became more common to quote the original words using a special typeface. At this time, the language of the Bard had not yet become fully authoritative, that is sacred; or, to use Bakhtin's words, *hieratic*, *calcified*. This process was to reach completion later on, after several editions of the Shakespearean canon, and the consequent increase in Shakespeare studies; then, the Shakespearean word achieved the full status of authoritative word, which

> permits no play with the context framing it, no play with its borders, no gradual and flexible transitions, no spontaneously creative stylizing variants on it. It enters our verbal consciousness as a compact and indivisible mass; one must either totally affirm it, or totally reject it. It is indissolubly fused with its authority – with

136 Among the many opinions, I would like to recall again at least that of Hazelton Spencer, *Shakespeare Improved* (New York: Ungar, 1927 [1963]).

137 M. M. Bakhtin, "Discourse in the Novel," in *The Dialogic Imagination* (Austin: University of Texas Press, 1981), 342.

138 Ibid., 343.

political power, an institution, a person – and it stands and falls together with that authority. One cannot divide it up – agree with one part, accept but not completely another part, reject utterly a third part.[139]

By doing so, Shakespearean language "indissolubly fuses with its authority", in this case, the person of the author, thus completing the process of the acquisition of authority that Shakespeare himself, as man, poet and genius, had already attained.

1.4.3 Mary Douglas, Purity and Danger

Graham Holderness suggests that Shakespeare is very similar to what anthropologists call a "culture hero":

> It is often believed that only primitive societies have myths: but the figure of Shakespeare is actually very similar to the "culture heroes" of anthropology: figures which may be legendary heroes, fabulised historical characters or mythological deities; but which exhibit, throughout the countless mythologies of world culture, certain common structural characteristics.[140]

If we transfer this into the realm of literature, we can see that Shakespeare is a culture hero deeply rooted in nature, and that the means through which he reached this role have "certain common structural characteristics" with rituals and religions that have been object of study of anthropology.

Many paratexts of the Shakespearean *alterations* made a claim to legitimacy on the grounds that they were adapting the Bard to the new age. They made this claim by using conventional rhetorical language – a ritual, in its strict sense, as ritual often assumes a religious tone. This semiotic system, which appears in the paratexts of the adaptations, is a turning point in the placement of Shakespeare at the highest point of English literature.

Contemporary anthropologists, whose socio-cultural observations can be used profitably in literary analysis, examine religious rituals and

139 Ibid.

140 Graham Holderness, "Bardolatry: or, The cultural materialist's guide to Stratford-upon-Avon" 11, in Graham Holerness (ed.), *The Shakespeare Myth*, Manchester: Manchester UP, 1988.

the realm of the sacred. Although Mary Douglas does not speak about literature or Shakespeare in *Purity and Danger*, her studies of cultural ideas and concepts can be applied to literature and Shakespeare specifically. Indeed, some of the concepts borrowed from contemporary anthropology significantly help to define the rising bardolatry that gradually created a discourse on the sacred, with Shakespeare as a god.

Purity and Danger, the text to which I mainly refer, is one of Douglas' earliest works. It includes a solid, profound study of concepts and ideas, which are later reiterated and expanded in subsequent studies. According to Douglas, one of the main characteristics of the sacred is *separation*:

> For instance, the Latin word *sacer* itself has this meaning of restriction through pertaining to the gods. And in some cases it may apply to desecration as well as to consecration. Similarly, the Hebrew root of k-d-sh, which is usually translated as Holy, is based on the idea of separation. Aware of the difficulty translating k-d-sh straight into Holy, Ronald Knox's version of the Old Testament uses "set apart." Thus the grand lines "Be ye Holy, Because I am Holy" are rather thinly rendered …[141]

Within the conventions of laudatory rhetoric in the paratexts of the adaptations, Shakespeare was identified, differentiated, and separated from all his contemporaries. The cases where other famous or not-so-famous playwrights were named alongside him were more frequent in the last decades of the seventeenth century; later on he was set apart, and eulogized without mentioning anybody else. This was a decisive step towards an abstract construction of the Bard from the concrete, that is, from the society and culture of the Elizabethan era in which he lived. Everything was meant to propel him to an absolute dimension transcending time and space, and this was attested by many famous affirmations of which only two will be quoted here "[Shakespeare] was not of an age, but for all time!"[142] and "[Shakespeare] had a universal mind,"[143] uttered by Ben Jonson and John Dryden, respectively.

The overall picture of Restoration paratexts reveals a situation in which Shakespeare began to be separated from everything that was not

141 Douglas, *Purity and Danger*, 10.

142 Ben Jonson, "To the memory of my beloved …".

143 John Dryden, "The Grounds of Criticism in Tragedy," *Troilus and Cressida* (London: 1679).

Shakespeare. In the early stage, in the second part of the seventeenth century, he was also separated from a part of himself, or to be more exact, from his language. Because in anthropology we are reminded that some primitive religions do not make a distinction between sanctity and impurity,[144] the fracture is, in reality, only apparent; the sacred element – Shakespeare – coexists with the impure element – language. In the first decades of the Restoration, the Bard was often removed from the element through which his work expressed itself, that is, through language. His adaptors pointed out that the problematic language was not Shakespeare's fault but reflected the age in which he lived. Absolved of guilt, the Bard was then ready to move towards a sainthood of literary kind. At the time, separation between author and work was regarded as possible. It was permissible to apply radical changes to the work after the playwright had given it to the company, and then years or decades later, when an adaptation of a past play took place. In the second half of the seventeenth century, merely updating the language, the usual manner in which alterations were made, was not regarded as undermining the profound philosophical, moral, and ethical meanings of the source work. Later, from the beginning of the eighteenth century onwards, some adaptations begin to pay more attention to Shakespeare's words, although they did so in a fragmentary manner. This idea was subsequently developed and endorsed by eighteenth-century editors, and in this way the process of praising and sacralizing the Bard's language became more consistent.

During the first decades of the Restoration, Shakespeare was separated from his words because they were deemed obscure, confused, dull, and dirty. In anthropological terms:

> As we know it, dirt is essentially disorder. There is no such thing as absolute dirt: it exists in the eye of the beholder … Dirt offends against order. Eliminating it is not a negative movement, but a positive effort to organise the environment.[145]

The above citation draws our attention to some other issues. In modern physics, it is common knowledge that point of view is a crucial element; connected to this is the fact that the observer influences the observed phenomenon. In our case, the Shakespearean adaptor perceives

144 Douglas, *Purity and Danger*, 13–14.
145 Ibid., 2.

the Bard's language as something that needs intervention, and so his actions attempt to create order in expression. Dirt, as well as beauty, is in the eye of the beholder. In the case of an *alteration*, the adaptor's effort is directed towards organizing the internal literary environment that is limited to a single work by Shakespeare, in order to combine form with content. Because the poetic substance is taken for granted as an *a priori*, it only remains to change the form of the imperfect language.

Acting against anything that appears dirty materially and idealistically is a "creative movement" through which human beings adapt their surroundings – even when they are cultural and literary – to fit their needs:

> In chasing dirt … we are not governed by anxiety to escape disease, but [we] are positively re-ordering our environment, making it conform to an idea. There is nothing fearful or unreasoning in our dirt-avoidance: it is a creative movement, an attempt to relate form to function, to make unity of experience.[146]

For the adaptor, the cleansing of Shakespeare's language is meant to assign him to a proper place in the cultural environment of the second half of the seventeenth century, and to make him accessible to the new culture and society of the time. The Bard's plays, therefore, were adapted to fit an idea – the idea that Restoration has of Shakespeare. As they were written originally, Shakespeare's works could not create an experience that could be assimilated by the man of the Restoration, and thus until the end of the century Shakespeare was altered to make him accessible to the public, and not vice versa. In this way, the public was not expected to change its mode of interpretation and perspective of values.

A change to Shakespeare's language is a creative action that brings along massive consequences. By its very nature, the theatrical word is simultaneously voice and action. Thus, any change made to it not only undermines the symbolic and semiotic system of the language, but also necessarily intervenes in the phonics and performative recitation. As a consequence, the adaptor's actions go beyond their original intentions (or at least, beyond those that are declared openly), which were meant simply to ascertain and paraphrase a language that is believed to be "difficult." Modifications to the dramatic language thus create a new

146 Ibid., 3.

universe of discourse that behaves differently and whose outcomes are profoundly different from those yielded in the source text. The pervasiveness of such a reshaping action is profound, as it often interacts with other interventions that alter characters and plot so that the final product is often very far removed from the primary source.

The Bard's adaptor, however, is not the only one associated with creative energy. The relationship is mutually dependent, because even the disordered Shakespearean model – indeed, precisely because of its nonorder – possesses creative power:

> Granted that disorder spoils pattern, it also provides the material of pattern. Order implies restriction; from all possible materials, a limited selection has been made and from all possible relations a limited set has been used. So disorder by implication is unlimited, no pattern has been realised in it, but its potential for patterning is indefinite. This is why, though we seek to create order, we do not simply condemn disorder. We recognise that it is destructive to existing patterns; also that it has potentiality. It symbolizes both danger and power.[147]

Since time immemorial, unboundedness and infinity have been considered divine attributes and so they can easily be linked to the disorder of the Shakespearean genius. The adaptor is both influenced by and reacts to the powerful and precarious fascination associated with the Bard: he takes a metaphorical drink from the textual sacred spring of Shakespeare, but not before having ordered the stream of his language and having remodeled it according to the tastes of the Restoration.

One of the methods of religious classification relied upon by contemporary anthropology is that of distinguishing them into primitive or advanced:

> If primitive, then rules of holiness and rules of uncleanness were undistinguishable; if advanced, then rules of uncleanness disappeared from religion.[148]

Thus, the bardolatry of the second half of the seventeenth century would seem to have at least one feature that connected it to a primitive religion, namely its lack of distinction between the sacred and the profane, the holy and the dirty and impure. As we shall see, Shakespeare is at once holy and

147 Ibid., 117.
148 Ibid., 14.

impure: his genius, his poetry, his value are praised, whereas his language is purified of the rhetorical excesses of the Elizabethan age. And by no means are these excesses softened by the creativity of the Bard, whose imagination is, in many places, defined as "wild" and "unrestricted," and whose linguistic production is not moderate, proportioned, or regularly articulated.

However, it is reasonable to think that, although perhaps unconsciously, the interest in, and appreciation of, Shakespeare in the Restoration derived precisely from these irregular qualities. In *The Psychoanalysis of Artistic Vision and Hearing* (1953),[149] Anton Ehrenzweig argued that a work of art enables us to go beyond conventions of regular experiences, and that aesthetic pleasure comes from the perception of what he calls inarticulate forms.

Thus, Shakespeare's sometimes inarticulate, dirty, and disconnected language necessitates purification and decontamination. As Douglas observes, an intervention such as this is not free of risk at the conceptual level since:

> Defilement is never an isolated event. It cannot occur except in view of a systematic ordering of ideas. Hence any piecemeal interpretation of the pollution rules of another culture is bound to fail. For the only way in which pollution ideas make sense is in reference to a total structure of thought, whose keystone, boundaries, margins and internal lines are held in relation by rituals of separation.[150]

The ideas on authorship in the Restoration allowed the adaptor a high degree of freedom, such that he could extensively change Shakespeare's language according to the audience tastes, neo-classical pseudo-Aristotelian rules, or both. At least until the beginning of the eighteenth century, there was a strong opposition to the possible contaminating effects of Shakespeare's language, which was changed, rewritten, updated, and modernized.

Through its changes, the process of purification is likely to make language poor and barren. Edward Ravenscroft, one of the Shakespearean adaptors who will be discussed in the chapter on paratext, uses a botanical metaphor, establishing a parallel between Shakespeare's text and a

149 Anton Ehrenzweig, *The Psychoanalysis of Artistic Vision and Hearing* (London: Routledge & Kegan Paul, 1953).

150 Douglas, *Purity and Danger*, 51.

garden. However, his selective decontamination ignores one of the principles upon which agriculture has been based for millennia, so as to sublimate it to the symbolic realm of the ritual and the religious. Douglas, in fact, observes that

> A garden is not a tapestry; if all the weeds are removed, the soil is impoverished. Somehow the gardener must preserve fertility by returning what he has taken out. The special kind of treatment which some religious accord to anomalies and abominations to make them powerful for good is like turning weeds and lawn cuttings into compost.[151]

Restoration bardolatry does not carry out this exchange and the results were sometimes recognized, even at the time, as negative. In some cases, the responsibility for the failure is shared with, or charged upon the French masters who are taken as models. John Dryden's reproachful words directed towards the dramatic models of France are surprisingly similar to those of Mary Douglas regarding religions that reach their ideal of purity: "It is part of our condition that the purity for which we strive and sacrifice so much turns out to be hard and dead as a stone when we get it."[152]

Thus, the process that comes from the ritual implications of textual refashioning becomes a discourse around the symbolic system of an English Elizabethan language perceived as tainted by an excess of rhetoric and figuration. But

> Just as the focus of all pollution symbolism is the body, the final problem to which the perspective of pollution leads is bodily disintegration. Death presents a challenge to any metaphorical system …[153]

so it is necessary to ask oneself about the type of response such a universe of discourse merits.

Remodeling the language is a technique that reinserts that which was once rejected as dirty and messy to renew the life of theater and Shakespeare. Restoration adaptations, however, responded to this in a rather unsatisfactory and transient way. From the beginning of the eighteenth century, there was a new trend that became more thoroughly developed

151 Ibid., 201–2.
152 Ibid., 199.
153 Ibid., 213.

from the 1720s and was pursued across the whole Shakespearean canon, and not just in single adaptations. Opposing the alteration of the Bard's plays, eighteenth-century editors developed a process of sacralizing his word. The eighteenth century thus reversed the apparent rupture between Author and Word that seemingly appears in the paratexts of the adaptations. The rupture is only apparent because the seeming negative attributes of impurity (filth and disorder) are actually also related to the sphere of the sacred, as anthropology shows.

Shakespearean adaptations from the period 1660–1737 can therefore be divided into two groups: one from 1660 until about 1701; another from about 1701 to 1737. In the first period Shakespeare is eulogized, and his language altered; the second group retains Shakespeare's eulogy, but his language starts to be preserved and restored. The first period is relevant from the point of view of bardolatry because it guarantees continuity to the presence of Shakespeare on the stage and on the page after the experience of the Commonwealth and the closing of theaters; the second, even though fragmentarily, presents the features that would come to characterize the activity of the editors of the Shakespeare canon.

2 Paratext I: The Peritext

2.1 Publisher's Peritext: Title Pages and Titles

2.1.1 Introductory Remarks

My discussion of peritexts of the Shakespearean adaptations follows the chronology of their printing rather than the date of their first stage representation (which might predate the printing date even by some years). This decision was determined by the fact that both publisher's and prefatorial peritext are specifically tied to the printed text and not to the staged text.

This is obviously not the case, however, for prologues and epilogues, both of which constitute the dramatic peritext. As recent studies have demonstrated,[154] during the Restoration, these two parts became increasingly important, and more varied in type. Their authors were sometimes the author of the play and sometimes not; they were sometimes staged when the curtain was up and sometimes when it was down; they could demonstrate tenuous or strong connections with the plays that they framed; they sometimes deliberately attempted to elicit the audience's goodwill, and so on. Sometimes they were only added to a later printed edition.

In Michael Dobson's view,[155] the adaptations from the Restoration and the eighteenth century play a fundamental role in establishing Shakespeare's place at the center of English literary culture. The present chapter aims to show how these groups of paratexts of the Shakespearean adaptations function as an important literary space in which bardolatry is particularly pronounced. It is a space in which the author – sometimes even as early as the front page – reveals his acknowledgment of the increasing

154 See, among others, Ennis and Slagle, *Prologues, Epilogues, Curtain-Raisers, and Afterpieces*, and Solomon, *Prologues and Epilogues of Restoration Theater*.

155 Dobson, *The Making of the National Poet*, 1–16.

authority of Shakespeare and his underlying reasons and principles for creating the *alteration*. Thus, it is where some of the fundamental characteristics defining the adapter's notion of Shakespeare are disseminated.

2.1.2 Title Pages and Titles

When a reader approaches a printed text, one of the first elements of the paratext that he or she encounters is what Genette calls the publisher's peritext, consisting of frontispiece/title page and title.

A chronological list is provided below of the adapted plays that show clear signs of their status as *alterations* from their outset. Of the thirty plus adaptations that emerged between 1660 and 1737, seven openly declared on the front page that they were altered texts of a Shakespearean play: all of them bear the Bard's name; all contains the word "alteration" (or similar), except *All for Love*, which uses "imitation"; moreover, the last three plays on the list employ the same formula, "altered from Shakespeare":

1. ALL for LOVE: OR, THE World well Lost. A TRAGEDY, As it is Acted at the THEATRE-ROYAL; And Written in Imitation of Shakespeare's Stile. By John Dryden, Servant to His Majesty.
2. Titus Andronicus, OR THE Rape of Lavinia. Acted at the Theatre Royall, A TRAGEDY, Alter'd from Mr SHAKESPEARS Work By Mr. Edw. Ravenscroft.
3. Measure for Measure, OR BEAUTY THE Best Advocate. As it is ACTED At the THEATRE in Lincolns-Inn-Fields. Written Originally by Mr. Shakespear: And now very much Alter'd; With Additions of several Entertainments of MUSICK.
4. K. HENRY IV WITH THE HUMOURS OF Sir John Falstaff. A TRAGI-COMEDY [As] it is Acted at the THEATRE in Little-Lincolns-Inn-Fields BY His Majesty's Servants. Revived, with Alterations. Written Originally by Mr. Shakespear.
5. THE SEQUEL OF HENRY the Fourth: With the Humours of Sir John Falstaffe, and Justice Shallow. As it is Acted by His MAJESTY's Company of Comedians, AT THE Theatre-Royal in Drury-Lane. Alter'd from Shakespear, by the late Mr. Betterton.
6. THE TRAGEDY OF King Richard the II; As it is Acted at the THEATRE IN LINCOLN's-INN-FIELDS. Alter'd from SHAKESPEAR, By Mr. Theobald.
7. KING HENRY VI. A TRAGEDY. As it is Acted at the Theatre-Royal in Drury-Lane, By His Majesty's Servants. Altered from Shakespear, in the Year 1720, By THEOPHILUS CIBBER.

From the outset, these seven plays present themselves as reworkings of an earlier play. In another seven examples, Shakespeare's authorship of the text is expressed implicitly through the title of the play, which is unmistakably Shakespearean (*Macbeth*, *Romeo and Juliet*, *The Tempest*, *Antony and Cleopatra*, *Timon of Athens*, *Troilus and Cressida*, *King Lear*). Thus, the total increases to fourteen plays, which is not far from half of the total number of adaptations that show a more-or-less explicit bond with the Bard.

There remains at least as many adaptations where the title page and title do not reveal any trace of their status as altered Shakespeare plays. However, the texts from this latter group should not be judged hastily, for they are not examples of adaptations that wish to present themselves as a new dramatic-textual entity in which there is an appropriation of Shakespeare that begins outside of the text, prior to the text, and in which the new author attempts to take the place of the Bard. In fact, many *alterations* of this group reveal signs of bardolatry and their own indebtedness to Shakespeare either in the prefatorial or the dramatic peritext.

2.2 Prefatorial Peritext: Dedicatory Epistles, Prefaces, Reader's Advisory, Theoretical Essays

2.2.1 Introductory Remarks

According to Genette, whose study is mainly focused on the novel, not on drama, the main part of the peritextual system is the prefatorial peritext, a vast group of paratexts consisting of dedicatory epistles, prefaces, readers' advisories, and theoretical essays.

In *Paratexts. Thresholds of Interpretation*, he states that the principal aim of the prefatorial peritext in French classical theater is to respond to its critics:[156] this situation does not differ greatly from what occurred in Restoration England. These responses to critics are carried out in different ways, most of which have been identified as follows:

156 Genette, *Paratexts. Thresholds of Interpretation*, 241.

> For example: I am not defending myself against critics, who are free to say what they want, but I am anxious to correct some errors … Or this: I accept criticism, but I observe that those who find fault with me contradict one another … Or this: what I am reproached for is what the best of the ancients have already done (implying: to attack me is to attack them). Or finally, and especially: the critics are overwhelmingly, against me, but the public is on my side.[157]

Since drama and English plays are not the focus of *Paratexts*, and because of the wide and different range of texts considered in it, it is not always possible to establish immediate connections with Genette's theory. In some other case, there is a clear exception, such as some of the arguments presented in the prefatory paratexts for the *captatio benevolentiae* of the work's addressee. In Shakespearean adaptations, the rhetoric of persuasion in this type of paratexts employs concepts and words such as "talent," "genius," and the like: words and concepts that Genette considers taboo. Thus, the French critic's observations regarding the prefatorial paratexts, which will be cited shortly and applied to the English theater of Restoration, are to be read backwards, much like the negatives of photographs are read:

> [in the prefatorial peritext] one refrains from dwelling on what could pass for a display of the author's *talent*. Among the numerous prefaces I had occasion to read when preparing for this study, none of them elaborated on either of these two themes: "Admire my style" or "Admire my craftsmanship." More general, the word *talent* is taboo. The word *genius* also, of course.[158]

The analysis of the dramatic peritexts below will show that one of the prevailing tendencies of bardolatry, especially in the first forty years of the Restoration, is to praise Shakespeare *in general*, and to criticize him *in particular* – his gifts are transcendent, his defects accidental; the author is thus adored for his abstract merits and, at the same time, exorcized for his concrete shortcomings – that is, some or some parts of his plays (in which the language and/or plot can be considered faulty).

The bardolatry that thus emerges from the prefatorial peritexts appears to have a voice that is multitonal, even ventriloquial. In some cases, resounding praise is counterpointed by strong criticism; however,

157 Ibid., 242.
158 Ibid., 198.

this is merely transitory because the voice of condemnation is slowly transformed into the voice of encomium, which gradually encompasses and assimilates the contradictory element.

2.2.2 1670–1687: From Davenant and Dryden's The Tempest to Ravenscroft's Titus Andronicus[159]

The preface to Davenant and Dryden's adaptation of *The Tempest* (1670), written by Dryden alone, begins by recognizing Shakespeare's authorship of the text and by expressing veneration and admiration for the poet: "It was originally Shakespear's: a *Poet* for whom he [Davenant] had particularly a high *veneration*, and whom he first taught me to *admire*." The tribute is made to the poet's invisible quality, not to his imperfect work. Shortly after, in fact, Dryden declared that "Sir William Davenant, as he was a man of quick and piercing imagination, soon found that somewhat might be added to the Design of Shakespear," thus assuming that his additions would improve the Bard's original plot. Moreover, Davenant commented on the scenes already adapted by Dryden: "sometimes he added whole Scenes together, which may as easily be distinguish'd from the rest, as true *Gold* from counterfeit by the weight." Here, an image of a precious mineral appears for the first time.[160] Gold, however, is not the Shakespearean word, nor does it even become that after Dryden adapted it; rather, it is created following a second process of refining carried out by Davenant. In this brief passage,[161] Dryden believes Davenant to possess greater skill

159 William Davenant and John Dryden, *The Tempest* (London, 1670); William Davenant, *The Tragedy of Hamlet Prince of Denmark* (London, 1676); Thomas Shadwell, *The History of Timon of Athens, the Man-Hater* (London, 1678); John Dryden, *All for Love: or, The World Well Lost* (London, 1678); John Dryden, *Troilus and Cressida, or, Truth Found Too Late* (London, 1679); John Crowne, *Henry the Sixth, The First Part. With the Murder of Humphrey Duke of Gloucester* (London, 1681); Nahum Tate, *The History of King Richard The Second Acted at the Theatre Royal, Under the Name of the Sicilian Usurper* (London, 1681); Nahum Tate, *The Ingratitude of a Common-Wealth: Or, the Fall of Caius Martius Coriolanus* (London, 1682); Nahum Tate, *The History of King Lear* (London, 1681); Edward Ravenscroft, *Titus Andronicus, or the Rape of Lavinia* (London, 1687).

160 Tate will, instead, speak of *jewels*.

161 As we shall see, his opinions on Shakespeare are inconsistent.

in dramatic poetry and, indirectly, elevates him above Shakespeare; his adaptation, mirroring the process of alchemy, has transformed the Bard's inert and *counterfeit* lexical material into *gold*. The catalyst, the fifth element, the philosopher's stone is the poetic quality, which Shakespeare undoubtedly possesses, as the opening praise confirms, but which, according to Dryden, Davenant possesses in greater quantity because of the results he has produced. Davenant, therefore, is not considered inferior to the Bard, and Dryden says that he is honored to have worked with such great masters in the final words of the preface ("joining my imperfections with the merit and name of Shakespear and Sir William Davenant").

Davenant's *Hamlet* (1676) is the first Shakespeare adaptation staged during the Restoration. The following is the complete foreword "To the reader":

> This play being too long to be conveniently Acted, such places as might be least prejudicial to the Plot or Sense, are left out upon the Stage: but that we may no way wrong the *imcomparable Author*, are here inserted according to the Original Copy with this Mark ' [italics mine].

Although Shakespeare is an incomparable author and, thus, superior to any other playwright, his play, as he apparently wrote it, is still too long to be staged conveniently and so some 800 lines were omitted from it. So as not to insult the Bard, these parts were nevertheless included in the printed edition and indicated by printed quotation marks at the beginning of the lines cut for performance. In addition to emphasizing the author/text dichotomy, the passage cited above also highlights the dichotomy of text-to-be-staged/text-to-be-read, which will later become more and more relevant. In other words, the latter dichotomy suggests that theatrical pace and conventions do not allow an integral stage representation; but the reader can appreciate the entire work, including the parts omitted for the stage representation, in the privacy and silence of his own house. This observation becomes quite clear when turning to Davenant's plays published in the *folio* edition. The separation of the two types of texts is indicated in the title page, which bears the title "The Works of Sr William Davenant Kt Consisting of Those which were formerly Printed, and Those which he *design'd for the Press*: Now Published Out of the Authors Originall Copies," a publication that excludes the adapted *Hamlet*, but includes Davenant's second adaptation, *The*

Law Against Lovers (which does not have the introductory paratextual apparatus).

Thomas Shadwell's title page "The history of Timon of Athens, the man-hater. As it is acted at the Dukes Theatre. *Made into a play*" [italics mine] (1678) leads one to believe that, before Shadwell, *Timon* was not a play, and that, in adapting it, it is Shadwell himself that gives it a shape that enables one to call it a play. This idea is reiterated in the final part of the work's dedicatory epistle to the Duke of Buckingham wherein the adapter presents his work as such to his patron, thus implicitly stating his opinion on Shakespeare and the source text:

> I am now to present your Grace with this History of Timon, which you were pleased to tell me you liked, and it is the more worthy of you, since it has the *inimitable* hand of Shakespear in it, which never made more *Masterly strokes* than in this. Yet I can truly say, I have made it into a Play. [italics mine]

The Bard's style is presumed inimitable on the basis that its perfection is unattainable, and his touches are more prominent in this work than in others; but his masterly strokes are scattered and therefore the play can only be called properly a play after the changes made by Shadwell. Shadwell expresses praise for the invisible quality of the creative genius that contrasts with the perfectibility of the visible, material word: once again, the work does not encompass in full the qualities of his quasi-divine creator.

In the preface to the adaptation *Antony and Cleopatra* (1678), Dryden employs some of the most approving tones ever towards Shakespeare. In the space of a few lines, there are several key points of bardolatry: deification ("Divine Shakespeare"),[162] conferment of the title of father of English dramatic poetry, natural genius, and even appreciation for the happiness of expression:

> 'tis almost a *Miracle* that much of his Language remains so pure; and that he who began Dramatique Poetry amongst us, untaught by any, and, as Ben Jonson tells us, without Learning, should by the force of his own *Genius* perform so much, that in a manner he has left no praise for any who come after him.[163] [italics mine]

162 Dryden, preface to *All for Love*.

163 Ibid.

It may sound odd that such a eulogy should stand side by side with reproach, "miracle" and "genius" next to "rubbish." Yet this is what happens when Dryden speaks of Shakespeare. In fact, the above praise to the purity of the Bard's language as a quasi *miracle* is soon clouded by the following condemnation to be found in *Troilus and Cressida*, where shadows of reproof are cast shade on Shakespeare's style. Indeed, these contradictory elements often exist in embarrassing proximity one to the other. In an examination of his contributions to the field of literary criticism, some critics have detected Dryden's ambivalent attitude towards the Bard. One of them who points out the contradictory nature of Dryden's position is Brian Vickers, who successfully highlights this critical oscillation in the volumes he edited dedicated to the review of Shakespearean criticism over time.[164]

It is not surprising therefore that Dryden claims the need he has to remove a "heap of rubbish"[165] from Shakespeare's *Troilus and Cressida* in order to model his adaptation, which was printed in 1679. Before coming to this claim, however, he cautiously praised the Bard by comparing him to Aeschylus, because the Greeks tributed as much "veneration" for him as the British did for their own playwright. "Reverence" for Shakespeare goes beyond the inherent difficulties connected to the English language, which, according to Dryden, unlike Greek, had not yet stabilized, but had, in any case, progressed much since the Elizabethan age. He could thus state that "the tongue in general is so much refin'd since Shakespear's time, that many of his words, and more of his Phrases, are scarce intelligible." This statement, together with "And of those [expressions] which we understand some are ungrammatical, others course [sic]; and his whole stile is so pester'd with Figurative expressions, that it is as affected as it is obscure," views the Bard's English as excessively rhetorical, obscure and very difficult to understand. This is even more true for the language of Shakespeare's early works, among

164 Brian Vickers, *Shakespeare, The Critical Heritage*, 6 vols. (London: Routledge & Kegan Paul, 1974). In fact, the introduction to the first volume states that "Dryden's references to Shakespeare is a curious sequence of ups and downs" (14) and that "Dryden's legacy [on Shakespeare] is a distinctly ambivalent one" (17).

165 This and the following citations are from John Dryden, preface to *Troilus and Cressida*.

which Dryden included *Troilus* (whereas the play is now usually dated at the beginning of the seventeenth century, which means approximately at the middle of the Shakespeare's career as playwright).

According to the adapter, the defects of outdated language are not the fault of the author, but of the time. Shakespeare is also relieved of other responsibilities, which are now attributed to the actors who printed the texts, such as the missing subdivision into acts and the large number of linguistic and typographical errors: "it is not divided into Acts: which fault I ascribe to the Actors, who Printed it after Shakespear's death; and that too, so carelessly, that a more uncorrect Copy I never saw." Overall, the Bard is met with more attacks than compliments. Indeed, the flame of poetic creation is soon weakened: some characters are not well developed, others are not treated according to the dictates of the tragic genre:

> For the Play it self, the Author seems to have begun it with some fire; the Characters of Pandarus and Thersites, are promising enough; but as if he grew weary of his task, after an Entrance or two, he lets 'em fall: and the later part of the Tragedy is nothing but a *confusion* of Drums and Trumpets, Excursions and Alarms. The chief persons, who give name to the Tragedy, are left alive: Cressida is false, and is not punish'd. Yet after all, because the Play was Shakespear's, and that there appear'd in some places of it, *the admirable Genius of the Author*; I undertook to remove that *heap of Rubbish*, under which many excellent thoughts lay wholly bury'd.[166] [italics mine]

As in other cases, Shakespeare's brilliance occasionally illuminates the work ("the Play was Shakespear's, and that there appear'd in some places of it"), but there remain large dark areas subject to improvement. Dryden's intervention is aimed at mending these widespread flaws. It includes a new and more robust plot, achieved by eliminating some characters, by better outlining some of those who remain, and by introducing a new one, Andromache, Hector's wife. The new plot is also achieved through the drastic reduction of scene changes, which in Shakespeare occurred frequently and were often disconnected from the play's main action ("no leaping from Troy to the Grecian Tents, and thence back again in the same Act"). Dryden's also aimed to clarify the original language; his action moves in two directions, sometimes he paraphrases

166 Dryden, preface, to *Troilus and Cressida.*

Shakespeare, sometimes he imitates Shakespeare's style. Compared to its source, the adapted language lacks purity, but gains in meaning:

> I need not say that I have *refin'd* his Language, which before was *obsolete*; but I am willing to acknowledg, that as I have often drawn his English nearer to our times so I have somtimes conform'd my own to his: & consequently, the Language is not altogether so *pure*, as it is significant.[167]

The paratext of the *Troilus and Cressida* adaptation includes the essay "The Grounds of Criticism in Tragedy," in which Shakespeare is once again attacked, this time on more than one front. Adhering to pseudo-Aristotelian rules,[168] Dryden expresses his disapproval of all the historical plays because they do not have a single plot: "As the Action ought to be one … This *condemns* all Shakespears Historical Plays, which are rather Chronicles represented, than Tragedies, and all double action of Plays." On the heels of Rymer, Dryden acknowledges that the plot's flaw almost extends to the whole canon: "How *defective* Shakespear and Fletcher have been in all their Plots, Mr. Rymer has discover'd in his Criticisms." The two playwrights are united by this fault, though it is more serious in the Bard; only in one comedy, *The Merry Wives of Windsor*, is the *plot* satisfactory from the point of view of the "rules":

> In the mechanic beauties of the Plot, which are the Observation of the three Unities, Time, Place, and Action, they are both *deficient*; but Shakespear most. Ben. Johnson reform'd those errors in his Comedies, yet one of Shakespear's was Regular before him: which is, The Merry Wives of Windsor.

The Bard is only appreciated for his concrete achievements such as the construction of his plays' characters: "Tis one of the excellencies of Shakespear, that the manners of his persons are generally apparent; and you see their bent and inclinations." And the example of King Henry IV

167 Ibid.

168 A simple reading of Aristotle's *Poetics* makes it clear that the treatise is not a prescribed text outlining rules to be followed. Rather, it is a descriptive essay of Greek tragedies written up to that time and recognizes their diversity. "Rules," "precepts," and "unities" are concepts deriving from a second reading of Aristotle's work, but are not, in reality, elaborated upon or displayed by the Greek philosopher. In fact, they are superstructures that are later developed. Thus, it is more accurate to speak of pseudo-Aristotelian rules, or neo-Classical rules.

supports this assertion: “But our Shakespear, having ascrib’d to Henry the Fourth the character of a King, and of a Father, gives him the perfect manners of each Relation, when either he transacts with his Son, or with his Subjects.” Because of this, the treatment of characters must be imitated: “So that in this part Shakespear is generally worth our Imitation.” Except for Jonson, however, who occupies the first place. Shakespeare is not the best, despite the large number of characters he created: “To return once more to Shakespear; no man ever drew so many characters, or general’y distinguished ’em better from one another, excepting only Johnson.”

Dryden’s final remarks concern style, which in his view is too obscure, unintelligible, and figurative. Although Shakespeare distinguishes clearly between the triumphant style and the sublime, he

> has his *failings*; but they are not so much in the passions themselves, as in his manner of expression: he often *obscures* his meaning by his words, and sometimes makes it *unintelligible*. I will not say of *so great a Poet*, that he distinguish’d not the *blown puffy stile*, from true *sublimity*; but I may venture to maintain that the *fury of his fancy* often transported him, beyond the bounds of Judgment, either in coyning of new words and phrases, or racking words which were in use, into the violence of a Catachresis: ’Tis not that I would explode the use of Metaphors from passions, for Longinus thinks ’em necessary to raise it; but to use ’em at every word, to say nothing without a Metaphor, a Simile, an Image, or description, is I doubt to smell a little too strongly of the Buskin.[169]

These characteristics differ from a style of phrasing that is bombastic, inflated, and pompous, which is typical of several playwrights, but not of the Bard,

> Wise men would be glad to find a little sence couch’d under all those *pompous words*; for *Bombast* is commonly the delight of that Audience, which loves Poetry, but understands it not: and as commonly has been the practice of those Writers, who not being able to infuse a natural passion into the mind, have made it their business to ply the ears, and to stun their judges by the noise. But Shakespear does not often thus; for the passions in his Scene between Brutus and Cassius are extreamly natural, the thoughts are such as arise from the matter, and the expression of ’em not viciously figurative. I cannot leave this Subject before I do justice to that *Divine Poet*, by giving you one of his passionate descriptions: ’tis of Richard the Second

169 Dryden, preface to *Troilus and Cressida*, n.p.

> when he was depos'd, and led in Triumph through the Streets of London by Henry of Bullingsbrook …[170]

In his preface and critical essay, Dryden displays an attitude that can be said to be, if not typical, quite widespread in his time. Dryden's paratext, in fact, outlines a common attitude among the adapters at the end of the seventeenth century. A study of the preface and critical essay of the poet laureate reveals that Shakespeare is praised as creator, author, poet, and genius ("*the admirable Genius of the Author*," "*so great a Poet*," "*Divine Poet*"), but simultaneously accused and exposed for some of his language and some flawed parts of his plays. Acting as a metaphor in literature, the body and the spirit, the symbolic-based oppositional dualism of Western Christian culture, is here foreshadowed emblematically. On one hand, the invisible spirit of the quasi-divine Shakespeare is perfect; on the other, the visible body – the *corpus* of texts – is an imperfect creation that is further corrupted by external agents. This binary opposition, subsumed by philosophical Aristotelian concepts of being-in-power and being-in-place, or more simply form versus substance, appears in the following image that separates pairs into dichotomies such as word and thought, unnecessary and necessary, nonvalue and value:

> If Shakespear were stript of all the Bombast in his passions, and dress'd in the most vulgar words, we should find the beauties of his thoughts remaining; if his embroideries were burnt down, there would still be *silver* at the bottom of the melting-pot.[171]

Dryden's concluding declaration stating that "Shakespear had an Universal mind" is thus inevitable, and its praise is significantly crystallized. To obtain a nonidealistic representation that transcends the absolute, but that at the very least also considers the second element of this type of conceptual chiasm, it is important to add a coda, which, I imagine, would sound something like this: "Shakespeare had an universal mind, *but a particular hand*."

During the period of the crisis unleashed by Titus Oates and referred to as the Popish Plot, John Crowne, in his work's dedicatory epistle to

170 Ibid.

171 Ibid.

Sir Charles Sedely, expressed his opinion on the Bard and on *2 Henry VI*, from which his adaptation (printed in 1681) proceeds:

> For though Shakespear be generally very delightful, he is not so always. His Volumn is all up-hill and down; Paradise was never more pleasant than some parts of it, nor Ireland and Greenland colder, and more uninbabirable then others. And I have undertaken to cultivate one of the most barren Places in it. The Trees are all Shrubs, and the Men Pigmies, nothing has any Spirit, or shape; the Cardinal is duller then ever Priest was.[172]

Once again, Shakespeare is "very delightful" when viewed from a general and abstract standpoint, while, from a concrete and particular angle, *2 Henry VI* is, on the whole, "one of the most barren Places" of his dramaturgical work.

The only change seems to come from the negative criticism of the Cardinal character. Given Crowne's reasons for composing the adaptation, which he expressed in the opening of his letter ("this Play is no indifferent Satyre upon the most pompous fortunate and potent Folly, that ever reigned over the minds of men, called Popery"),[173] it is not surprising that the Shakespearean counterpart is branded as "duller then ever" and, in the adaptation, transformed into a villain without a conscience.

In the dedicatory epistle to the patron of Nahum Tate's *Richard II* (1681) it is revealed that its staging was prohibited only three days after its appearance in theaters ("Silenc'd on the Third Day").[174] With good reason, the adapter was quite opposed to this decision, given that it was from the third day of the representation, that the playwright began to benefit from the income from a percentage of box office revenues, after the expenses incurred by the theater are covered. The censorship was triggered by political motives, despite the fact that the play "still retains the *immortal Spirit* of its first-Father,"[175] and that the Bard was generally considered a neutral and impartial playwright. As is customary, Shakespeare's invisible quality, immortal spirit, and poetic flame are taken into account, but also this time it is embodied in a *history* that is

172 John Crowne, "Epistle Dedicatory," *Henry the Sixth*, n.p.

173 Ibid.

174 Nahum Tate, "Epistle Dedicatory," *The History of King Richard The Second*, n.p.

175 Ibid.

perfectible at least. Indeed, in the new *Richard II* the patron, his first reader, will find "*some Master Touches* of our Shakespear, that will Vie with the best Roman Poets,"[176] while the rest will be altered. Therefore the Bard can compete with the classics but only in well defined places in the text; these passages are saved by Tate and incorporated into his adaptation; the rest is altered.

The changes made by Tate follow a clear design. As he does not accept the crude realism of the original – "Our Shakespear in this Tragedy, bated none of his Characters an Ace of the Chronicle; he took care to she 'em no worse Men than They were, but represents them never a jot better," the characters are changed, among which the first is Richard II. In fact, Tate says of the King: "My Design was to engage the pitty of the Audience for him in his Distresses, which I cou'd never have compass'd had I not before shewn him a Wise, Active and Just Prince." Tate's alterations are of two different kinds, at least; sometimes he changes an existing scene, such as when he mitigates the harsh accusatory words of the King's opponents, or when he presents as temporary the King's acquisition of the Gaunt family's annuity; sometimes he adds a brand new scene, such as the one before Richard's deposition, in an attempt to remove the sense of weakness and fragility of an anointed King, very much present in Shakespeare.

In the dedicatory epistle of his adaptation of *Coriolanus* (1682), Tate acknowledges his debt towards Shakespeare through metaphorical language:

> I have not yet another Plea for Pardon, since I impose not on your Lordship's Protection a work merely of my own Compiling; having in this Adventure Launcht out in Shakespear's Bottom. Much of what is offered here, is Fruit that grew in the *Richness of his Soil*; and what ever the Superstructure prove, it was my good fortune to *build upon a Rock*.[177]

Nature and fertility, frequently associated with Shakespeare, allow the adaptation to achieve the ripeness of a fruit, grown thanks to the richness of the soil. Then is a shift to the sacred, with a reference to the Bible, Matthew's Gospel, 7:24–25, Jesus' speaking:

---

176 Ibid.

177 Nahum Tate, "Epistle Dedicatory," *The Ingratitude of a Common-Wealth*, n.p.

24 Therefore everyone who hears these words of Mine and acts on them, may be compared to a wise man who built his house on the rock.
25 And the rain fell, and the floods came, and the winds blew and slammed against that house; and yet it did not fall, for it had been founded on the rock.

A shift that notwithstanding the persistence of the natural element "rock," shifts the semantic field to architecture, in a crystallized expression meaning "constructing on solid foundations," where "superstructure" is the Shakespearean alteration. The source text is seen as a base, an origin that is *natural* and *divine*, while the adapted play is a human work of art whose solidity is guaranteed by its foundations. As in other cases, Shakespeare is linked with Nature and fruitfulness and with the sacred word of the son of the Christian God.

In the dedicatory epistle to his adaptation of *King Lear* (1681), Tate perceives "Shakespear's Creating Fancy"[178] as excessive, overabundant, disordered, and only the Bard fortunately uses the language that expresses it:

> The Images and Language are so odd and surprising, and yet so agreeable and proper, that whilst we grant that none but Shakespear cou'd have form'd such Conceptions, yet we are satisfied that they were the only Things in the World that ought to be said on those Occasions.[179]

For this reason Tate abundantly employs a less archaic style – one that is stylistically and metaphorically more somber; he will use "less Quaintness of Expression."[180]

The expression used to define Shakespeare's *Lear*, "a Heap of Jewels, unstrung and unpolisht,"[181] has been met with success, and is often drawn upon to describe the perception of Shakespeare's plays during the Restoration. The full metaphor runs as follows: "I found the whole to answer your Account of it, a Heap of Jewels, unstrung and unpolisht; yet so dazling in their Disorder, that I soon perceiv'd I had seiz'd a Treasure."[182] The Bard's words are like a pile of precious

178 Nahum Tate, "Epistle Dedicatory," *The History of King Lear*, n.p.
179 Ibid.
180 Ibid.
181 Ibid.
182 Ibid.

stones that are unworked and do not have the smooth appearance of a jewel, yet they are brilliant in their *natural* chaos.

A similar configuration of oppositional dualism is to be found in Edward Ravenscroft's adaptation of *Titus Andronicus* (1687). Ravenscroft's bardolatry starts from different premises but it achieves analogous results. Although tradition attributes authorship of *Titus* to Shakespeare, the adapter denies this attribution, and evaluates the play as overall very poor, although, he admits, there are some parts that should not be completely forgotten. In the premise to the reader, Ravenscroft states the following:

> I have been told by some anciently conversant with the Stage, that *it was not Originally his* [Shakespeare's], but brought by a private Author to be Acted, and he only gave some *Master-touches* to one or two of the Principal Parts or Characters; this I am apt to believe, because *'tis the most incorrect and indigested piece in all his Works*; *It seems rather a heap of Rubbish then a Structure.* – However as if some great Building had been design'd, in the removal we found many Large and Square Stones both usefull and Ornamental to the Fabrick, as now Modell'd ...[183]

In this example, the exaltation of Shakespeare's genius assumes a slightly new form. Ravenscroft does not praise a great poet who has created an imperfect work but a great poet who has perfected somebody else's originally mediocre work: Shakespeare's "Master-touches"[184] are the parts that come to constitute the best "Large and Square Stones"[185] gathered and employed in the adaptation. His crude opinion on *Titus*, which is straightforwardly defined "a heap of Rubbish,"[186] is by no means referable to Shakespeare because Ravenscroft erroneously does not consider the Bard author of the play; it echoes Dryden's opinion of *Troilus and Cressida*, where Shakespeare was undoubtedly called under judgment.

There is a résumé of the architectural theme seen in *Coriolanus*, but here it is simplified and devoid of religious undertone. There is now only a "great building" whose removal has brought to light some "large and square stones" that can be reused as ornaments for the new house; the foundation lies elsewhere and is not sacred.

183 Edward Ravenscroft, "To the Reader," *Titus Andronicus*, n.p.

184 Ibid.

185 Ibid.

186 Ibid.

2.2.3 1700–1703: An Historical Play and Three Comedies[187]

The eighteenth century immediately starts with a change, and not only because the death of Dryden. Colley Cibber's preface to his *alteration* to *Richard III* marks a turning point in the perception of Shakespeare's language. The print edition of the adaptation is significantly dated 1700, and in it, the author inserts a reference to Dryden. The edition is noteworthy as it is for a reading public: through typographical symbols Cibber is careful to enable his readers to make an immediate distinction between what is Shakespeare's, either his original word, or his paraphrased word by the adaptor, and what is not Shakespeare's – that is, Cibber's new words. The shift in the linguistic perception of the Bard is thus ratified: the source style is no longer altered in profound and pervasive ways but is otherwise taken as a reference and model. Shakespeare's language is no longer adapted to fit the Restoration one; rather, it is the other way round, it is the adaptor's language that changes to accommodate the pre-existing source. This operation is not simple:

> I have done my best to imitate his Style, and manner of thinking: If I have fail'd, I have still this comfort, that our best living Author in his imitation of Shakespear's Style only writ Great and Masterly.[188]

Cibber foreshadowed an attitude that would develop throughout the century and beyond. It represented the early stage of a new approach to Shakespeare's word that, before the end of the decade, would witness the first of many eighteenth-century editions in the Shakespearean canon. In 1709, Nicholas Rowe published *The Works of William Shakespear*, setting a trend that would be followed by many editions in the eighteenth century.[189]

---

187 Colley Cibber, *The Tragical History of King Richard III* (London, 1700); George Granville, *The Jew of Venice. A Comedy* (London, 1701); John Dennis, *The Comical Gallant: or the Amours of Sir John Falstaffe. A Comedy* (London, 1702); William Burnaby, *Love Betray'd; or, The Agreeable Disappointment. A Comedy* (London, 1703).

188 Cibber, preface to *The Tragical History of King Richard III*, n.p.

189 Alexander Pope, Lewis Theobald, Thomas Hammer, William Warburton, Samuel Johnson, Edward Capell, George Steevens, Isaac Reed, Edmond Malone, and Ambrose Eccles.

In 1701, George Granville adapted *The Merchant of Venice*. The reader's advisory counts *The Jew of Venice* among the long list of Shakespearean adaptations – "too many to mention"[190] – following, in part, the lead of *Richard III* regarding typographical symbols. In fact:

> The Reader may please moreover to take Notice, (that nothing may be imputed to Shakespear which may seem unworthy of him) that such Lines as appear to be markt, are Lines added, to make good the Connexion where there was a necessity to leave out; in which all imaginable Care has been taken to imitate the same fashion of Period, and turn of Stile and Thought with the Original.[191]

The above passage sheds light on the author's willingness, analogous to Cibber's, to identify clearly and separate the Shakespearean parts from those that are not Shakespearean. The distinction was meant not only to associate the Bard with the best parts of the play but also to emphasize that there were two separate authors. It signaled the beginning of a change in literary appropriation, now more conscious and respectful of the textual authority on which it relied on. It also moved in the direction of the recognition of the intellectual property of a work, which, before the end of the decade, led to the drafting of the first English copyright law, the Statute of Anne, which sees the light in the same year of Rowe's *Works of William Shakespeare*, 1709.

Thanks to the measures dictated by the new intellectual sensitivity, every reader of the new text could find changes made to Shakespeare's texts easily:

> What other Alterations have been requisite as to the change of Words, or single Lines, the Conduct of Incidents, and Method of Action throughout the whole Piece, to bring it into the Form and Compass of a Play, would be superfluous to examin, every Reader being able to satisfy himself, if he thinks fit, by comparing.[192]

Following the same course of action taken by Shadwell in his *Timon*, Granville stated that the changes were meant to enable the Shakespearean play to assume a form, dimension, and order that was originally lacking: "to bring it into the Form and Compass of a Play." In fact, according to the expectations of that time, in order to be a true play, a dramatic

190 George Granville, "Advertisement to the Reader," *The Jew of Venice*, n.p.

191 Ibid.

192 Ibid.

text had to follow the neoclassical rules advanced by the French theater, whose diffusion could not be completely ignored by English playwrights.

The dedicatory epistle to John Dennis' *The Comical Gallant* (1702) opens with the fears of the author regarding the reception of his adaptation of *The Merry Wives of Windsor*:

> When I first communicated the design which I had of altering this Comedy of Shakespear, I found that I should have two sorts of People to deal with, who would equally endeavour to obstruct my success. The one believed it to be so admirable, that nothing ought to be added to it; the others fancied it to be so despicable, that any ones time would be lost upon it.[193]

The picture above where two groups stand against the adaptor's plays for opposite reasons may have been quite real, but undoubtedly is a great dialectical hypothesis that enables him to find a third way, a path between the two extremes. Dennis, in fact, concludes his argument by declaring that:

> Thus, Sir, I have endeavoured to convey two things by you to the General Reader, the one, that this Comedy is not so Despicable as to be Incapable of Improvement; the other, that it is not so admirable, as not to stand in need of any.[194]

The adapter begins with the reasons why the comedy ought to be appreciated ("That this Comedy was not despicable, I guess'd for several Reasons"):[195] the primary points are external – that is, they came from somebody else's judgment of the play such as the true appreciation of it expressed by Elizabeth I and other individuals thereafter, during Charles I's age; the secondary points are internal, that is, of the play itself such as the "three or four extraordinary Characters … truly Comical"[196] (he does not mention which ones), and to the vague "happy touches"[197] (he does not say where). On the whole, it cannot be called an "admirable" play, as there are opportunities to make improvements to it: "It was for the above-named reasons, that I thought this by no means a despicable Comedy. And it was for the Reasons which follow, that I believed it not so admirable, but that it might receive improvement."[198] These reasons are external:

193 John Dennis, epistle dedicatory, *The Comical Gallant*, n.p.
194 Ibid.
195 Ibid.
196 Ibid.
197 Ibid.
198 Ibid.

the comedy was written in fourteen days ("in so short a time as this Play was writ, nothing could be done that is perfect"),[199] and its stagings in the Restoration period were not successful ("this Comedy had never upon Revivals had any great success, and that particularly when it was Revived in King Charles the Seconds time").[200] Dennis's opinion does not seem to be first hand: he appeals to third-party opinions of an impressionist kind to motivate both the qualities and the defects of the play. It appears that there is no textual or theatrical critical motivation resulting from personal reflection, thus the adjectives "despicable" and "admirable" are the polar opposites of a sophistic reasoning that ends with the predictable conclusion of the necessity of intervening with an adaptation.

Before concluding, however, Dennis expresses praise for Shakespeare and criticism for his work, following an attitude that is quite widespread, as we have seen. In fact, the adapter explains that his critique "is not said in the least with a design to derogate from Shakespear's *merit*, who performed more than any one else could have done in so short a time. In the alteration I have endeavoured to Correct the foresaid *Errours*,"[201] thus giving *merit* to Shakespeare and excusing him for the *errors* resulting from the quickness with which he composed the work (due to the haste, they are not his fault). The Bard is now a playwright "whose Reputation has been long established,"[202] and yet *The Merry Wives of Windsor* "has strange Defects"[203] that will make it intolerable to the public of the eighteenth-century theater, which cannot be indifferent to the neoclassical principles: "[it] will come to be less endured as the Stage grows more Regular."[204] Observing the French pseudo-Aristotelian rules, Dennis attacks the lack of unity of action in the source play:

> For there are no less than three Actions in it that are independent one of another, which divide and distract the minds of an Audience, there is more than one insignificant Scene, which has nothing to do with any other part of the Play, which is enough to obstruct and stifle the Action.[205]

199 Ibid.
200 Ibid.
201 Ibid.
202 Ibid.
203 Ibid.
204 Ibid.
205 Ibid.

Shakespeare's style is also, once again, under attack: "The Style in some places is stiff and forced and affected, whereas the Dialogue in Comedy ought to be as free as the air."[206] Dennis directed his greatest effort to improve the dialogue: "I have above all things endeavoured to make the Dialogue as easie and free as I could."[207]

However, Dennis' tenuous argumentative dialectic collapses when he admits the true guiding principle for his changes: "In short, I have alter'd every thing which I dislik'd, and retain'd every thing which I or my Friends approved of." These words leave little doubt concerning the strength of his critical convictions and his motivations.

Following Cibber and Granville, William Burnaby, in the preface to *Love Betray'd* (1703), the adaptation of *Twelfth Night*, also claims to use typographical symbols to separate Shakespeare's words from those that are not Shakespeare's. In his adaptation the Bard's language is quantitatively minimal, but Shakespeare's unaltered lines are so well known that the reader would very easily recognize them anyway, even without any typographical mark:

> Part of the Tale of this Play, I took from Shakespear, and about Fifty of the Lines; Those that are his, I have mark'd with Inverted Comma's, to distinguish 'em from what are mine. I endeavour'd where I had occasion to introduce any of 'em, to make 'em look as little like Strangers as possible, but am afraid (tho' a Military Critick did me the honour to say I had plunder'd all from Shakspear) that they wou'd easily be known without my Note of distinction.[208]

2.2.4 1720–1723: Historical Plays and Roman Plays[209]

In the dedicatory epistle to the Duke of Newcastle in *The Invader of his Country* (1720), an adaptation of *Coriolanus*, John Dennis states that

206 Ibid.

207 Ibid.

208 William Burnaby, preface to *Love Betray'd*, n.p.

209 John Dennis, *The Invader of His Country, or The Fatal Resentment, a Tragedy* (London, 1720); Lewis Theobald, *The Tragedy of King Richard III, alter'd from Shakespear* (London, 1720); Aaron Hill, *King Henry The Fifth, or The Conquest of France by the English, a Tragedy* (London, 1723); Ambrose Philips, *Humfrey Duke of Gloucester, a Tragedy* (London, 1723).

his play is an *alteration* without reference to the rhetoric of bardolatry: "I take the Liberty to Dedicate to Your Grace The Invader of his Country, which is the Coriolanus of Shakespear alter'd by me."[210] In a concise and simple manner, Dennis acknowledges his debt to the Shakesperean source by employing words that are very similar to those used in the editorial peritexts of the title pages and titles.

In the dedicatory epistle to the Count of Orrery for the adaptation of *Richard II* (1720), Lewis Theobald used the metaphor of blood, understood symbolically as a bond of kinship, to describe the relationship between the adapted text and the author of the source text in poetic terms. To better elicit compassion, this began with the adaptation ("orphan child")[211] and from there went back to the illustrious father ("Great Parent")[212] through a parentage bond that was assured by the "strong Lines of her Family":[213]

> I now presume to recommend to your Care an Orphan Child of Shakespear; … Whatever Disguise I may have put upon Her, I hope, She retains those strong Lines of her Family, which may entitle Her, as a Descendant from that Great Parent, to Your generous Protection.[214]

The purity of the bloodline comes to convey a double referent: one is internal, being the adapted play and Shakespeare; one is external, being the noble lineage of the patron to which the play is dedicated. The implicit common symbolic likeness is hoped to guarantee the "orphan child" another "great parent." Both physically and metaphorically, this element – blood – is a cornerstone of many religions, including Christianity. Thus, this dedicatory epistle indirectly participates in the universe of discourse idolatrizing the Bard through religious and sacred imagery.

In the opening of the preface, Theobald acknowledges his indebtedness to Shakespeare's source: "I must, like an honest Man, begin first with my largest Debts, and make a Sort of Compensation for the Helps which I have borrowed from Shakespear."[215] He then proceeds using a

210 John Dennis, "Epistle Dedicatory," *The Invader of His Country*, n.p.
211 Lewis Theobald, "Epistle Dedicatory," *The Tragedy of King Richard II*, n.p.
212 Ibid.
213 Ibid.
214 Ibid.
215 Ibid.

Dryden-like bardolatry that acknowledges the Bard's highest merits as well as his concrete faults.

Indeed, Shakespeare is exalted by conferring to him the title of "Father of the British Stage, who founded, rais'd, and modell'd it,"[216] while his plays are relegated to a lower status, and *Richard II* is no exception. Theobald explains his intervention in the original Shakespeare, to whom he credits only the occasional "scatter'd Beauties,"[217] as a necessity to make the play more regular; that is, to make it more compliant with the principle of *decorum* for the characters, and of pseudo-Aristotelian unity for the plot:

> The many scatter'd Beauties, which I have long admir'd in His Life and Death of K. Richard the II, induced me to think they would have stronger Charms, if they were interuoven in a regular Fable. For this Purpose, I have made some Innovations upon History and Shakespear ... In these, and such Instances, I think there may be reserv'd a discretionary Power of Variation, either for maintaining the Unity of Action, or supporting the Dignity of the Characters.[218]

His bardolatry, therefore, still idolizes Shakespeare and praises his invisible and general qualities ("The Strenght, and Vigour, of his Fancy"; "the Delicacy of his Spirit"),[219] but it does not hold Shakespeare's visible output in the form of text or word in such high regard:

> The Strength, and Vigour, of his Fancy have been confess'd, and admir'd, in the extravagant and supernatural Characters of his own Creation, such as his Caliban, Witches, &c. And give me Leave to take Notice of the Delicacy of his Spirit in One Instance; because the Observation has not, that I know of, ever yet been started by Any body. No Dramatic Poet, before Shakespear, in any Language that I know, or remember, has heighten'd his Distress from the Concurrence of the Heavens, as He has done in his Lear.[220]

Both text and speech – the concrete materializations of the creative genius – are perceived as misleading, excessive, and almost a byproduct of excess of flair and imagination. This disorder, however, can be seen

216 Ibid.
217 Ibid.
218 Ibid.
219 Ibid.
220 Ibid.

in a more positive light if viewed alongside Homer, as even the first and greatest poets of all Western culture possessed this kind of flaw:

> Shakespear is allowed by All to have had the most wonderful Genius, and the warmest imagination, of any Poet since the Name of Homer. As these Qualities led him to say, and express, many Things sublimely, figuratively, and elegantly; so they often forc'd him out of his Way, upon false Images, hard Metaphors, and Flights, where the Eye of Judgment cannot trace him. This Fault He has in common with All great Wits: Homer is accus'd of It by the Antients.[221]

A classic among the Classics, the author of the *Iliad* and the *Odyssey* offers Theobald an opportunity to present some counterevidence demonstrating the Bard's knowledge of the Classics: ("I could, with the greatest Ease imaginable, produce above 500 Passages from these Plays to evidence his Intimacy with the Latin Classicks").[222] The opponents are in a no-win situation, either they acknowledge Shakespeare's learning or praise him even more for his bond with Nature and Wit. Anyone who denies the learning of the Bard is in fact indirectly praising Shakespeare for "his Wit and Natural Parts":

> The Second Motive, which I had for setting to Work on this Story, was, that it would afford me an Opportunity, in confessing my Obligations to Shakespear, of doing him some Justice upon the Points of his Learning, and Acquaintance with the Antients: Both which have not only been contested, but even denied him in positive Terms. Perhaps, in robbing Him of these Secondary Aids, they might design a Compliment to the Force, and Extensiveness, of his Wit and Natural Parts.[223]

A necessary consequence is that Ben Jonson is faulted for enabling the notion of a Shakespeare who is unacquainted with the Classics:

> They, who affirm that Shakespear was wholly unacquainted with the Antients, beg the Question; and, perhaps, have been unreasonably led into that Error by the false Opinion of Some of his Contemporaries, and the falser Interpretation of their Meaning by Some Moderns. Ben Johnson seems to be the Original from whence they copy One after Another; and the farther from Him, still the more erroneously.[224]

---

221 Ibid.

222 Ibid.

223 Ibid.

224 Ibid.

For preciseness' sake, in the paratexts of the first Shakespearean *folio* of 1623, Jonson declared that the Bard had "small Latine, and lesse Greeke," and not that "Shakespear was *wholly* unacquainted with the Antients" – something that Theobald must have been aware of when saying "the farther from him [Jonson] still the more erroneously." In fact, he proceeds in this line of thought when he points out that "It is very evident, that Ben [Jonson] allows him some Share of Knowledge in both these learned Languages."[225] Theobald himself declares his aim: to "present Shakespear to be a better Scholar, than his Countrymen yet have been willing to acknowledge Him,"[226] a quest that, if pushed too far, could attribute to Shakespeare a wide humanistic learning, which he actually did not possess, and therefore hypothesizing a hypercorrection that does not reflect reality as it falls into the opposite extreme.

Among the conceptual nuclei that have so far appeared in the present discussion on bardolatry, the figure of Shakespeare emerges from the above paratext as the *English Homer*, an epithet that will later on crystallize and become formulaic over time. This is another step towards positioning Shakespeare at the center of English culture, thus elevating him to the status of a cultural hero, and giving "the English Homer" an eternal place among the English epithets alongside those coined by Homer himself in his native language such as "rosy-fingered Dawn," "swift-footed Achilles," and many others.

Theobald's paratext is not only a defense of the Bard's learning, but also a contribution to bardolatry. Dryden was another who highly praised Shakespeare, as we have seen, but in Theobald the negative critiques of the Bard are much less prominent than those of Dryden. In fact, throughout the two prefatory texts, there are several expressions of encomium tributed to Shakespeare celebrating different aspects of the "father of the British stage," whose "most wonderful genius," is creator of some "scattered beauties" in his play(s); the "strenght [sic] and vigour of his fancy," "delicacy of his spirit," "warmest imagination," and "wit" undoubtedly make him the greatest poet, the "English Homer," as we have just seen.

In the preface to the reader in the 1723 adaptation of *King Henry V*, Aaron Hill openly declares his debt to Shakespeare, articulating his

225 Ibid.
226 Ibid.

veneration of the Bard using a widespread common rhetoric that is not original, either in terms or in concepts. Laudatory adjectives are not innovative, neither is the image of a new written version as a new dress or fabric; nor least of all the poetic declaration that would use Shakespearean foundations to create a new dramatic building that is at the same time both true to and better than the textual source which founds it:

> The inimitable, and immortal, Shakespeare, about a hundred and thirty Years since, wrote a Play, on this Subject, and call'd it, The Life of King Henry, the Fifth: – Mine is a New Fabrick, yet I built on His Foundation; and the Reader, I am afraid, will, too easily, discover, without the Help of a Comparison, in what Places I am indebted to him.[227]

The last play of this group is *Humfrey Duke of Gloucester*, an *alteration* of *2 Henry VI* (1723). Ambrose Philips is one of the four adapters[228] who identify and separate Shakespeare's word from that which is not Shakespeare's. In this case intervention is not shown by the use of typographical symbols but is declared in a statement listing the Shakespearean textual places, which have been either faithfully borrowed or lightly paraphrased. Philips places this statement before the dramatic text, in the reader's advisory:

> They, who have read Shakespear's Second Part of Henry VI may, probably, recollect most of the Passages, I have borrowed from Him, either Word for Word, or with some small Alteration. Nevertheless, that I may not be thought unwilling to Acknowledge my Obligation to so great a Poet; I desire my Readers will place to his Account, One or Two Hints, and One intire Line, in the 24th Page, where Eleanor's Penance is related: Four Lines, in the 38th Page, where Beaufort speaks of Gloucester's Popularity: Three Parts in Four of the Description of the Duke's dead Body, in Page 71: And about Seventeen Lines in the last Scene; some of which are so very beautifull, that it may be questioned, whether there be any Passages, in Shakespear, that deserve greater Commendation.[229]

227 Aaron Hill, "Preface to the Reader," *King Henry The Fifth*, n.p.

228 The other three adapters are Colley Cibber, George Granville, and William Burnaby.

229 Ambrose Philips, "To the Reader," *Humfrey Duke of Gloucester*, n.p.

2.2.5 Conclusions

In the first decades of Restoration, the general picture of bardolatry emerging from the various prefatory peritexts is not completely homogeneous. This situation can partly be ascribed to the many hands that had their part in it (especially as one of them is Dryden's).

On the one side, there are praises for a sublime Shakespeare, which becomes a concept transcending time and materiality: the man, author, and poet, is a quasi-divine figure, a genius that pertains to an eternal super celestial sphere. On the other side, there are reproaches for a flawed work (or rather parts of it), which is an object inextricably rooted in time and materiality; language is the thing to blame, as it is the means through which the work takes shape. Why a perfect creator creates in an imperfect way is never explained.

Another explanation for this situation can be found if we bear in mind that there was a lively literary debate, at the time, discussing neoclassical theory, so this may well have affected the opinions of some critics and adapters on the specific issue of language regarding Shakespeare. Seen from an historical perspective, this ambivalence was only temporary: the attacks on Shakespeare's language were specific and more frequent at the time when the literary debate on the principles of neoclassicism was at its strongest. It vanished as time passed, eventually reaching the point where absolute praise was given to the works of Shakespeare.

A third possible reason for the temporary condemnation of Shakespeare's language in the second part of the seventeenth century can be explained with an even more broadly cultural theory. According to this theory, each age affirms itself by opposition and negation towards the preceding one, and the closer is the time, the stronger is the movement against the preceding age.

Restoration society and culture had to affirm themselves by opposition to what preceded them – the Elizabethan age (here considered in its broadest time span). After the return of Charles II to the throne, as time passed, the drive against what was considered a barbarous time and an obscure language weakened, and the elements that were previously stigmatized begin to be absorbed in a process that would lead them to be fully accepted.

In fact, some adaptations published from the beginning of the eighteenth century point towards a new approach to the Bard that would be further developed by Rowe and the editors of the Shakespearean canon who followed him. The earlier attitude to the Bard's language freely and deeply intervened on the text; it brought clarity at the expenses of polyphony and polysemy.

Cibber, Granville, and Burnaby, and then Bullock and Philips, brought increasing attention and care to the Shakespearean word itself and, consequently, different ideas regarding adaptation. Source text was highlighted, marked, and separated from adapted text. There were no longer the changes and alterations made to the language of the early Restoration period, when the aim was to paraphrase and simplify Shakespeare with the result that the complexity and richness of Shakespeare's polysemy at the philosophical and poetic level was flattened or even removed outright. At the conceptual level, the new approach introduced, although in a rudimentary and imperfect manner, some of the principles that would subsequently be developed and perfected, beginning with Rowe's edition of the Shakespearean canon in 1709.

The contrast between Shakespeare and his word, between the Bard and his language, thus gradually disappeared, thanks in part to the change of cultural attitudes in the eighteenth century, which would eventually give rise to philology.

2.3 Dramatic Peritext: Prologues and Epilogues

2.3.1 Introductory Remarks

Before concluding my discussion on the peritexts, it will be worth analyzing the dramatic peritext, with special attention to the prologue and epilogue (and omitting stage directions). The parts comprising the prefatorial peritext are addressed to the patron and the reader, and function as the presentation and introduction for the text to be read: thus, they frame the written record of the play. The prologue and epilogue are usually much closer to the play itself and, enclosing it, constitute its extremes:

thus, they comprise the internal framework of the play. Sometimes read when the curtain is down, they address the theater's audience to request their favor: acting as a *captatio benevolentiae*, they perform a function similar to the dedicatory epistle so as to eventually receive the addressees' concrete financial support, whether directly from the patron to the author in the form of a grant, or indirectly from the theater to the playwright in the form of a percentage of the revenues from repeating performances.

Regarding Shakespearean adaptations, at least, the two elements of the dramatic peritext of the Restoration are branded differently from their counterparts in the preceding age: in some instances, they are allographs because they are not written by the playwright. Their main aim is to gain the public's favour. My analysis, however, does not examine these elements, but, like the study of the editorial and prefatory peritext, it investigates the relation between the peritextual element (the prologue and epilogue) and the construction of Shakespeare as a cultural icon.

2.3.2 The Tempest; Troilus and Cressida; The History and Fall of Caius Marius; The Misery of Civil War[230]

Dryden's relevance as Shakespeare's critic is now widely accepted; Nicholas Rowe supports this view when he includes Dryden's prologue to the adaptation of *The Tempest* in the prefatory essay of his first volume of the *Works of Shakespear*, "Some account of the life, & c. of Mr. William Shakespear," which appeared in 1709, 39 years after Davenant and Dryden's adaptation, and 9 years after the death of the latter.

Dryden alone wrote the prologue to this altered version of *The Tempest*. It is a paean sung in honor of Shakespeare; as in a triptych sanctifying his superiority the Bard, taught by none, is placed first among Fletcher and Jonson, to whom he imparted wit and art respectively. The first playwright is a poet of the immediate perception of nature, the

230 William Davenant, and John Dryden, *The Tempest, or The Enchanted Island, A Comedy* (London, 1670); John Dryden, *Troilus and Cressida, or Truth Found too Late* (London, 1679); Thomas Otway, *The History and Fall of Caius Marius, A Tragedy* (London, 1680); John Crowne, *The Misery of Civil War, A Tragedy* (London, 1680).

second of perception re-elaborated by man, and the third of perception mediated by nature through man.

The verses in the opening rhyming couplet present a natural metaphor of tree, root and branches that acknowledges the original textual source of the adaptation:

> As when a Tree's cut down the secret root
> Lives under ground, and thence new Branches shoot
> So, from old Shakespear's *honour'd dust*, this day
> Springs up and buds a new reviving Play.
> Shakespear, who (*taught by none*) did first impart
> To Fletcher *Wit*, to labouring Johnson *Art*.
> He, *Monarch-like*, gave those his subjects law,
> And is that *Nature* which they paint and draw. (vv. 1–8)[231]

Shakespeare's dust is to be honored because the Bard was the king of poets ("*Monarch-like*"); as a king, his power that comes from God is divine and sacred ("Shakespear's pow'r is sacred as a King's," v. 24).

His greatness is such that Jonson and Fletcher may outperform all other playwrights simply gathering the drops of ink falling from his pen: "If they have since out-writ all other men, / 'Tis with the *drops* which fell from Shakespear's Pen" (vv. 13–14). With some imagination we may establish a connection with the Holy Graal, the cup in which Joseph of Arimathea saved some drops of Christ's blood, and create a new imagery where Shakespeare is Christ, Joseph is Jonson and Fletcher, and blood is ink. The poetic creation – the miracle of Shakespeare – is made possible through ink; likewise the creation of a new world – the miracle of Christ – is made possible through blood. Both are unique and unrepeatable, and so is their work: "… Shakespear's Magick could not copy'd be, / Within that Circle none durst walk but he" (vv. 19–20).

The dramatic peritext of the *Troilus and Cressida* adaptation is a very consistent piece of bardolatry. Here Shakespeare is not discussed; it is the very Bard himself who speaks, embodied by Betterton who is "Representing the Ghost of Shakespear." The Bard rises from the realm of shadows, where he stands out from the other poets thanks to the eternity of his poetry, towards which other poets strive to revive their withered vein:

231 William Davenant, and John Dryden, prologue to *The Tempest*, n.p.

See, my lov'd Britons, see your Shakespeare rise,
An awfull ghost confess'd to human eyes!
Unnam'd, methinks, distinguishe'd I had been
From other shades, by this *eternal green*,
About whose *wreaths* the vulgar Poets strive,
And with a touch, their wither'd Bays revive. (vv. 1–6)[232]

The verses that follow these opening couplets reiterate some concepts already expressed in the prefatorial peritext: that is, Shakespeare's alleged absence of literary culture and unfamiliarity with the Greek and Latin classics, his belonging to a confused and barbaric age, the presence of instances of such excellence that makes poetry inalterable:

Untaught, unpractis'd, in a *barbarous Age*,
I found not, but created first the Stage.
And, if I drain'd no Greek and Latin store,
'Twas, that my own abundance gave me more.
On foreign trade I needed not rely
Like fruitful Britain, rich without supply.
In this my rough-drawn Play, you shall behold
Some Master-strokes, so manly and so bold
That he, who meant to alter, found 'em such
He shook; and thought it *Sacrilege* to touch. (vv. 7–16)[233]

It is well worth noting the term "Sacrilege," because it reveals religious overtones common to many other paratexts operating within the conventions of the laudatory rhetoric of the Bard. Here, the amount of sacred words used in the play by Shakespeare that are worth keeping are represented by a few "Master-Strokes" only; as we know, as time passes, these few words will increase until they comprise the whole text. Dryden's *Troilus and Cressida* dates back to the end of the 1670s, so this adaptation can be counted among the precursors of the seventeenth-century spirit animating the editors of the Shakespearean canon, whose aim was to preserve the word of the Bard. These editors began to search, defend, and appreciate Shakespeare's language in a process that, as it slowly defined itself over time, would move from fragmentation to unity, as dealing with the language not of the single play, but of Shakespeare's whole dramatic production.

232 John Dryden, prologue to *Troilus and Cressida*, n.p.
233 Ibid.

There's more. Shakespeare is also said to be the creator of English theater and drama, as if it had not existed before him: "I found not, but created first the Stage" (8). He stands out as a godlike demiurgical figure: there was nobody before him, nobody with him (Jonson and Fletcher are not mentioned), nobody after him "Now, where are the successours to my name? / What bring they to fill out a Poets fame?" (17–18).

The beginning of the prologue, logically and semantically connected to the following v. 12, is very powerful, and deserves a detailed account. Dryden forges a strong bond between Britain and Shakespeare, taking a decisive step towards "the making of the national poet," to use Michael Dobson's words. From the metrical point of view, the neat half-line caesura sustains the simple yet elegant rhetorical play, an anaphora (see/see) immediately followed by an antithesis (my/your), whose aim is to merge Britons (and Britain) with Shakespeare. A few lines later, the ghost regains and reinforces the bond with a simile that transfers the qualities of Britain to himself: "Like fruitfull Britain, rich without supply" (12). It would be harder to be more concise if one wanted to unite concepts of homeland, fruitfulness, richness, and the national poet. This is one of the clearest cases of bardolatry in which Shakespeare is Britain.

The Prologue to *The History and Fall of Caius Marius* shows, like the previous prologue by Dryden, evident features of bardolatry. The quotation below is "a glowing homage to Shakespeare, whom Otway has imitated in part of his play."[234] He declares that the Bard is the best poet of his time:

> Our Shakespear wrote too in an Age as blest,
> The happiest Poet of his time and *best.*
> A gracious Prince's Favour chear'd his Muse,
> A constant Favour he ne'r fear'd to lose.
> Therefore he wrote with *Fancy unconfin'd,*
> And *Thoughts* that were *Immortal* as his *Mind.*
> And from the Crop of his luxuriant Pen
> E're since succeeding Poets humbly glean.
> Though much the most unworthy of the Throng,
> Our this-day's Poet fears h' has done him wrong.
> Like greedy Beggars that steal Sheaves away,

234 Pierre Danchin, ed., *The Prologues and Epilogues of the Restoration 1660–1700: A Complete Edition* (Nancy: Publications Université Nancy II, 1981–88), II, iii, 206.

> You'll find h' has rifled him of half a Play.
> Amidst this baser Dross you'll see it shine
> Most beautifull, amazing, and *Divine*. (vv. 20–33)[235]

It is possible to perceive lexical echoes of expressions also encountered in Dryden such as "Fancy unconfin'd" and "fury of his fancy,"[236] or "luxuriant Pen" and "abundance/fruitfull/rich,"[237] referring to recurrent lexica of bardolatry.

There is a return to praising the transcendent eternal Shakespeare – that is, a "Mind" creating "Thoughts" that are immortal. In this case, the contingent element – the *play* – his creation, is also eulogized. Although not considered as a whole, the original parts "shine/Most beautifull, amazing, and Divine" as a reflection of the godlike quality of the Bard, and rise above the "baser Dross" of the other, more recent parts of the adaptation. This is another case where lexica relating to the sacred continue to be apparent; initially, they were only connected to the creator, but here their connection with the created element begins to show more clearly. After its first performance in October 1679, *The History and Fall of Caius Marius* was also privately staged at Southwick House, Richard Norton's seat in Hampshire, in the middle[238] or summer[239] of 1708 rather than in 1687. On this occasion, a different prologue introduces the play. Shakespeare and his work are both commended, as this is a

> … Play
> Whose stock by y.e Great Shakespeares Hand was set
> In whom all Nature all y.e Graces met
> With Charming Verdure did its Branches shoot
> And tho yet Wild it bore Dilicious fruit (14–18)

The Bard's poetic creation is eulogized: his great hand wrote a play where all nature and poetic graces are encompassed; it is a delicious

235 Thomas Otway, prologue to *The History of the Fall of Caius Marius*, n.p.

236 Dryden, "The Grounds of Criticism in Tragedy." We also see this echoes, earlier, in John Milton's *L'Allegro*: "… Shakespeare, Fancy's child, / Warble[s] his native wood-notes wild" (vv. 133–4) (Oxford: Oxford Clarendon Press, 1893), 8.

237 Prologue of *Troilus and Cressida*, discussed above.

238 Danchin, ed. *The Prologues and Epilogues of the Restoration 1660–1700*, 45.

239 Pierre Danchin, ed, *Prologues and Epilogues of the Eighteenth Century: A Complete Edition*, 4 vols. (Nancy: Presses Universitaires de Nancy, 1990) I, i, 408.

fruit. But the growth of this play is also wild, and therefore it is unsurprising if grafting may bring improvement, or if transplanting can help flourishing:

> Grafted by Outways Art it still Improv'd
> And in y.e Nicest Court was praisd & Lov'd
> Transplanted here by Judicious Care
> A Skillfull hand has made it flourish here (19–22)

The semantic field of the sacred encountered in the first prologue of *Caius Marius* is also to be found in the prologue to John Crowne's *The Misery of Civil War*, where the term "Divine" appears, an term attributed to Shakespeare that begins to take the form of a formulaic epithet. In this case, Crowne, the author of this adaptation of *2 Henry VI*, employs this term to claim his total authorship of the work, whereas the Bard, according to him, did not contribute at all to the text's new construction: "For by his feeble Skill 'tis built alone, / The *Divine* Shakespeare did not lay one Stone."[240]

2.3.3 2 Henry VI; King Richard the Second; King Lear; The Ingratitude of a Common-Wealth[241]

Henry VI: The First Part, with the Murder of Humphrey Duke of Gloucester is Crowne's adaptation of *2 Henry VI*, written after *The Misery of Civil War*, which adapted *1 Henry VI*. Unlike his first adaptation, in the prologue of his second adaptation Crowne now admits the Shakespearean source using a botanical metaphor: the overall written *corpus* of plays is a kitchen garden while the individual plays comprising this *corpus* are plants, which are considered immortal. It is worth noting that, in this case, it is not the Bard but his plays that are depicted as eternal.

240 John Crowne, prologue to *The Misery of the Civil War*, n.p.

241 John Crowne, *Henry the Sixth, The First Part, with the Murder of Humphrey Duke of Gloucester* (London, 1681); Nahum Tate, *The History of King Richard The Second, Acted at the Theatre Royal, Under the Name of the Sicilian Usurper* (London, 1681); Nahum Tate, *The History of King Lear* (London, 1681); Nahum Tate, *The Ingratitude of a Common-Wealth, or The Fall of Caius Martius Coriolanus* (London, 1682).

To make the adaptation even more appealing to the tastes of the time, Crowne adds "vinegar" (34) to the smooth, "oyly" (32) words of Shakespeare – that is to say an antipapist satire, as is evident in the concluding part of the Prologue:

> To day we bring old gather'd Herbs, 'tis true,
> But such as in sweet Shakespears Garden grew.
> And all his Plants *immortal* you esteem,
> Your Mouthes are *never* out of taste with him.
> Howe're to make your Appetites more keen,
> Not only oyly Words are sprinkled in;
> But what to please you gives us better hope,
> A little vinegar against the Pope. (vv. 27–34)[242]

The plea for the audience's favor is based here on the dimension of eternity of plays that are "plants immortal" (29), "never out of taste" (30) from which the author made his adaptation, and which he hoped would bring along also more material returns, due to their likely success in an age where there was growing public influence in determining the triumph or failure of a play, and, consequently, the eventual financial return for the author.

In the epilogue, an equestrian metaphor was used to reiterate the same theme, with a fear that the adaptation, despite originally coming from the Bard, "Shackspears breed" (v. 7),[243] and therefore endowed with "Mettle, Courage, Shape, or Speed" (8), would not, in any case, gain the public's favor:

> Now some fine things perhaps you think to hear,
> But he who did reform this Play does swear
> He'll not bestow rich Trappings on a *Horse*,
> That will want Breath to run a Three-days Course;
> And be turn'd off by Gallants of the Town,
> For Citizens and their Wives to Hackney on.
> Not that a Barb that's come of *Shackspears breed*,
> Can e're want Mettle, Courage, Shape, or Speed;
> But you have Poetry so long rides Post,
> That your delight in Riding now is lost. (vv. 1–10)[244]

242 John Crowne, prologue to *Henry the Sixth, The First Part*, n.p.

243 Ibid., Epilogue, n.p.

244 Ibid.

Tate exhibited a similar sense of apprehension in his epilogue to *Richard II*, in which he was even less flattering towards the public, whose capacities to judge he seriously questioned. Perhaps he feared a negative response towards a historical play that, before the closure of theaters, was "famous Sense" (v. 4):[245]

> Now we expect to hear our rare Blades say
> Dam' me, I see no Sense in this dull Play;
> Tho much of it our abler Judges know,
> *Was famous Sense* 'bove *Forty Years ago*.
> Sometimes we fail to Please for want of Witt
> Ith' Play – but more for want on't in the Pitt;
> For many a ruin'd Poëts Work 'twou'd Save,
> Had you but half the Sense you think you have. (vv. 1–8)[246]

In the prologue to the adaptation of *King Lear*, "Shakespear's praise" (13) was developed by the connection between a reference to the sacred and to nature with its abundance using a metaphor that established a correspondence between flowers and play. Tate hopes success for his adaptation "since in *rich* Shakespear's *soil* it grew" (8); the "*plenteous* Flow'rs" (14) that are the play "a Pow'r *Divine* first made 'em Grow" (16), so even a "course Hand" (15) may easily succeed in composing a "Garland" (14) out of them.

In accordance with the spirit of the age, the (radical) changes introduced by Tate[247] aimed to make "Morals" (19) more evident and introduce "Order" (12) where it was not present. Order was the link that joined a fracture between the Bard, "Divine," and his play "this Heap of Flow'rs." Though the power that created the flowers comprising the play was divine, the order of their composition was not – this is how Tate justified his job:

> Yet hopes, since in *rich* Shakespear's *soil* it grew,
> 'Twill relish yet with those whose Tasts are True,
> And his Ambition is to please a Few.
> If then this Heap of Flow'rs-shall chance to wear
> Fresh Beauty in the Order they now bear,
> Ev'n this Shakespear's *Praise*; each Rustick knows

245 Nahum Tate, epilogue to *The History of King Richard The Second*, n.p.

246 Ibid.

247 Love between Edgar and Cordelia, and a happy ending to the play.

'Mongst *plenteous* Flow'rs a Garland to Compose,
Which strung by his course Hand may fairer Show,
But 'twas a *Pow'r Divine* first made 'em Grow. (vv. 8–16)[248]

In the epilogue of the same tragedy, the adapter called on the public to distinguish between what was Shakespearean and what was not, inviting it to criticize the altered parts but also to recognize the original "many Master-Touches" (another recurrent expression of praise) that "shine" (22). It was hoped that the adaptation would meet the audience's favor thanks to its solid grounding upon the lawful authority of the "great Shakespear's Right" (24), but if even this should be not sufficient to render the whole representation pleasant, Tate called for a reversal of logic through which then the "Play" can condemn the "Judgement" of the public and not vice versa:

Well – since y'are All for blustring in the Pit,
This Play's Reviver humbly do's admit
Your abs'lute Pow'r to damn his Part of it;
But still so many *Master-Touches* shine
Of that vast Hand that first laid this Design,
That in great Shakespear's Right, He's bold to say
If you like nothing you have seen to Day
The Play your Judgment damns, not you the Play. (vv. 19–26)[249]

The prologue to *The Ingratitude of a Common-Wealth*, Tate's adaptation of *Coriolanus*, written by Sir George Raynsford, "stresses the fact that the play is founded on Shakespeare (vv. 10–15)."[250] Shakespearean praise is displayed with an intermingling of holiness, *imagery* of precious elements, and financial references:

Yet he presumes we may be safe to Day,
Since Shakespear gave Foundation to the Play:
'Tis Alter'd – and his *sacred* Ghost appeas'd;
I wish you All as easily were Pleas'd:
He only ventures to make *Gold* from Oar,
And turn to *Money*, what lay dead before. (vv. 10–15)[251]

---

248 Nahum Tate, prologue, *The History of King Lear*, n.p.

249 Ibid., epilogue, n.p. = [Nahum Tate, epilogue, *The History of King Lear*, n.p.].

250 Danchin, II, iii, 349.

251 Nahum Tate, prologue to *The Ingratitude of a Common-Wealth*, n.p.

There are two motives that have already appeared. The first is "Shakespear ... Ghost" (11–12), which is here again evoked, and which, as is customary, is qualified with adjectives referring to the religious-sacred sphere. The second is "To make Gold from Oar" (14): despite the transcendent perfection of the Bard, his creations can still be perfected, improved, and refined: the dramatic source is like a raw mineral from which it is possible to extract, if adequately treated and purified, the most noble of all metals. "Gold" belongs to the same semantic field of economic-financial value as "Money": the attempt to draw material benefit from this adaptation of *Coriolanus* is explicit.

2.3.4 The Jew of Venice; The Comical Gallant; The Sequel of Henry IV; The Invader of his Country[252]

The prologue to George Granville's *The Jew of Venice* uses a new form that is no longer a monologue but a dialogue, thus resurrecting not only Shakespeare but also Dryden through the *mise-en-scène* of a dialogue between the two playwrights. Although the form is new, the rhetoric is not because it reiterates concepts that so far have been shown to be common: the two are poet laureates (according to the initial stage direction: "The Ghosts of Shakespear and Dryden arise Crown'd with Lawrel");[253] the Bard is defined according to religious terminology ("reverend Shakespear");[254] moreover, he is associated with Nature, and thus if the public does not appreciate the play it is because they are too far removed from Nature ("They know not Nature, for they tast not Thee");[255] and the Elizabethan age is considered more primitive and backwards than the present one ("These Crimes unknown, in our less polisht Age").[256]

252 George Granville, *The Jew of Venice, a Comedy* (London, 1701); John Dennis, *The Comical Gallant: or The Amours of Sir John Falstaffe, a Comedy* (London, 1702); Thomas Betterton, *The Sequel of Henry the Fourth, with the Humours of Sir John Falstaffe, and Justice Shallow* (London, [1719]); John Dennis, *The Invader of His Country, or the Fatal Resentment, a Tragedy* (London, 1720).

253 George Granville, prologue to *The Jew of Venice*, n.p.

254 Ibid., v. 1.

255 Ibid., v. 13.

256 Ibid., v. 26.

Finally, Granville uses Shakespeare's voice to bring prestige to himself. When he describes *The Merchant of Venice* as a play that is a mere draft of "rude Sketches [of] pencil,"[257] he is being rather modest from a critical standpoint, given that he considers the Bard's play as something imperfect and perfectible. In contrast, he is innovative in his decision to not attribute to Shakespeare the usual "Master stroakes," which he reserves for himself instead. Granville, however, goes further by also attributing to himself a "faultless hand,"[258] which, during those times, was very rarely recognized in others, including the Bard. Granville thus displays an excessive and narcissistic sense of self-satisfaction:

> The first rude Sketches Shakespear's Pencil drew,
> But all the shining *Master stroakes* are new.
> This Play, ye Criticks, shall your Fury stand,
> Adorn'd and rescu'd by a *faultless Hand*. (vv. 37–40)[259]

In the Prologue to the adaptation of *The Merry Wives of Windsor*, Dennis' praise of Shakespeare is muted, outwardly attributing the comedy's imperfections to the speed with which it was written, and yet demonstrating appreciation for the final product:

> But Shakespear's Play in fourteen days was writ,
> And in that space to make all just and fit,
> Was an attempt surpassing human Wit.
> Yet our *great* Shakespear's *matchless* Muse was such,
> None e're in so small time perform'd so much. (vv. 11–15)[260]

Not long after, however, the conclusion of the prologue to *The Comical Gallant* reveals the adapter's true position, which is reminiscent of the main critical course of action seen here thus far. Granville expresses an obsequious and religious admiration for the poet and creator, employing rhetoric that is by now standard ("master touches," "Sacriledge").[261] This rhetoric acts as a counterpoint to the *play*, which is criticized for its many *errors* that require *correction* in order to obtain a *uniform* and

257 Ibid., v. 37.
258 Ibid., v. 40.
259 Ibid.
260 John Dennis, prologue to *The Comical Gallant*, n.p.
261 Ibid., vv. 21–22.

normal dramatic text that follows the principles of *Art* (neoclassical), and not only those of Nature (Shakespearean):

His *master touches*, so exact, so true,
We thought it *Sacriledge* to change for new,
Except a very few which ne're could joyn,
In the same just and *uniform* design.
His haste some *errors* caus'd, and some neglect,
Which we with care have labour'd to *correct*,
Then since to please we have try'd our little *Art*,
We hope you'll pardon ours for Shakespear's part. (vv. 21–28)[262]

Thomas Betterton's adaptation *The Sequel of Henry IV*[263] comes with not one, but two prologues, none of which is written by the adapter himself. The first, written by Sewell, presents the Bard as the father of English theater and as a playwright who blends serious and tragic elements of war with Falstaff's light and comedic elements: "Shakspear who gave our English Stage its Birth,/Here makes a medley Scene of War, and Mirth" (vv. 1–2).[264] When the Bard does not follow neoclassical rules ("If sometimes, devious from old Rules be strays,/And treads a-wry from Aristotle's ways"),[265] he cannot be blamed. In his apologia, Sewell does not accuse the man, but the times, exclaiming this directly to the pubic: "Yet you great Judges, sometimes wink at Crimes,/Most were not his, but Errors of the Times!" (vv. 21–22).[266]

Through a fencing metaphor, the eulogy accords strength and power to the coarse and confused language of Shakespeare, rendering all apologias superfluous, as the value of the Bard's creation is confirmed by the past and present success of his dramaturgy both as a staged representation and a printed text:

Like *wanton* Fencers, some *rude* Stroaks he made,
To show the *strength* and *toughness* of his Blade.
But all Apologies for him are wrong,
He proves his *Value*, by his lasting long. (vv. 25–28)[267]

262 Ibid.
263 Thomas Betterton, *The Sequel of Henry the Fourth*.
264 Ibid., "Prologue by Mr. Sewell," n.p.
265 Ibid., vv. 9–10.
266 Ibid.
267 Ibid.

The second prologue, written by Roussillon, is memorable only for its mention of Shakespeare's immortality:

> To touch the ungenerous Breast with conscious Shame,
> To warm the Heart with Love of virtuous Fame,
> To check the raging Passions of the Mind,
> To move the Soul, and civilize Mankind,
> To lash the Crimes of a degenerate Age,
> Were the first Labours of the infant Stage:
> For this the ancient buskin'd Heroes fought,
> And Terence, and *immortal* Shakespear wrote. (vv. 1–8)[268]

In the prologue to his adaptation of *Coriolanus*, titled *The Invader of his Country*, Dennis describes the play as a "grafting" of Shakespeare's text, thus using a metaphor belonging to the semantic field of gardening, an area that has already appeared in the course of this study.

The usual "Master-strokes" to the Bard, which are by now fairly expected, "in wild confusion lye" (v. 4),[269] and necessitate control that will bring "order" to the play. The opening verses of the prologue confirm this concept in couplets:

> The Tragedy we represent to Day
> Is but a Grafting upon Shakespear's Play,
> In whose Original we may descry,
> Where Master-strokes in wild Confusion lye,
> Here brought to as much Order as we can
> Reduce those Beauties upon Shakespear's Plan. (vv. 1–6)[270]

Dennis continues by explicitly confirming what transpires in several epitexts of adaptations, that is, that Nature trumps Art, and so Shakespeare trumps neoclassical Rules:

> And from his Plan we dar'd not to depart,
> Least Nature should be lost in Quest of Art:
> And Art had been attain'd with too much Cost,
> Had Shakespear's Beauties in the Search been lost. (vv. 7–10)[271]

---

268 Ibid., "Prologue Design'd to be Spoke," by G. Roussillon.

269 John Dennis, prologue to *The Invader of His Country*, n.p.

270 Ibid.

271 Ibid.

2.3.5 The Tragedy of King Richard the II; Love in a Forest; Henry V; The Universal Passion[272]

In the prologue to his adaptation of *Richard II*, Theobald acknowledges his debt to the Bard and reserves the only adjective of praise, "immortal," for him. Immediately after, there is a recurrent image of a Shakespeare who seems to have only drafted the historical play ("this Tale began")[273] in a style and with a plot that are both still rough ("wrote it in a rude, Historick Plan"):[274]

> Immortal Shakespear on this Tale began,
> And wrote it in a rude, Historick Plan,
> On his rich Fund our Author builds his Play,
> Keeps all his Gold, and throws his Dross away;
> Safe in this Aid, he can no Thunder dread,
> Fenc'd with the God's own Laurel round his Head. (vv. 22–27)[275]

Evidently, the text is a sort of naturally rich mine but, as is customary, the precious material is separated and refined, as gold is separated from slag and dirt. The metaphor of the precious metal that needs to be distilled from impurities is by now a cliché, and also appears in the prologue to *Love in a Forest* (1723), Charles Johnson's adaptation of *As You Like It,* and *A Midsummer Night's Dream*:

> In Honour to his Name, and this learn'd Age,
> Once more your much lov'd Shakespear treads the Stage.
> Another Work from that great Hand appears,
> His Ore's refin'd, but not impar'd by Years. (vv. 1–4)[276]

The connection of Shakespeare with Nature is not original either. Although learned individuals describe it coldly, the Bard is able to render

272 Lewis Theobald, *The Tragedy of King Richard II, alter'd from Shakespear* (London, 1720); Charles Johnson, *Love in a Forest, A Comedy* (London, 1723); Aaron Hill, *King Henry The Fifth, or The Conquest of France By the English, A Tragedy* (London, 1723); James Miller, *The Universal Passion, A Comedy* (London, 1737).

273 Lewis Theobald, prologue, *The Tragedy of King Richard II*, v. 2, n.p.

274 Ibid., v. 23.

275 Ibid.

276 Charles Johnson, prologue, *Love in a Forest*, n.p.

it real thanks to his interior poetic ardor. Shakespeare is able to achieve admiration for his many sacred natural Truths because he himself is "irregularly" great:

> Those sacred Truths our Sages coldly tell
> In languid Prose; as He describes – we feel.
> He looks all Nature thro'; strikes at a Heat
> Her various Forms, irregularly Great. (vv. 5–8)[277]

Here, the religious-sacred sphere ("Those sacred Truths") has Nature as a point of reference, and in Nature, the Bard is a prophet because he possesses a complete understanding and vision of it ("He looks all Nature thro'"). And in the Bard, the poetic flame burns freely with neither limits nor restrictions ("Heat … irregularly Great").

The adaptor nonetheless accords himself some merit, for he harmonized Shakespeare's lyre, formalized his metric scheme, and introduced neoclassical unity to the dramatic plot:

> His whole Ambition does, at most, aspire
> To tune the sacred Bard's immortal Lyre;
> The Scene from Time and Error to restore,
> And give the Stage, from Shakespear one Play more. (vv. 37–40)[278]

The Bard is sacred, his Lyre immortal, but, as a rule, his Theater is mistaken and requires corrective intervention.

The prologue to Hill's adaptation of *King Henry V* draws attention to the prestige tied to the Bard, a superior genius of theater ("tow'ring Genius of the Stage")[279] whose name alone rouses and fixes the spectator's attention and whose greatness theater recognizes with a sense of fear mixed with reverence. Anyone who tries his hand at Shakespeare's muse will only be defeated because the Bard is superior:

> From Wit's old Ruins, shadow'd o'er with Bays,
> We draw some rich Remains of Shakespear's Praise.
> Shakespear! – the Sound bids charm'd Attention wake:
> And our aw'd Scenes, with conscious Reve'rence, Shake!

277 Ibid.

278 Ibid.

279 Aaron Hill, prologue to *King Henry The Fifth*, v. 19, n.p.

Arduous the Task, to mix with Shakespear's Muse!
Rash Game! where All, who play, are sure to lose.
Yet – what our Author cou'd, he dar'd to try:
And kept the fiery Pillar in his Eye.
Led by such Light, as wou'd not let him stray,
He pick'd our Stars, from Shakespear's milky Way. (vv. 1–10)[280]

In the final couplet, Hill enters the sphere of the heavens and the afterlife as he declares that his *alteration* of *Henry V* selects and employs only some of the brilliant and numinous fragments written by Shakespeare, only a few selected stars from the vast starry white sea of the Milky Way. These stars are the points of reference in the chaotic world of war of Henry V:

Hid, in the Cloud of Battle, Shakespear's Care,
Blind, with the Dust of War, o'erlook'd the Fair:
Fond of their Fame, we shew their Influence, here,
And place 'em, twinkling through War's smokey Sphere.
Without their Aid, we lose Love's quick'ning Charms;
And sullen Virtue mopes, in steril Arms.
Now, rightly mix'd, th' enliven'd Passions move:
Love softens War, – and War invigo'rates Love. (vv. 11–18)[281]

In *The Universal Passion* (1737), adaptation of *Much Ado About Nothing*, James Miller understands the difficulty of the task he has undertaken, as no muse can have a sweeter song or can rise as high as that of Shakespeare:

But conscious how unequal to the Task,
Our Bard scarce dares your Clemency to ask:
What Muse so sweet that can like Shakespear's sing!
What Pinions soar like Shakespear's Eagle Wing! (vv. 17–20)[282]

In parting, the prologue implores the public's compassion to save the new comedy by employing the image of the adapted/orphaned text and a source/father (that is, Shakespeare) text that was encountered earlier:

280 Ibid.
281 Ibid.
282 James Miller, prologue to *The Universal Passion*, n.p.

"To your Protection Shakespear's Offspring take,/And save the Orphan for the Father's Sake" (vv. 32–33).[283]

2.3.6 Conclusion

In some cases the two constituent elements of the dramatic peritext reappear to demonstrate more concisely concepts that have already been expressed in the publisher's or prefatorial peritext, but are repeated due to the different audiences to whom they are addressed. It should not come as a surprise, therefore, that there is a sporadic recurrence of the dichotomy that exalts Shakespeare poet-creator and, at the same time, condemns the created poetic work. In the case of prologues and epilogues, however, the dramatic peritext becomes a textual space for a bardolatry that is declaimed without, or only slightly, a counterpoint; its voice is therefore clearer.

From a general overview of the peritexts of Shakespearean adaptations as a whole, it follows that such an element has thus had an important role in the elevation of Shakespeare to the status of cultural hero, not to mention its contribution to shaping those conceptual superstructures through which we observe the Bard today. Some of these operate at the subconscious level, while some others are overtly present and exert a powerful influence. Shakespeare, then, is configured not only as a playwright, but also as poet, genius, nature, natural genius, fantasy, imagination, and much more. But above all, as time passes, his failures and flaws are integrated and assimilated by a discourse with religious-sacred overtones that chooses the Bard as its idol. This begins to manifest itself well before Restoration, in the first *folio* edition of his plays, in 1623. As we know Jonson, in fact, had said at that time that Shakespeare "*He was not of an age, but for all time*!" – a statement that proved to be quite prophetic.

283 Ibid.

3 Paratext II: The Epitext

3.1 Introductory Remarks

If Genette's vast category of the paratext is subdivided into its constituent parts – the peritext and epitext – even when considering only the quantitative data, it is clear that the latter has attracted far more attention among scholars. In their seminal studies on Shakespearean criticism, John Munro[284] and Augustus Ralli[285] demonstrated that epitexts are, in fact, predominant, whereas peritexts are rarely found, if not altogether absent. In the 1970s, Brian Vickers subsequently attempted to rectify this lacuna,[286] and this book is a further step in the same direction.

In the present chapter, my purpose is to complete the review of the paratexts with more instances of bardolatry belonging to the field of epitext. Despite the fairly regular frequentation of this category by literary critics, I have decided to include it for completeness sake, hopefully integrating it with new or relatively unknown texts.

3.2 Pre-Restoration (1598–1647): *Palladis Tamia*, the *First Folio*, and other texts

In 1598, when *Palladis Tamia* was published, Shakespeare was already considered among the best English poets. In the section titled "A

284 John Munro, ed., *The Shakespearean Allusion-Book: A Collection of Allusions to Shakespeare from 1591 to 1700*, 2 vols. (London: Oxford University Press, 1909 [1932]).

285 Augustus Ralli, *A History of Shakespearean Criticism* (London: Oxford University Press, 1932).

286 Brian Vickers, ed., *Shakespeare. The Critical Heritage*, 6 vols. (London: Routledge & Kegan Paul, 1974).

comparatiue discourse of our English poets, with the Greeke, Latine, and Italian Poets," Francis Meres documents the greatest poets belonging to the three cultures for each branch of poetry. Although the title of "God of English Poets" is accorded to Chaucer ("Chaucer is accounted the God of English Poets"),[287] the honor is quite an empty title because it is not confirmed in any of the poetic categories identified by Meres.

The Bard's name appears a total of nine times, and is listed in five different categories: in all dramatic poetry (comedy and tragedy),[288] and thus in lyrical,[289] tragic,[290] comic,[291] and elegiac poetry, the last of which is meant to be love poetry.[292] In the remaining passages, Shakespeare is widely praised, and is judged among those who have contributed greatly to enriching the language.[293] Indeed, if the Muses spoke English, they would use "Shakespeares fine filed phrase."[294] The Bard is also placed alongside two classical Latin poets: Ovid, for his sonnets and poems *Venus and Adonis* and *Lucrece*;[295] and Horace, for the overall poetic worth of his compositions.[296]

Meres paints a picture of a Shakespeare, who, after a decade of activity, already found himself in company of the foremost poets of his time. Although at that moment he was not the leader, nor was he worshipped, in the following decades he would quickly progress, ascending Mount Parnassus, sharing the peak with Jonson and Fletcher to form a triumvirate of poetry, before becoming the one and the greatest.

287 Francis Meres, *Palladis Tamia* (London, 1598), 279r.

288 Ibid., 282r.

289 Ibid., 283r.

290 Ibid.

291 Ibid., 283v.

292 Ibid., 284r.

293 "The English tongue mightily enriched, and gorgeouslie inuested in rare ornaments and resplendent abiliments by sir Philip Sidney, Spencer, Daniel, Drayton, Warner, Shakespeare, Marlow, and Chapman." Meres, *Palladis Tamia,* 280r.

294 Ibid., 282r.

295 "The sweete wittie soule of Ouid liues in mellifluous & hony-tongued Shakespeare, witnes his Venus and Adonis, his Lucrece, his sugred Sonnets among his priuate friends, & c." Meres, *Palladis Tamia,* 281v–282r.

296 "And as Horace saith of his; Exegi monumentu aere perennius … so say I seuerally of sir Philip Sidneys, Spencers Daniels, Draytons, Shakespeares, and Warners workes." Meres, *Palladis Tamia,* 282r–282v.

About two decades later, and only seven years after Shakespeare's death, evidence of the sacred aura characterizing bardolatry can be found in the dedicatory epistle in *First Folio*[297] by John Heminge and Henry Condell, who addressed the epistle to the patrons of the work William Earl of Pembroke and Philip Earl of Montgomery. In the letter, the religious dimension involves both the direct beneficiaries of the work and the literary object that is configured as a gift, thus linking Baudelairean *correspondences* to a classic twentieth-century anthropological work, the seminal "Essai sur le don," by Marcel Mauss,[298] where the sacral dimension of the gift and the persons involved in the exchange that surrounds it are discussed with great insight.

The actors-editors express awe for their noble patrons, towards whom "no man to come neere your L.L. but with a kind of religious addresse."[299] Within the rhetorical conventions of patronage, they thus conferred a fictional divine or semidivine character to the recipients of the work. It is as though they were presenting a gift to a deity in a ritual of fertility:

> Country hands reach foorth milke, creame, fruites, or what they have: and many Nations (we have heard) that had not gummes & incense, obtained their requests with a leavened Cake. It was no fault to approach their Gods, by what meanes they could: And the most, though meanest, of things are made more precious, when they are dedicated to Temples. In that name therefore, we most humbly consecrate to your H.H. these remaines of your servant Shakespeare.[300]

In the *First Folio*, Ben Jonson's *To the memory of my beloved, The Author Mr. William Shakespeare*, written in memory and praise of the Bard, also

297 John Heminge and Henry Condell, "To the most Noble and Incomparable of Brethen. William Earle of Pembroke, &c. Lord Chamberlaine to the Kings most Excellent Maiesty. And Philip Earle of Montgomery, &c. Gentleman of his Maiesties Bed-Chamber. Both Knights of the most Noble Order of the Garter, and our singular good Lords," in William Shakespeare, *Mr. William Shakespeares Comedies, Histories, and Tragedies* (London, 1623).

298 Marcel Mauss. *The Gift. The Form and Reason for Exchange in Archaic Societies*. (London: Routledge Classics, 1990 [2002]). Originally published as "Essai sur le don. Forme et raison de l'échange dans les sociétés archaïques," in *L'Année Sociologique* (1923–4).

299 William Shakespeare, *Mr. William Shakespeares Comedies, Histories, and Tragedies*, A2v.

300 Ibid.

exhibits a pervasive eulogistic character. For a work of the laudatory kind, however, it lingers unusually long before high praises are accorded to the Bard. The poem is structured into four parts: an introduction, a praise of Shakespeare, a praise of Britain, and a peroration; the first and last parts occupy eight couplets each, and the central two parts twelve couplets each, for a total of eighty lines. It is worth noting that the introduction does not include praises, and indeed presents a suspicious number of negative seeds such as envy, ignorance, (blind) affection, (crafty) malice, and concludes with despising words such as "bawd," "whore" and "ill fortune." With some effort, Jonson finally begins his praise of the Bard at verse 17 ("I, therefore will begin"). From here and henceforth in the text, Shakespeare is praised as a soul of the age, a wonder of the stage, and so on, nationalistically linking him to Britain, and comparing him with the greatest poets of all ages, especially the Classics Greek and Latin, and the contemporary English ones.

The harshness of Jonson's opening lines was not pardoned and left some traces. Seventy years after the *First Folio*, in his preface to the translation of Giovenale's *Satire* (1693), Dryden articulates feelings of hostility somewhat similar to those found in *To the memory of my beloved* attacking Jonson, whose work is described as "An Insolent, Sparing, and Invidious Panegyrick."[301] At the beginning of the eighteenth century, Rowe would express the same opinion and would paint a bleaker picture of Jonson[302] in the paratext to his edition of the Shakespeare canon.

Jonson's lines "He was not of an age, but for all time!" and "And though thou hadst little Latine, and lesse Greeke" are among the most

301 John Dryden, preface to *The Satyrs of Decimus Junius Juvenalis, and of Aulius Persius Flaccus* (London, 1726), n.p.

302 "Ben [Jonson] was naturally Proud and Insolent, and in the Days of his Reputation did so far take upon him the Supremacy in Wit that he could not but look with an evil Eye upon any one that seem'd to stand in Competition with him. And if at times he has affected to commend him [Shakespeare] it has always been with some Reserve, insinuating Uncorrectness, a careless manner of Writing, and Want of Judgement. The Praise of seldom altering or blotting out what he writ, which was given him by the Players who were the first Pubicators of his Works after his Death, was what Jonson could not bear." Nicholas Rowe, "Some Accont of the Life, & c of Mr. William Shakespeare," in William Shakespeare, *The Works of William Shakespeare* (London, 1709), xiii.

quoted because they contribute to establishing the image of an absolute, eternal, and timeless Shakespeare. And, of course, "natural" because he was born a natural poet, gifted with natural poetic fire, and was a poet of human nature.

In the *Folio*, after the Jonsonian "To the memory of my beloved the author," there is another paratext eulogizing Shakespeare. The verses by Leonard Digges praise the Bard, promising him eternal life thanks to his poetry ("Be sure, our Shakespeare, thou canst never dye/But crown'd with Lawrell, live eternally" [vv. 21–2]).[303] Immortality through poetry is a *topos* that can be traced to the dawn of Western literature but it must be remembered that such an attribute is intrinsic to divinities and gods and is thus connected to the religious sphere of human life. With the evolution of civilization in later ages and the development of a literary culture, the concept moves from the sacred to the profane, becoming the prerogative of poetic genius.

In 1630[304] John Milton composed an epitaph[305] in honor of Shakespeare, which appeared in the *Second Folio*. Unlike those in Jonson, Milton's opening lines more obviously express the sacred meaning that Shakespeare, whose bones were venerated as relics of a saint, began to assume little more than a decade after his death:

> What neede my *Shakespeare* for his honour'd bones,
> The labour of an Age, in piled stones
> Or that his hallo'w Reliques should be hid
> Under a starre-ypointing Pyramid? (vv. 1–4)

In the same epitaph, Milton praised the ease with which Shakespeare creates poetry ("For whil'st to th' shame of slow-endevouring Art/Thy easie numbers flow …," vv. 9–10), an attribute that would increase its frequency and intensity decade after decade. This quality was further reiterated in *L'Allegro*:

303 Leonard Digges, "To the Memorie of the deceased Author Maister W. Shakespeare," in Wiliiam Shakespeare, *Mr. William Shakespeares Comedies, Histories, and Tragedies*, n.p.

304 John Milton, *Milton's Poems* (London, 1645).

305 John Milton, "An Epitaph on the admirable Dramaticke Poet, W. Shakespeare," *Second Folio* (London, 1632).

Then to the well-trod stage anon,
If *Johnson*'s learned sock be on,
Or sweetest *Shakespeare*, Fancy's child,
Warble his native wood-notes wild (vv. 131–34)[306]

Here, the key words are *fancy* and *wild*, because they are a reflection of the Bard's relationship with creativity and freedom of the poetic word, which is opposed to rules; something that is typically English and in contrast to Jonson's erudite style, which is steeped in the Greek and Latin Classics.

The religious-sacred aura also occurs in works by minor authors such as Thomas Terrent's *Jonsonus Virbius*, printed in London in 1638:

Nec geminos vates, nec Te Shakspeare filebo,
Aut quicquid sacri nostros conjecit in annos
Consilium Fatii. (vv. 6–8)[307]

[Nor the twin poets,[308] nor you Shakespeare I shall be silent on,
Or whichever other sacred name Fortune's will
Has given to our time.]

In these years, then, Shakespeare's language was still deemed harmonious and melodious, but this view changed a few years later when, at the beginning of the Restoration, it would start to be perceived as antiquated and obsolete. But in 1640, in his reader advisory,[309] John Benson still described the Bard's poems as "excellent and sweetely composed Poems," pure and "everliving Workes."[310]

> in your perusall you shall find them Seren, cleere and elegantly plaine, such gentle straines as shall recreate and not perplexe your braine, no intricate or cloudy stuffe to puzzell intellect, but perfect eloquence.[311]

In the same edition of Shakespeare's poems, Leonard Digges's[312] funeral oration reiterated the image of a natural and illiterate Bard, whose

306 John Milton, *L'Allegro*.
307 Thomas Terrent, *Jonsonus Virbius* (London, 1638).
308 Beaumont and Fletcher.
309 John Benson, "To the Reader," *Shakespeare's Poems* (London, 1640).
310 Ibid., n.p.
311 Ibid., n.p.
312 Digges, "Upon Maister William Shakespeare, the Deceased Author, and his Poems," *Shakespeare's Poems*, n.p.

poetry is innate[313] and whose name is eternal. He repeated in part what had already been expressed in the *First Folio*:

> Poets are borne not made, when I would prove
> This truth, the glad remembrance I must love
> Of never dying Shakespeare, who alone,
> Is argument enough to make that one.
>
> ...
>
> Next Nature onely helpet him, for looke thorow
> This whole Booke, thou shalt find he doth not borrow
> One phrase from Greeks, nor Latins imitate,
> Nor once from vulgar Languages Translate,
> Nor Plagiari-like from others gleane. (vv. 1–4; 11–15)[314]

John Warren even better represented the depiction of the concept of immortality of the writer through poetry in his verses dedicated to the Bard titled "Of Mr. William Shakespeare":

> These learned Poems amongs't thine after-birth,
> Than makes thy name immortall on the earth,
> Will make the learned still admire to see
> The Muses gifts so fully infused on thee. (vv. 5–8)[315]

On August 8, 1643, *Northern Nuntio*, a royalist newspaper published in York, reported that an atheist was expelled from Nottingham because he believed Shakespeare's plays to be more authoritative than the Gospels: "God [was] gloried in the contrary, setting Shakespear's plays at a better pitch of authority than the Gospel of Christ."[316] In 1649, a written work in defense of the legitimacy of the execution of the King claims that such an act would not have been necessary "[h]ad [Charles I] but studied Scripture half so much as [he studied] Ben Johnson or Shakespeare."[317]

---

313 About 20 years later, Thomas Fuller also expresses this idea using similar words: "He was an eminent instance of the truth of that Rule, Poeta not fid, sed nascitur; one is not made, but born a Poet." Thomas Fuller, *The Histories of the Worthies of England* (Warwickshire, 1662), 126.

314 Digges, "Upon Maister William Shakespeare," *Shakespeare's Poems*, n.p.

315 John Warren, "Of Mr. William Shakespeare," *Shakespeare's Poems*, n.p.

316 *Northern Nuntio*, August 8, 1643.

317 John Cook, *King Charls his Case; or, an Appeal to all Rational Men, Concerning his Tryal* (London, 1649), 13.

These two small examples further show how Shakespeare's word was compared to, if not considered equal or superior to, the Sacred Scriptures, before the mid-seventeenth century.

The last paratext of this section praises the peaks of Shakespeare's versification, at the same time exposing the unevenness of his style. In the introductory paratexts of the *First Folio of the Beaumont and Fletcher's Works* (1647), John Berkenhead's poem composed in honor of the two playwrights has time to briefly describe the Bard using a simile comparing him to the tide of the seas, implying that his style had many high points, but was also irregular and erratic: "Brave Shakespeare flow'd, yet has his Ebbings too, / Often above Himselfe, sometimes below."[318] Earlier, in another natural simile, Berkenhead compared the Bard to the overflowing river Nile; when it exceeds and outdoes boundaries, thus surpassing all limits, at the same time it fertilizes all the soil it touches.

3.3 From Fuller to Langbaine[319] (1662–1699)

In 1662 Thomas Fuller expressed the idea of Shakespeare's innate genius with a metaphor employing the imagery of a precious stone:

> Indeed his Learning was very little, so that, as *Cornish diamonds* are not polished by any Lapidary, but are pointed and smoothed even as they are taken out of the Earth, so *nature* it self was all the *art* which was used upon him.

318 Francis Beaumont and John Fletcher, *Comedies and Tragedies* (London, 1647).

319 Fuller, *Histories of the Worthies of England*; Richard Flecknoe, "A Short Discourse of the English Stage," *Love's Kingdom, A Pastoral Trage-Comedy, With a Short Treatise of the English Stage* (London, 1664); Samuel Pepys, *Diary*, 2 vols. (London, 1825); Margaret Cavendish, *CCXI Sociable Letters* (London, 1664); John Dryden, *An Essay of Dramatick Poesie* (London, 1668), and *A Defence of the Epilogue, Or, An Essay on the Dramatique Poetry of the Last Age* (London, 1672); Nahum Tate, preface to *The Loyal General* (London, 1680); Robert Gould, *The Play-House, A Satyr* (London, 1685); Gerard Langbaine, *Momus Triumphans* (London, 1687), *An Account of the English Dramatick Poets* (London, 1691), and *The Lives and the Characters of the English Dramatick Poets* (London, 1699).

About twenty years later, Tate would reuse the metaphor, making it famous, to describe the Bard's original play with respect to his adaptation, which he modified to accommodate the public's taste and the Restoration's theatrical space.

In 1664, Richard Flecknoe's "A Short Discourse" appeared as a paratext in *Love's Kingdome*, an adaptation of *Love's Dominion* by the same author. Flecknoe praised Shakespeare for his qualities as a writer gifted for all genres: "For Playes, Shakespear was one of the first, who invented the Dramatick Stile, from dull History to quick Comedy, upon whom Johnson refined."[320] Jonson, however, was not considered superior to the Bard as his higher degree of *refineness* became an excess of *elaborateness*.

After discussing Beaumont and Fletcher, Flecknoe commented on Suckling's *Aglaura*; the play triggers a parallel with the Bard that echoes the image of Shakespeare's work as a lush and wild garden, as we have already seen when discussing the prologues and epilogues of the adaptations:

> 'twas full of fine flowers, but they seemed rather stuck, then growing there, as another of *Shakespear's* writings, that 'twas a fine Garden, but it wanted weeding.[321]

If Shakespeare and Jonson are brought into direct comparison, Flecknoe chooses the Bard; consistently, between Nature and Art the first one is preferred:

> To compare our English Dramatick Poets together (without taxing them) *Shakespear* excelled in a natural Vein, *Fletcher* in Wit, and *Johnson* in Gravity and ponderousness of Style; whose onely fault was, he was too elaborate; and had he mixt less erudition with his Playes, they had been more pleasant and delightful then they are. Comparing him with *Shakespear*, you shall see the difference between Nature and Art; and with *Fletcher*, the difference betwixt Wit and Judgement: Wit being an exuberant thing, like *Nilus*, never more commendable then when it overflowes; but Judgement a stayed and reposed thing, always containing it self within its bounds and limits.[322]

320 Flecknoe, *A Short Discourse of the English Stage*, iii.

321 Ibid., iii–iv.

322 Ibid., v.

Like many others, the image of the Nile river overflowing beyond the "bounds and limits" of its bed is a natural image linked to fluidity and abundance, and even if here it is immediately connected to Fletcher, it is often a symbol of Shakespeare's creative genius, which is becoming more and more configured as thoroughly laudable ("commendable"), not reprehensible or abhorrent. Overflow and exaggeration are the excess, surplus and significant supplement of Shakespeare's protean and polysemic versification, which also creates a unique and rich idiolect in constant renewal while it crosses and breaks down normative barriers of the current language.

Another point that Flecknoe highlights is the link between dramatic writing and theatrical acting, between playwright and actor. Bardolatry owes much, though not all, to the printed page; in the first decades of the Restoration actors, especially Betterton, held the fame of Shakespeare high. Indeed, up to the mid-eighteenth century, when the literacy was significantly higher than in the preceding age, the greatest contributors to the construction of Shakespeare as a cultural icon were the leading actors protagonists of the Restoration. Thomas Betterton is one such contributor.

Gary Taylor refers to this link several times, as in the following example:

> This association between the success of a particular performer and the fortunes of a play in the repertoire was not confined to Betterton or the Restoration period. The same thing happened in the eighteenth century, when the twenty-four-year-old David Garrick catapulted both himself and Richard the Third into stardom, simultaneously. A role is a meeting place for an actor and a play; if the actor triumphs so does the play.[323]

If the actor triumphs, so does the play, and consequently the playwright. Such is the Bard's case: "in the restoration of Shakespeare's reputation, publisher followed; actors led."[324] Indeed, whereas in the seventeenth century theater stimulated printing, in the eighteenth century the opposite occurred,[325] a change that took place around the 1720s when "the

323 Gary Taylor, *Reinventing Shakespeare* (Oxford: Oxford UP, 1989), 22.

324 Ibid., 33.

325 "In the seventeenth century the popularity of Shakespeare's plays with audiences had stimulated the publication of reading editions. In the eighteenth century, their popularity with readers stimulated new productions. Actors now followed." Taylor, *Reinventing Shakespeare*, 94.

center of English culture was shifting from performance to print – and Shakespeare went with it."[326]

Now, let us return to "A Short Discourse," where Flecknoe acknowledges that the happy union between playwright and actor is particularly significant in the Elizabethan era, and produces results superior to those in the period in which he writes:

> It was the happiness of the Actors of those Times to have such Poets as these to instruct them, and write for them; and no less of those Poets to have such docile and excellent Actors to Act their Playes, as a *Field* or a *Burbridge*; of whom we may say, that he was a delightful *Proteus*, so wholly transforming himself into his Part and putting off himself with his Cloathes, as be never (not so much as in the Tyring-house) assum'd himself again until the Play was done: there being as much difference betwixt him and one of our common Actors, as between a Ballad-singer who onely mouths it, and an excellent singer, who knows all his Graces, and can artfully vary and modulate his Voice, even to know how much breath he is to give to every syllable.[327]

The relevance of good acting for the rise bardolatry is also revealed in a very often-quoted text. The diary of Samuel Pepy confirms the importance of gifted and charismatic actors and actresses and the connection that acting has with the success (or the failure) of the play. Pepys dedicates several passages to Betterton, the main actor of the period, especially to his performance in *Hamlet*, in which he plays the protagonist and his performance is excellent, time after time. Suffice it to remember:

> 1661. AUGUST 24. – To the Opera, and there saw "Hamlet, Prince of Denmarke," done with scenes very well, but above all, Betterton did the Prince's parts beyond imagination. (Vol. I, p. 342)
>
> 1663. MAY 28. – By water to the Royall Theatre; but that was so full they told us we could have no room. And so to the Duke's house; and there saw "Hamlett" done, giving us fresh reason never to think enough of Betterton. (Vol. II, p. 224)
>
> 1668. AUGUST 31. – To the Duke of York's playhouse, and saw "Hamlet," which we have not seen this year before, or more, and mightily pleased with it, but above all with Betterton, the best part, I believe, that ever man acted. (Vol. V., p. 347)[328]

---

326 Ibid., 62.

327 Flecknoe, *A Short Discourse of the English Stage*, vi–vii.

328 Samuel Pepys and Henry B. Weatley, eds., *The Diary of Samuel Pepys*, 8 vols. (London: G. Bell & Sons, 1913).

However, not everyone's opinion is the same, as John Evelyn shows a negative estimation of the tragedy set in Elsinore:

> 1661. NOVEMBER 26. – I saw Hamlet Prince of Denmark played, but now the old plays began to discuss this refined age, since his majesties being so long abroad. (Vol. I, p. 342)[329]

For *Macbeth*, Pepys had similar praise as for *Hamlet*. In the Scottish play Betterton once again had the role of the protagonist; and Pepys' eulogy for the actors stands out even more. When Betterton was on stage:

> 1666. DECEMBER 28. – To the Duke's house, and there saw "Macbeth" excellently acted, and a most excellent play for variety. (Vol. IV, p. 195)[330]
>
> 1667. JANUARY 7. – To the Duke's house, and saw "Macbeth," which though I saw it lately, yet appears a most excellent play in all respects, but especially in divertissement, though it be a deep tragedy; which is a strange perfection in a tragedy, it being most proper here, and suitable. (Vol. IV, p. 202)[331]

When Betterton was not on the stage:

> 1667. OCTOBER 16. – To the Duke of York's house; … and I was vexed to see Young who is but a bad actor at best act Macbeth in the room of Betterton, who, poor man! is sick: but Lord! what a prejudice it wrought in me against the whole play, and every body else agreed in disliking this fellow. Thence home, and there find my wife gone home; because of this fellow's acting of the part, she went out of the house again. (Vol. V, p. 57)[332]
>
> 1667. NOVEMBER 6. – With my wife to a play, and the girl – "Macbeth," which we still like mightily, though mighty short of the content we used to have when Betterton acted, who is still sick. (Vol. V, p. 86)[333]

In the same years in which Pepys recorded notes in his diary, Margaret Cavendish wrote many letters, which were gathered and published in London in 1664 under the title *CCXI Sociable Letters written by the Thrice Noble, Illustrious, and Excellent Princess, The Lady Marchioness*

329 John Evelyn and William Bray, eds., *Memoirs and Diary*, vol. 1 (London, 1819), 342.

330 Samuel Pepys and Henry B. Weatley, eds., *The Diary of Samuel Pepys*, IV, 195.

331 Ibid., IV, 202.

332 Ibid., V, 57.

333 Ibid., V, 86.

of Newcastle. A passage from Cavendish's letter CXXIII is significant in its outpouring of appreciation for Shakespeare, for whom words denoting the naturalness and universality of his gifts – that is, their inherent and all-encompassing nature – are still crucial:

> Indeed *Shakespear* had a clear judgement, a quick wit, a spreading fancy, a subtil observation, a deep apprehension, and a most eloquent elocution; truly, he was a natural orator, as well as a natural poet, and he was not an orator to speak well only on some subjects, as lawyers …; but *Shakespear*'s wit and eloquence was general, for an upon all subjects.[334]

In his essay on dramatic poetry written in 1668, John Dryden anticipates several points that he discusses more extensively in "The Grounds of Criticism in Tragedy," which forms part of the paratext of the *Troilus and Cressida* (1679) adaptation. The annotations are brief and touch upon various topics: general praise, which defines Shakespeare as the father of English dramatic poetry ("Shakespeare was the Homer, or Father of our Dramatick Poets");[335] specific praise which concerns character profiles ("The variety and greatness of characters which are derived to us by Shakespeare and Fletcher"),[336] and the plot structure ("I could produce even in Shakespeare's and Fletcher's Works, some Playes which are almost exactly form'd; as the Merry Wives of Windsor, and the Scornful Lady").[337] All this praise, however, comes with some criticism for the language ("Shakespeare's language is likewise a little obsolete").[338]

The following passage typifies the widespread attitude towards the Bard during the Restoration: general praise for the man and poet, exaltation of his naturalness, combined with negative criticism for some specific passages concerning use of language that is now perceived as irritating and excessively rich:

> To begin then with *Shakespeare*; he was the man who of all Modern, and perhaps Ancient Poets, had the largest and most comprehensive soul. All the Images of Nature were still present to him, and he drew them not laboriously, but luckily: when he describes any thing, you more than see it, you feel it too. Those who accuse

334 Cavendish, *CCXI Sociable Letters,* n.p.

335 Dryden, *An Essay of Dramatick Poesie,* 50.

336 Ibid., 45–9.

337 Ibid.

338 Ibid.

> him to have wanted learning, give him the greater commendation: he was naturally learn'd; he needed not the spectacles of Books to read Nature; he look'd inwards, and found her there. I cannot say he is everywhere alike; were he so, I should do him injury to compare him with the greatest of Mankind. He is many times flat, insipid; his Comick wit degenerating into clenches, his serious swelling into Bombast. But he is always great, when some great occasion is presented to him.[339]

In his essay written in defense of the epilogue (1672), Dryden demonstrates Shakespeare's irregular style, which reaches sublime heights as well as depths of triviality:

> *Shakespeare*, who many times has written better than any Poet, in any Language, is yet so far from writing Wit always, or expressing that Wit according to the Dignity of the Subject, that he writes in many places, below – the dullest Writer of ours, or of any precedent Age. Never did any author precipitate himself from such heights of thought to so low expressions, as he often does. He is the very *Janus* of Poets, he wears, almost every where two faces: and you have scarce begun to admire the one, ere you despise the other.[340]

In the preface to his original tragedy *The Loyal General* (1680), Nahum Tate gives expression to another widespread attitude towards Shakespeare during the Restoration: that is, the tendency to minimize Shakespeare's errors and faults so as to better praise his gifts and qualities. In fact, although Tate deems it essential for a great poet to have knowledge of the Classics, he makes an exception for the Bard:

> What I have already asserted concerning the necessity of Learning to make a compleat Poet, may seem inconsistent with my reverence for our Shakespeare. – Cujus amor semper mihi crescit in Horas.[341]

The Play-House is a satire on theater composed in 1685 by Robert Gould, printed after the turn of the century in 1709 in *Works*, a collection of his writings. *The Play-House*'s relevance lies in its clear representation of the Restoration years in which Shakespeare shares the throne as king of poets with Jonson and Fletcher to form a true poetic triumvirate, in

---

339 Ibid.

340 Dryden, *A Defence of the Epilogue, Or, An Essay on the Dramatique Poetry of the Last Age,* 167–75.

341 Nahum Tate, preface to *The Loyal General,* n.p.

common imagery of the time.[342] Sacred and immortal, the three bards are greeted with reverence:

> Hail Sacred Bards! Hail ye Immortal Three!
> The British Muses Great Triumviri!
> Secure of Fame, You on Stage will live!
> Whilst we have Wits to hear, and they have Praise to give.[343]

Langbaine wrote three treatises between 1687 and 1699. The aim of the first, titled *Momus Triumphans* (1687), was outlined in the preface by the author: as a literary critic and biographer, Langbaine attempted to trace and show examples of plagiarism in English drama by revealing the sources of plays, which are often not declared by the playwrights, especially when the source of inspiration for their muse is not famous. *Momus Triumphans* is a pioneer treatise whose legacy is recognized only after many decades. Regarding the work on Shakespeare, in fact, his total creative originality, motivated by his alleged ignorance or little knowledge of classical culture, has been uncritically affirmed many times during the eighteenth century.

In the period immediately prior to the closure of theaters, the leading names are Shakespeare, Fletcher, and Jonson; their relevance makes them stand out from the general classification following the alphabetical order of the plays:

> This Catalogue was printed *Alphabetically*, as to the Names of the *Plays*, but *promiscuously* as to those of the *Authors*, (*Shakespeare*, *Fletcher*, *Johnson*, and some others of the most voluminous Authors excepted) each Authors name being placed over against each Play that he writ, and still repeated with every several Play, till a new Author came on.[344]

On Shakespeare and Jonson, Langbaine shows that both were inspired by imitating the Greek and Latin Classics, "Shakespear and Johnson indeed imitated these Illustrious Men I have cited."[345] On Shakespeare and Fletcher, Langbaine shows that their undisputed cultural popularity

342 This image is then used by others, including Langbaine, who, in his *Momus Triumphans*, uses it in the third part dedicated to John Dryden.

343 Gould, *The Play-House,* n.p.

344 Langbaine, preface to *Momus Triumphans,* iii.

345 Ibid., ix.

and pervasiveness was such that, if one should cite them, the quotation would be immediately recognized:

> 'Tis true indeed, what is borrow'd from *Shakespeare* or *Fletcher*, is usually owned by our Poets, because every one would be able to convict them for Theft, should they endeavour to conceal it. But in what has been stolen from Authors not so generally known, as *Murston*, *Middleton*, *Massenger & c.* we find our Poets playing the parts of *Bathyllus* to *Virgil*, and robbing them of that Fame, which is as justly their due, as the Reward of the Emperour Augustus had promised to the Author of that known Distich affixed on the Court Gate, was to Virgil.[346]

In 1691, some years after *Momus Triumphans*, Langbaine publishes another work that broadens and deepens the main concept of his first publication, namely the search for sources of English dramatic texts. *An Account of the English Dramatick Poets* presents in a descriptive form what had already appeared as a simple and synthetic summary list in the earlier publication: in *An Account* for each author, Langbaine gives an overview of the various plays and he prefaces each one with a brief generic introduction about the playwright.

Speaking of Shakespeare in the introduction of *An Account*, Langbaine begins in the best tradition of praise: the Bard is "one of the most Eminent Poets of his Time."[347] He then moves to one of many variations on the theme of the Art/Nature dualism, which is solved as usual with the latter prevailing: "his Natural Genius to Poetry was so excellent, that like those Diamonds, which are found in Cornwall, Nature had little, or no occasion for the Assistance of Art to polish it."[348] In agreement with this position, Shakespeare's learning is thus deemed good, but not excellent:

> The Truth is, 'tis agreed on by most, that his Learning was not extraordinary; and I am apt to believe, that his Skill in the *French* and *Italian* Tongues, exceeded his Knowledge in the *Roman* Language.[349]

Langabine expresses general praise for many works by Shakespeare, refusing to substantiate and document the individual and specific level: the absolute excellence of the Bard's compositions begins to take shape

346 Ibid., xi.
347 Langbaine, *An Account of the English Dramatick Poets,* 453.
348 Ibid.
349 Ibid.

as a tradition supported by "many great men"; a step in the path to become an article of faith, a dogma, an existing *a priori* fact that requires no explanation:

> the Excellency of his Compositions, in all Kinds of it: … it would be superfluous in me to endeavour to particularise what most deserves praise in him, after so many Great Men have given him their several Testimonials of his Merit; so I should think I were guilty of an Injury beyond pardon to his Memory, should I so far disparage it, as to bring his Wit in competition with any of our Age.[350]

Because Langbaine considers Shakespearean plays the best ever written in the English language, the status of the Bard begins to surpass that of Jonson and Fletcher, the other two great contemporary playwrights:

> I esteem his Plays beyond any that have ever been published in our Language: and tho' I extreamly admire *Johnson* and *Fletcher*; yet I must still aver, that when in competition with *Shakespear*, I must apply to them what *Justus Lipsius* writ in his Letter to *Andreas Schottus*, concerning *Terence* and *Plautus*, when compar'd; *Teremtium amo, admirer, sed Plautum magis*.[351]

Moreover, in line with the primary aim of the treatise, the uncovering of the literary sources of plays, Langbaine lashes out at Ravenscroft, who is guilty of having appropriated Shakespeare's *Titus Andronicus* and adapted it while openly denying authorship to the Bard. He thus proposes a new forced prologue to Ravenscroft to insert in the *alteration*, which would recognize the literary source of the text. The opening lines of the Prologue by Langbaine contain hints of a sacred bardolatry:

> *To day the Poet does not fear your Rage,*
> Shakespear *by him reviv'd now treads the Stage:*
> *Under his sacred Lawrels he sits down*
> *Safe, from the blast of any Criticks Frown.*
> *Like other Poets, he'll not proudly scorn*
> *To own, that he but winnow'd* Shakespear'*s Corn;*
> *So far he was from robbing him of 's Treasure,*
> *That he did add his own, to make full Measure.*[352]

350 Ibid., 453–4.
351 Ibid., 454.
352 Ibid., 465.

Finally, it is interesting to note that the approach used by Langbaine is medieval and not scientific, as it relies on the *auctoritas* of the great literary personalities of the near past. Langbaine passively accepts this tradition and does not dare to oppose the "so many Great Men that have given him [Shakespeare] their several Testimonials of his Merit."[353] The same line of thought can be detected in a categorical statement about the Bard's cultural background: "The Truth is, 'tis agreed on by most, that his Learning was not extraordinary,"[354] which reflects a lack of personal investigation, and a blind acceptance of the widespread current position on the subject.

In Langbaine's third treatise *The Lives and Characters of the English Dramatick Poets* (1699), the excavation work to uncover the sources of plays is supplemented by an introductory discourse that provides miscellaneous information on every playwright considered; by doing so, Langbaine uses a structure that he had previously employed in *An Account*.

In *The Lives and Characters*, Langbaine's comment undoubtedly contributes to the cultural construction of bardolatry ("the greatest Poet that ever trod the Stage"), and also claims that Shakespeare had excellent knowledge of the Classics – at least of the Latin classics ("Latin … he understood … perfectly"):

> He was both Player and Poet; but the greatest Poet that ever trod the Stage, I am of Opinion, in spight of Mr. Johnson, and others from him, that though perhaps he might not be that Critic in Latin and Greek as Ben; yet that he understood the former, so well as perfectly to be Master of their Histories, for in all his Roman Characters he has nicely followed History, and you find his *Brutus*, his *Cassius*, his *Anthony*, and his *Caesar*, his *Coriolanus & c.* just as the Historians of those times describe 'em.[355]

A chronological brief review of the three treatises shows how Langbaine's opinion of Shakespeare becomes more laudatory over time. In the first treatise, *Momus Triumphans*, the Bard is one of the leading playwrights for production ("the most voluminous Authors") and popularity ("Authors … generally known"), but he still does not stand out as towering above the other poet playwrights. In the second treatise, *An Account*,

353 Ibid., 454.
354 Ibid., 453.
355 Langbaine, *The Lives and Characters* 126.

Shakespeare gains the first position among the other literary figures. Finally, in the third treatise, *The Lives and Characters*, Langbaine gives Shakespeare the title of greatest of the poets.

In this last work, Langbaine's consideration of Shakespeare's knowledge of the Classics has increased: at first "his Learning was not extraordinary; … his skill in the French and Italian Tongues, exceeded his knowledge in the Roman Language," but now his knowledge somehow has grown: "he understood [Latin] so well, so well as perfectly to be Master of their Histories." Likewise, Shakespeare's status as a poet moves from one of a relevant role of co-protagonist, to one of a principal protagonist: if at first he was "one of the most Eminent Poets of his Time" he is now "the greatest Poet that ever trod the Stage."

3.4 The Rymer Controversy[356]

Thomas Rymer is the first during the Restoration to speak totally against Shakespeare, though only in regards to *Othello* and, less effectively, to *Julius Caesar*. His criticism is limited in scope because it questions neither the Bard nor his poetry *tout-court*, but remains essentially limited to the tragedy of the Moor of Venice. As in the case of Collier, as we shall later see, the attack against Shakespeare brings about responses in defense of the Bard carried out by Dennis, Dryden, and Gildon.

356 Thomas Rymer, *The Tragedies of the Last Age* (London, 1677); John Dryden, "Heads of an Answer to Rymer," (London,1677); Francis Beaumont and John Fletcher, *Comedies and Tragedies Written by Francis Beaumont and John Fletcher Gentlemen* (London, 1711); Thomas Rymer, *A Short View of Tragedy* (London, 1693); John Dennis, *The Impartial Critick, Or, Some Observations Upon A Late Book, Entitled a Short View of Tragedy, Written by Mr. Rymer* (London, 1693), *The Advancement and Reformation of Modern Poetry* (London, 1701), "To the Right and Honourable My Lord Radcliffe," *Examen Poeticum: Being the Third Part of Miscellany Poems* (London, 1693), and "Letter to Dennis," March 3, 1694, *The Select Works of Mr. John Dennis* (London, 1718); Charles Gildon, "Some Reflections on Mr. Rymer's Short View of Tragedy," *Miscellaneous Letters and Essays* (London, 1694).

In 1677, in *The Tragedies of the Last Age*, Rymer attacks the best tragedies of the pre-Restoration period: three by Beaumont and Fletcher, two by Shakespeare, and one by Jonson:

> The choicest and most applauded *English Tragedies* of this last age; as *Rollo*; *A King and no King*; the *Maids Tragedy* by *Beaumont* and *Fletcher*; *Othello*, and *Julius Caesar*, by *Shakespear*; and *Cataline* by worthy *Ben* [Jonson].[357]

Dryden's defense, a letter-essay published posthumously in 1711 in the preface to Tonson's edition of Beaumont and Fletcher's *Folio*, is an immediate response to Rymer's attack and defends Shakespeare and Fletcher across the board. On the characters in the plays, Dryden counters that "they are neither so many nor so various in Sophocles and Euripides, as in Shakespeare and Fletcher";[358] about the language, he states that "Homer excels Virgil, Virgil all other ancient Poets, and Shakespeare all Modern Poets";[359] finally, in praising Shakespeare's tragedies, he concludes with a citation by Frenchman René Rapin, a Jesuit, poet, and treatise writer who is well known in England:[360]

> *Rapin*'s Words are Remarkable: "'Tis not the admirable Intrigue, the surprising Events, and extraordinary Incidents that make the Beauty of a Tragedy, 'tis the Discourses, when they are Natural and Passionate." So are *Shakespeare*'s.[361]

A decade-and-a-half later, in 1693, in *A Short View of Tragedy*, Rymer condemns the tragedies not discussed in his earlier treatise, reflecting extensively on the tragedy of the Moor of Venice. Beginning with the four constituent parts of a play, namely *fable*, *characters*, *thought* and

357 Rymer, *The Tragedies of the Last Age* 1–2.

358 Beaumont, preface to *Comedies and Tragedies,* n.p.

359 Ibid.

360 Rapin's first poem is *Eclogæ Sacræ* (1659), which earned him the name of second Theocritus; he then writes *Hortorum Libri IV* (1665) which are translated into English in 1673 and 1706. These two works place him among the greatest poets who wrote in Latin. His most noted critical essays are *Observations sur les poèmes d'Horace et de Virgile* (1669), *Rèflexions sur l'usage de l'èloquence de ce temps* (1672), and *Rèflexions sur la poètique d'Aristote et sur les ouvrages des poètes anciens et modernes* (1674). The last work was translated into English by Rymer, who added a preface that he wrote in defense of pseudo-Aristotelian unity.

361 Beaumont, preface to *Comedies and Tragedies,* n.p.

expression, the author criticizes *Othello* point by point. The plot is only a "phantom of a Fable,"[362] which Shakespeare changes from the source "always, unfortunately, for the worse";[363] although the moral teachings can be instructive ("The Moral, sure, of this Fable is very instructive"),[364] the tragedy suffers from a long series of elements that would destroy its credibility ("And, certainly, never was any Play fraught, like this of *Othello*, with improbabilities")[365] (which are all specified by Rymer). The harshest opinions are also more general in nature; regarding the tragic style of *Othello*, Rymer states that:

> In the *Neighing* of an Horse, or in the growling of a Mastiff, there is a meaning, there is as lively expression, and, may I say, more humanity, than many times in the Tragical flights of *Shakespear*.[366]

Whereas the overall assessment of the work denies its specific tragic character.

> There is in this Play, some burlesk, some humour, and ramble of Comical Wit, some show, and some Mimickry to divert the spectators: but the tragical part is, plainly none other, than a Bloody farce, without salt or flavour.[367]

All the accusations against *Othello* are, according to Rymer, of crimes against nature and philosophy; in the case of *Julius Caesar*, he also adds history:

> But here he sins not against Nature and Philosophy only, but against the most known History, and the memory of the Noblest Romans, that ought to be sacred to all Posterity.[368]

This wave of accusations causes many to rise up in defense of Shakespeare. In the same year of *A Short View*, Dennis publishes *The Impartial Critick*[369] in which he answers that "contrary to Mr. Rymer's assertion,

362 Rymer, *A Short View*, 86.
363 Ibid., 87.
364 Ibid., 89.
365 Ibid., 92.
366 Ibid., 95–6.
367 Ibid., 146.
368 Ibid., 148.
369 See above for publication details.

Shakespeare was a great Genius."[370] His overall attitude towards the Bard is, however, rather indecisive, an attribute that has something in common with Dryden's attitude, even if Dennis possess it to a higher degree. In 1701, in fact, in *The Advancement and Reformation of Modern Poetry* he seems to have changed ideas. Or, at least, he has reduced Shakespeare's status, which is now deemed much more inferior to the Classics ("I prefer ... the Grecian Tragedies ... to our celebrated English Tragedies"):[371] *Julius Caesar*, in particular, is nonreligious as it does not follow pseudo-Aristotelian rules, and its moral is rather dubious (indeed, it is defined as *extravagant*, *irregular*, *irreligious*, as well as *an empty amusement or a scandalous and pernicious libel upon the government of the world*).[372]

In the paratexts of *Examen Poeticum*, Dryden instead responds with a dedicatory epistle "To the Right Honourable My Lord Radcliffe,"[373] in which he pays homage to the venerable tradition of Shakespeare and Jonson, unrivalled masters ("Peace to the Venerable Shades of Shakespeare, and Ben Jonson. None of the Living will presume to have any competition with them: as they were our Predecessors so they were our Masters").[374] Even in a private letter addressed to Dennis,[375] Dryden states that Shakespeare was a genius in composing tragedies ("Tragedy. Shakespeare had a Genius for it"),[376] and that his genius is a superior attribute that enables him to rise above any criticism ("Genius alone is a greater Virtue [if I may so call it] than all other Qualifications put together").[377]

Charles Gildon, however, provides a more extensive and detailed response, which is published about a year after Rymer's work, and employs the same weapons used by his adversary, thus beginning with a comparison with the Classical writers. In 1694 he published a book containing several writings, including one in defense of theater; in this work, titled "Some Reflections on Mr. Rymer's *Short View of Tragedy*,

370 Dennis, *The Impartial Critick,* 50.

371 Dennis, *The Advancement and Reformation,* 6.

372 Ibid.

373 Dryden, *Examen Poeticum,* A6r.

374 Ibid.

375 "Letter to Dennis," II, 504.

376 Ibid.

377 Ibid.

and an Attempt at a Vindication of Shakespear, in an Essay directed to John Dryden Esq."[378] there is an obvious bardolatrous tone demonstrated by numerous adjectives and recognizable qualities attributed to Shakespeare.[379]

If the religious overtones in the veneration that is tributed to the Bard is only a distant resonance ("the Excellence I find in Shakespear himself, commands a juster veneration"),[380] it is because Gildon focuses more closely on poetic genius, which is linked to the military hero by way of pseudo-Aristotelian rules, freedom, and the concept of limit. Immersing his arguments in a nationalistic anti-French context, he states that neoclassical rules are a confinement that genius cannot bear for its natural inclination towards freedom, infinity, and boundlessness. Its actions, be they literary or military, are irregular in a noble way and cannot be judged according to the criteria by which the rest of humanity is evaluated. The hero, in battle as in poetry, is at a higher level. Here follows the passage in full:

> A nice Observation of the Rules, is a Confinement a great *Genius* cannot bear, which naturally covets Liberty; and tho' the *French*, whose *Genius*, as well as Language, is not throng enough to rise to the Majesty of Poetry, are easier reduc'd within the Disciple of Rules, and have perhaps of late years, more exactly observ'd 'em. Yet I never yet met with any Englishman, who would prefer their Poetry to ours. All that is great of Humane things, makes a nearer approach to the *Eternal Perfection* of Greatness, and extends as much as possible its limits toward being Boundless: 'Tis not govern'd by Common Rules and Methods, but Glories in a *Noble Irregularity*; and this is not only in Writings, but Actions of some Men. *Alexander*, *Caesar*, *Alcibiades*, &c, seem'd actuated by other Principles than the common maxims that govern the *Rest* of Humane Kind; and in them the greatest Virtues have been mixt with great Vices, as well as the Writings of *Shakespear*; yet are they granted *Heroes*, and so must He be confess'd a Poet: The Heroes Race are like *Achilles*.[381]

Thus, despite his flaws, the Bard is elevated to the status of a cultural hero, much in the same way that Caesar or Achilles rise to become heroes of history. Achilles was praised by Homer, whose poetic qualities come

378 Charles Gildon, *Miscellaneous Letters and Essays,* 64–118.

379 Shakespeare is a *genius* (90), *incomparable* (64), *inimitable* (73), *admirable* (83); he has *excellence of expression* (113), and is the fullest expression of *beauties and perfections* (65) and *harmonious majesty* (115).

380 Gildon, *Miscellaneous Letters,* 85.

381 Ibid., 91–2.

alive again in Shakespeare. His at times difficult language is not flawed due to his individual idiolect, but to the natural passage of time and the evolution of language. The historical dimension that considers language diachronically was not a widespread critical perspective during that time, when, instead, opinions prevailed that were more or less impressionistic and personal. However, these could acknowledge that language has undergone "a great alteration" with the passing of time:

> *Shakespears* Numbers carry such an Harmonious Majesty, that what *Rapin* and some other Critics say of *Homer*, is justly his due; they give a noble Beauty to the meanest things. 'Tis true, the Words he sometimes uses, by their obsoleteness renders some of his expressions a little dark, but then we must remember the great alteration our language has undergone since his time.[382]

3.5 Jeremy Collier and the Two Disputes[383]

Among the antitheater treatises of the time, the most famous has the aim to unravel the *disorder*[384] of English theater ("discover … the Disorders of the English Stage").[385] Taken as a whole, *A Short View* does not speak against Shakespeare in an excessively scathing manner, especially if compared with the cutting remarks directed at other playwrights who were more or less contemporaries of the Bard.

382 Ibid., 115.

383 Jeremy Collier, *A Short View of the Immorality and Profaneness of the English Stage* (London, 1698); Elkanah Settle, *A Farther Defence of Dramatick Poetry* (London, 1698); George Ridpath, *The Stage Condemn'd* (London, 1698); James Drake, *The Antient and Modern Stages Survey'd* (London, 1699); Jeremy Collier, *A Defence of the Short View of the Immorality and Profaneness of the English Stage* (London, 1699); *Visits from the Shades* (London, 1704); Arthur Belford, *Serious Reflections on the Scandalous Abuse and Effects of the Stage* (London, 1705), *A Serious Remonstrance in Behalf of the Christian Religion* (London, 1719), and *A Sermon Preached in the Parish-Church of St. Butolph's Aldgate* (London, 1730).

384 Some contemporary anthropological studies, including those by Mary Douglas, have linked disorder, filth, separateness, to the sacrum, and have shown ways in which these concepts can be applied to studies in literature.

385 Collier, *A Short View*, 233.

Collier's greatest criticism is directed at some of the plays' characters. According to Collier, the quality of the woman is "modesty," which blends coyness, modesty, discretion, and bashfulness, and is considered socially respectable behavior. This quality is excellently represented in the scene from Euripides' *Phaedra* since "She keeps her Modesty even after she has lost her Wits."[386] In *Hamlet* the plot unravels differently, and, consequently, corresponds to the negative opinion in *A Short View* about plot and character:

> Had *Shakespear* secur'd this point for his young Virgin *Ophelia*, the *Play* had been better contriv'd. Since he was resolv'd to drown the Lady like a Kitten, he should have set her a swimming a little sooner. To keep her alive only to sully her Reputation, and discover the Rankness of her Breath, was very cruel.[387]

Here, Collier seems to be attacking Shakespeare by using a reverent tone ("the Play had been better contriv'd"), which is maintained also in his review of Falstaff, for whom admiration becomes disappointment:

> In the mean time I shall take a Testimony or two from *Shakespear*. And here we may observe the admir'd *Falstaffe* goes off in Disappointment. He is thrown out of Favour as being a Rake, and dies like a Rat behind the Hangings. The Pleasure he had given, would not excuse him. The *Poet* was not so partial, as to let his Humour compound for his Lewdness.[388]

In the above citation, it is important to note that Collier mistakes Polonius for Falstaff because it is the latter that dies in his bed delirious, as is narrated in Act II, Scene iii of *Henry V*. Beyond this, Shakespeare is criticized for having used the comic to exaggerate the character's filth and licentiousness. Continuing with his character analysis but moving to a more general level, Collier expresses his satisfaction with the way in which Shakespeare treats the clergy:

> *Shakespear* takes the Freedom to represent the Clergy in several of his *Plays*: But for the most part he holds up the *Function*, and makes them neither Act, nor Suffer any thing unhandsome.[389]

386 Ibid., 10.

387 Ibid.

388 Ibid., 154.

389 Ibid., 125.

Various characters were used as examples. These include an extensive discussion about *Sir John Oldcastle*, which Collier erroneously considers Shakespearean. Aside from this error, Collier's overall opinion of the Bard reveals less hostility than to the more recent English playwrights: "So that upon the whole, Shakespear is by much the gentiler Enemy."[390]

Even from a linguistic standpoint, the accusations directed at the Bard are gentle. Regarding the licentiousness and obscenity of his language, Collier states:

> As for Shakespear, he is too guilty to make an Evidence: But I think he gains not much by his Misbehaviour; He has commonly Plautus's Fate, where there is most Smut, there is least Sense.[391]

In this way, *smut* and *sense* are inversely proportional to each other, which means that when one increases the other decreases; thus, a high degree of obscenity brings along a low understandability, and vice versa.

Finally, in the paragraph dedicated to "Cursing and Swearing" in the second chapter, the Bard's style is actually quite esteemed: "Shakespear is comparatively sober."[392] This view places Shakespeare beneath Jonson but above several other playwrights who are defined as "particularly rampant and scandalous,"[393] among whose works Collier mentions *The Old Batchelor*, *The Double Dealer*, *Love for Love*, *The Provoked Wife*, and *The Relapse* as particularly indecent.

Collier's work sparks a wide literary debate. The period of the first dispute covers 1698–1700, and was very lively and productive. Among the many responses to *A Short View*, one by Elkanah Settle[394] in 1698 showed its opposition to Collier by citing five Shakespearean tragedies among the seven most significant plays in the Restoration period:

> Here the shortest way to tell you what *will* please an *English* Audience, I think, is to look back and see what *has* pleased them. And here let us first take a view

390 Ibid., 126. This view remains unchanged in the later *A Defence of the Short View* (1699), in which Collier says "The Short View, &c. takes notice that Shakespear, though to blame, was a Genteeler Enemy than the Relapser [John Vanbrugh]" 79.

391 Collier, *A Short View,* 50.

392 Ibid., 57.

393 Ibid.

394 In *Shakespeare, The Critical Heritage*, Vickers believes instead that this citation is anonymous or that it was perhaps written by Edward Filmer (II, 89).

> of our best English Tragedies, as our *Hamlet*, *Mackbeth*, *Julius Caesar*, *Oedipus*, *Alexander*, *Timon of Athens*, *Moor of Venice*, and all the rest of our most shining Pieces.[395]

If we recall Gary Taylor's position, this statement further testifies to the primacy of Shakespeare's plays in theaters, the major channel of diffusion of the plays until well into the first half of the eighteenth century; as we know, the spread of printing and public readership still had a marginal role in the second half of the seventeenth century, although it gradually and consistently grew, decade after decade.

In the same year, 1698, George Ridpath defended the *Short View* in his *The Stage Condem'd*, in which he sadly cited the following observation made in the antitheatrical treatise *Histriomastix* (1632) written by the puritan William Prynne:

> Mr. *Prin* tells us in his Book before mentioned, in two Years time there were above 40,000 Play Books printed: They became more vendible than the choicest Sermons: Grew up from Quarto's to Folio's; were printed on far better Paper than most of the Octavo or Quarto Bibles, and were more saleable than they. And *Shakespeers* Plays in particular were printed in the best Paper.[396]

It is worth noting that there is a return to the paradigm of the sacred, which Ridpath combines with the commercial dimension of book sales, noting with regret that secular texts sold better than sermons. In particular, Shakespeare, whose works were printed on the best paper available, was being culturally disseminated even before theaters were closed in 1642. In several cases, the Bard was associated with the sphere of the sacred; in this particular case, at least according to Prynne's opinion, repeated by Ridpath, Shakespearean texts went beyond it and even rose above it.[397]

Collier's allegations against Shakespeare are rejected point by point in James Drake's *The Antient and Modern Stages Survey'd* (1699). In his defense of *Hamlet*, Drake spoke of the moral lesson deriving from the tragedy, and of its conclusion according to the principles of poetic justice:

395 Settle, *A Farther Defence,* 32.

396 Ridpath, *The Stage Condemn'd,* 10.

397 Let us recall the same situation related in *Northern Nuntio*, as well as the remark by John Cook about Charles I in *King Charls his Case*.

> Whatever defects the Criticks may find in this Fable, the Moral of it is excellent. Here was a Murther privately committed, strangely discover'd, and wonderfully punish'd. Nothing in Antiquity can rival this Plot for the admirable distribution of Poetic Justice. The Criminals are not only brought to execution, but they are taken in their own Toyls, their own Stratagems recoyl upon 'em, and they are involv'd themselves in that mischief and ruine, which they had projected for *Hamlet*.[398]

Drake believed that the attack on Ophelia in *A Short View* was triggered by the song "To morrow is St Valentine's day," which Colliers considered obscene. Consequently, Collier regretted the late death of the character, which also carried the weight of "the excuse of madness for Self-murther."[399] Ophelia's defense, however, was not grounded in objectivity, and became a simple attack on Collier's cognitive faculties, thus decreasing Drake's credibility: "Mr. Collier is deceived by a bad Nose, or a rotten Tooth of his own"[400] and "It may therefore be worth while to enquire, whether the fault lies in her Mouth, or his Nose."[401]

As in other examples, the bardolatry emerging from in Drake's treatise has tracts of indecisiveness. The gloss on p. 201 states that "Shakespear preferr'd to all the rest of the English Dramatics," while the corresponding passage begins with "I must still think [Shakespeare] the Proto-Dramatist of England, tho he fell short of the Art of Johnson and the Conversation of Beaumont and Fletcher,"[402] and then continues:

> Upon that account he wants many of their Graces, yet his Beauties make large amends for his Defects, and Nature has richly provided him with the materials, tho his unkind Fortune denied him the Art of managing them to the best Advantage.[403]

On the whole, this assessment balances precariously between lack of grace and amending beauties, nature and art; and Shakespeare's faults are not his own, but are ascribed to unkind fortune.

However, the tragic plays of the Bard are praised and even judged superior to those of Classical Antiquity, in addition to being widely known and applauded by the public of the time:

398 Drake, *The Antient and Modern Stages Survey'd,* 204.
399 Ibid., 295.
400 Ibid., 202.
401 Ibid., 293.
402 Ibid., 201.
403 Ibid., 201–2.

> The Tragedies of this Author in general are Moral and Instructive, and many of 'em such, as the best of Antiquity can't equal in that respect. His *King Lear*, *Timon of Athens*, *Macbeth*, and some others are so remarkable upon that score, that 'twou'd be impertinent to trouble the Reader with a minute examination of Plays so generally known and approved.[404]

This stance is rather original, as it praises the material creation, the work itself, which a quite uncommon. In fact, a general overview of the system of paratexts shows a tendency towards a different, if not opposed, direction – the exaltation of the Bard and the condemnation of his plays, a trend that is especially evident in the second half of the seventeenth century.

After a couple of years, the debate around Collier's text resumed; however, the period of the second dispute (1703–1708) arising from *A Short View* did not produce such valuable results, at least as far as the construction of Shakespeare as a hero of English culture is concerned. The only passage in which the Bard is mentioned, an isolated passage, is found in Dialogue VI of *Visits from the Shades* (1704), in which Ben Jonson, the character of the dialogue, relates that:

> I have kept a Correspondence with your Theater for these forty Years, and could never yet find any of you come to the perfection of *Shakespear*, and, to speak without vaunting, any thing comparable to my *Volpone*, or *Silent Woman*.[405]

In all other texts deriving from the dispute, the Bard's name is virtually absent. The only works in which there is an indirect reference to Shakespeare belong to Arthur Bedford. In his preface to *Serious Reflections*,[406] Bedford attacks the plays *Macbeth* and *The Tempest* because they are a "mocking [of] the Almighty Power of God, who alone commands the winds and the seas, and they obey him."[407] In 1719 Bedford returns to this subject in the subsequent and more thorough work *A Serious Remonstrance*,[408] in which he notes that *Sauny the Scot*, John Lacy's adaptation of *The Taming of the Shrew*, "is full of most dreadful

404 Ibid., 206.
405 Anonymous, *Visits from the Shades,* 38.
406 Bedford, *Serious Reflection.*
407 Ibid., vii.
408 Bedford, *A Serious Remonstrance.*

oaths, and horrid curses,"[409] and concludes that the Bard's play is better because "the original in Shakespear is free from cursing."[410] In the appendix of *A Sermon*, which was printed in 1730, but includes concepts that date back to earlier periods, he reflects upon *Macbeth* criticizing it because it does not discourage the use of witchcraft or magic ("There is no discouragement of witchcraft or magick").[411] After giving examples referring to the characters of Macbeth, Banquo, and Macduff, and in spite of the popularity of the play ("I have dwelt the longer on this play, as being one most frequently acted"),[412] Bedford concludes with a negative assessment: "the antidote is too weak for the poison, or rather in this case is no antidote at all."[413]

The passages cited above show that only minimal references to Shakespeare are made; the Bard is never brought to the defendant's seat in the period of the second dispute arising from Collier's treatise.

3.6 From Wright to Felton, Traversing *Roscius Anglicanus* and *The Tatler*[414]

In the preface to the dialogue in *Historia Histrionica* (1699), a work cast in the form of a dialogue between two abstract figures, Lovewit and Trueman, James Wright compares plays with portraits, and, displaying a great sense of history, recognizes that each age has its own style, which differs from the preceding and subsequent age. This chronological perspective,

409 Ibid., 371.

410 Ibid.

411 Bedford, *A Sermon Preached* 35.

412 Ibid., 38.

413 Ibid., 38–9.

414 James Wright, *Historia Histrionica, An Historical Account of the English-Stage* (London, 1699); [Charles Gildon?] *A Comparison Between the Two Stages* (London, 1702); George Farquhar, "A Discourse Upon Comedy, In Reference to the English Stage," *Works,* 2 vols. (London, 1711); John Downes, *Roscius Anglicanus, Or An Historical Review of the Stage* (London, 1708); Richard Steele, *The Tatler* No. 71, 20 (September 1709); Henry Felton, *A Dissertation on Reading the Classics, and Forming a Just Style. Written in the Year 1709* (London, 1713).

however, has not attracted many critics, especially after that some Shakespearean studies, until quite recently, have introduced and developed in various ways an unhistorical and unchronological discourse of absolutes and transcendental truths. The following is Wright's passage:

> For plays are exactly like portraits, drawn in the garb and fashion of the time when painted. You see one habit in the times of Charles I. another quite different from that, both for men and women, in Queen Elizabeth's time; another under Henry the Eight different from both, and so backward all various. And in the several fashions of behaviour and conversation there is as much mutability as in that of clothes.[415]

With regard to Shakespeare specifically, the dialogue between Lovewit and Truman only makes a small contribution to the overall picture of bardolatry. The only reference worth noting is the following; a simple sentence stating that Shakespeare had more expertise in writing than in acting:

> TRUMAN. What I can at present recollect I'll tell you, *Shakespear*, (who as I have heard, was much a better Poet, than a Player) *Burbadge*, *Hemmings*, and others of the Older fort, were Dead before I knew the Town.[416]

One of the most significant passages refers to Jonson and to the changes made by Wright's contemporary playwrights to Elizabethan plays; these can also be applied to Shakespeare:

> TRUMAN. *Ben. Johnson?* How dare you name *Ben. Johnson* in these times? When we have such a crowd of Poets of a quite different Genius; the least of which thinks himself as well able to correct *Ben. Johnson*, as he could a Country School Mistress that taught to spell.
>
> LOVEWIT. We have indeed, Poets of a different Genius; so are the Plays: But in my Opinion, they are all of 'em (some few excepted) as much inferior to those of former Times, as the Actors now in being (generally speaking) are, compared to *Hart*, *Mohum*, *Burt*, *Lacy*, *Clun*, and *Shatterel*; for I can reach no farther backward.[417]

The picture that emerges is not exciting. Creation, production and performance were considered inferior to the previous period; by negative

415 Wright, preface to *Historia Histrionica,* n.p.
416 Ibid., 4.
417 Ibid., 2.

inference, Shakespeare, his plays, and the actors who represented them on stage were better than those of the Restoration.

Anonymous or by Charles Gildon,[418] printed in 1702, *A Comparison between the Two Stages* is a treatise written in dialogue form with three interlocutors: two gentlemen, Ramble and Sullen, and a literary critic, Chagrin. It exalts Shakespeare; general praises are expressed by Chagrin:

> *CRITICK.* I think the People were never more in the right; for no Author ever writ with that Felicity, or had such a prodigious compass of Thought …[419]

In terms of dramatic genres, the Bard's mastery is praised in a similar way in the category of historical dramas:

> *CRITICK* … and tho' some of those Plays that *Batterton* Acted were Historical, and consequently highly irregular, yet they never fail'd to please; tho' its one of the hardest things in the World to make an Historical Play diverting.[420]

He subsequently adds that:

> *CRITICK* … *Shakespear* wou'd not ha' told his Story at that rate; his relation of Battles and Triumphs are his Master pieces, and 'tis the best occasion a Poet can have to display himself.[421]

The other two canonical dramatic genres, comedy and tragedy, are lauded in a similar tone, as eulogized by Sullen: "Shakespear [is] sublime in the first [tragedy], and always natural in the latter [comedy]."[422]

While it is true that a study of bardolatry often begins at the textual level, the present study primarily intends to reveal the paratextual dimension of this phenomenon. Bardolatry, it should be noted, can also be considered at the extratextual level, in particular in the performance. As we have already seen in Pepys' *Diary*, the rhetorical questions about the value of actors in determining the success of a play and a playwright offer some food for thought:

---

418 S. B. Wells, "An Eighteenth Century Attribution," *Journal of English and Germanic Philology* 38 (1939): 239–46. Here, Wells supposes that it was written by Charles Gildon.

419 [Gildon?] *A Comparison between the Two Stages,* 42.

420 Ibid., 42–3.

421 Ibid., 87.

422 Ibid., 57.

> *CRITICK* … Upon the Stage it may appear well, but he [Rowe] had some of the best Tragedians in the World to Act it, and who knows not the Advantage a Play receives from their Mouths? Who knows not the effect of *Batterton*'s fine Action? Who is not charmed with Mrs. *Barry*? What Beauty do they not give every thing they represent? What Beauty do they not give every thing they represent? Still don't mistake me Gentlemen; I am not solliciting against the Poet's Merit, but am insinuating t'ee how many indifferent Play has had good success when these Persons have been concern'd in it.[423]

If great acting renders great an *indifferent play* by an *indifferent dramatist*, then the effect is only amplified if the play is acknowledged as a masterpiece and is by a playwright who belongs to a group of recognized masters such as Jonson, Fletcher, or Shakespeare.

Thus far bardolatry in *A Comparison* is altogether moderate, but there is a passage, cited below in full, in which Sullen imagines Betterton rapt in a prayer to Shakespeare. The episode is clearly permeated by a religious quality wherein the Bard is king of heaven:

> *O* Shakespear, Shakespear! *What have our Sins brought upon us! We have renounc'd the ways which thou hast taught us, and are degenerated into Infamy and Corruption: Look down from thy Throne on* Mount Parnassus, *and take commiseration on thy Sons now fallen in Misery: Let down a Beam of thy brightness upon this our forlorn* Theatre; *let thy Spirit dwell with us, let thy Influence be upon our Poets, let the Streams of thy* Helicon *glide along by* Lincolns-Inn-Fields, *and fructifie our Soil as the Waters of the* Nile *make fruitful the barren Banks of* Egypt. He rose, and rose much comforted: With that he falls to work about his Design, opens the Volume and picks our two or three of *Shakespears* Plays; and now, says he, I'll seague it away ifaith: Blessed be the Relicks of this Saint; they're more precious than those at *Loretto*, and a Penny that comes in from so pious a Shrine must needs prosper. The whim fell in very luckily with the humour of the People, and every body run now to renew their acquaintance with *Shakespear*.[424]

The Bard, therefore, is Master, King of Poets, and he resides in heaven. His divine status is reinforced with the anaphoric repetition of the deictic possessive "thy," which appears six times within close range ("*thy* Throne on Mount Parnassus"; "*thy* Sons now fallen"; "a Beam of *thy* Brightness"; "let *thy* Spirit dwell with us"; "let *thy* Influence be upon our Poets"; "let the Streams of *thy* Helicon … fructifie our Soil"). The

423 Ibid., 190.

424 Ibid., 42.

deifying perspective, which invokes mercy and requests a guiding light for its children fallen from heavenly grace, is portrayed in the more concrete (and pagan) setting with Mount Parnassus and the Helicon River.

The following metaphor is even more significant: "two or three of Shakespears Plays" become "Blessed … Relicks of this Saint" and a "pious … Shrine." Since the publication date for *A Comparison* is 1702, this treatise immerses itself among the seeds, which can no longer be considered isolated and unique, of a bardolatry that has already been well developed throughout the whole of the seventeenth century. Like others at the beginning of the eighteenth century, Sullen's voice moves Shakespeare's work closer to the sacred, qualifying it as relic and shrine. In this way, he becomes part of the trend that begins to move the core of the veneration for the Bard towards his versification and material output, the play.

Over time, Shakespeare's versification and poetics gain so much reputation and are so consolidated that their weight is same as that of Aristotle. George Farquhar believes this, and proposes an *ipse dixit* comparison between the two in which the Bard would be triumphant. In his "A Discourse upon Comedy," he in fact states that:

> It must be so, because Aristotle said it. Now I say it must be otherwise, because Shakespeare said it, and I'm sure that Shakespeare was the greatest Poet of the two.[425]

Roscius Anglicanus, John Downes' celebrated treatise on theater printed in 1708, focuses on the production, staging, and performance of plays. Shakespeare's greatness also emerges in the great actors who represent the tragic, comic or historical heroes of the Bard's plays. This is particularly true at least until the first decades of the eighteenth century, a time when the printing press begins to proliferate and the printed page become more and more widespread. As we know, until the late seventeenth century, Shakespeare's reputation is highly indebted to performance in theaters:

> As confirmed by Downes, Thomas Betterton is among the first great Shakespearean actors:

425 Farquhar, "A Discourse upon Comedy," I, 78.

> *Hamlet* being Perform'd by Mr. *Betterton*, Sir *William* (having seen Mr. *Taylor* of the *Black-Fryars* Company Act it, who being Instructed by the Author Mr. *Shakspeur*) taught Mr. *Betterton* in every Particle of it; which by his exact Performance of it, gain'd him Esteem and Reputations, Superlative to all other Plays… No succeeding Tragedy for several Years got more Reputation, or Money to the Company than this.[426]

Along with the noted passage on *Hamlet* cited above, it is important to add another, with a similar tone, on *Henry VIII*:

> The part of the King was so right and justly done by Mr. *Betterton*, he being Instructed in it by Sir *William*, who had it from Old Mr. *Lowen*, that had his Instructions from Mr. *Shakespear* himself, that I dare and will aver, none can, or will come near him in this Age, in the performance of that part: … It continu'd Acting 15 Days together with general Applause.[427]

Similar admiration, if not altogether superior, is expressed in *The Tatler* when Betterton has almost arrived at the end of his career; despite his age, the power of his acting is still impressive – "a force of action in perfection." A year before his death, 1709, in number 71, one in fact reads:

> Had you been to Night at the Play-house you had seen the Force of Action in Perfection. Your admir'd Mr. Betterton behav'd himself so well that tho' now about Seventy he acted Youth; and by the prevalent Power of proper Manner, Gesture and Voice, appear'd through the whole Drama a Youth of great Expectation, Vivacity, and Enterprize. [The *To be or not to be* soliloquy, the closet scene, the ghost scene, Ophelia's funeral] are each of them Circumstances which dwell strongly upon the Minds of the Audience, and would certainly affect their Behaviour an any parallel Occasions in their own Lives.[428]

Thus, through Betterton, *Hamlet* and Shakespeare remain in the minds and memory of the audience thanks to the acting ability of the great actor, who is able to impress upon the public's conscience a play's most memorable scenes, which endure in memory and are remembered as models of ethical behavior for real life, which one can refer to.

---

426 Downes, *Roscius Anglicanus,* 21.

427 Ibid., 24.

428 Steele, *The Tatler*, No. 71, September 20, 1709.

Henry Felton's popular[429] treatise *A Dissertation on Reading the Classics*,[430] includes a passage with a very high level of bardolatry. In fact, its exaltation of Shakespeare's *genius*, *nature*, and *wit* is so great that it even surpasses the praise found in Margaret Cavendish's letter CXIII cited above:

> Shakespeare is a wonderful Genius, a single Instance of the Force of Nature, and the Strength of Wit. Nothing can be greater and more lively than his Thoughts; nothing nobler and more forcible than his Expression. The Fire of his Fancy breaketh out into his Words and sets his Reader on a Flame. He maketh the Blood run cold or warm, and is so admirable a Master of the Passions that he raises Your Courage, Your Pity, and Your Fear, at his Pleasure; but he delighteth most in Terror.[431]

3.7 The First Editors of the Shakespeare Canon[432]

This section examines the contributions of the first three editors of the Shakespeare canon, plus two essays by Charles Gildon appearing in an unauthorized book intended to cover the lacuna in Nicholas Rowe's edition. The chronological span is quite wide, covering over two decades from 1709 to 1733, and the contributions are not always found in a prefatory position in the Shakespearean edition, but for clearness' sake, I have decide to discuss the various contributions grouping them under a single category.

---

429 Felton's *A Dissertation on Reading the Classics, and Forming a Just Style*, written in 1709 and printed in 1713 for the first time, records five editions in 40 years between 1713 and 1753.

430 Please see above for publication information.

431 Felton, *A Dissertation,* 212–13.

432 Nicholas Rowe, "Some Account of the Life, &c of Mr. William Shakespeare," *The Works of William Shakespeare* (London, 1709); Charles Gildon, "An Essay on the Art, Rise and Progress of the Stage in Greece, Rome and England," and "Remarks on the Plays of Shakespeare," *The Works of Mr. William Shakespeare. Volume the Seventh* (London, 1710); Lewis Theobald, *The Censor,* No. 70, April 2, 1717; Alexander Pope, *The Works of Shakespeare, Collated and Corrected* (London, 1725); Lewis Theobald, *Shakespeare Restored* (London, 1726), and *The Works of Shakespeare, Collated with the Oldest Copies, and Corrected, with Notes, Explanatory and Critical* (London, 1733).

In London, in 1709, Tonson published the first edition of the Shakespeare canon appearing after the four *Folios*. It was edited by Rowe, who, in the prefatorial peritexts to the first volume, wrote an essay on the Bard that focused on the biography of the author.

In Shakespeare, Rowe admired "that fire, impetuosity, and even beautiful extravagance,"[433] his "fire and strength of imagination"[434] that fortunately had *not* been softened by the presence of Classical culture. Proceeding thus, Rowe transformed a flaw into a quality. Regarding the Bard's other main shortcoming, his failure to comply with pseudo-Aristotelian rules, another, although not new, defensive strategy was adopted: the opinion that the Elizabethan period was an uncivilized and primitive age ("Shakespeare liv'd under a kind of mere light of nature"; "we are to consider him as a man that liv'd in a state of almost universal license and ignorance").[435] Thus, the fault did not lie with the individual, but with the society and time in which he lived.

Rowe acknowledged Shakespeare's greatness and genius, qualities that could allow the Bard to surpass the Classics: "the natural bent of his own great genius, equal, if not superior, to some of the best of [the Classics]."[436] His praises for Shakespeare were for his general style: as when he defended the Bard from Rymer proclaiming that "[Shakespeare is] a Man Excellent on most Occasions, and whom all the World ever was and will be inclin'd to have an Esteem and Veneration for,"[437] thus enabling certain widespread sacred overtones to transpire; or as when discussing the Bard's dramatic writing, where Shakespeare excels across the board ("'Tis not very easie to determine which way of writing he was most excellent in").[438]

A year later, a spurious "volume seven" appeared including poems by the Bard and two extended essays by Charles Gildon, "An Essay on the Art, Rise and Progress of the Stage in Greece, Rome and England," and "Remarks on the Plays of Shakespeare." In the first essay, Gildon claimed to use a neutral critical approach, which, beginning

433 Rowe, "Some Account of the Life," iii.
434 Ibid., vii.
435 Ibid., xxvi.
436 Ibid., iii.
437 Ibid., xv.
438 Ibid., xvii.

from neoclassical precepts, brought to light both the author's *errors* and *perfections*, since there was a group of zealots who praise Shakespeare blindly and uncritically:

> As I shall give many more Examples of his Beauties than those few which his Editor has but very slightly glanc'd on his Life, so shall I lay down such Rules of Art that the Reader may be able to distinguish his Errors from his Perfections, now too much and too unjustly confounded by the foolish Biggotry of his blind and partial Adorers.[439]

If, then, Gildon intended to distance himself from the "foolish biggotry of [Shakespeare's] blind and partial adorers," his position on the Bard's knowledge of the Classics was not completely free from tones of praise. In his opinion, Shakespeare was a genius and a miracle of the age he lived in; he did not know the Classics, but if he had known them, he would have been their equal because the rules of Antiquity would not have spoiled his natural genius, which enabled him to produce excellent writings:

> 'Tis my opinion that if Shakespeare had had those Advantages of Learning which the perfect Knowledge of the Ancients wou'd have given him, so great a Genius as his wou'd have made him a very dangerous Rival in Fame to the greatest Poets of Antiquity, so far am I from seeing how this Knowledge cou'd either have curb'd, confin'd, or spoil'd the natural Excellence of his Writings. For tho' I must always think out Author a Miracle for the Age he liv'd in yet I am oblig'd, in Justice to Reason and Art, to confess that he does not come up to the Ancients in all the Beauties of the Drama.[440]

Gildon observed Shakespeare through the lens of art and the rules of the Classics, and it would seem that this kept him from using more appreciative tones, suggesting that this much genius is excessive, and needs to be mitigated. In the following passage, the characters' manners and diction are excellent, but this is immediately juxtaposed with the plot, which is very often faulty in the Bard's case:

> Nature enabl'd Shakespeare to succeed in the Manners and Diction often to Perfection, but he cou'd never by his Force of Genius or Nature vanquish the barbarous

439 Gildon, "An Essay on the Art," ii.
440 Ibid., iii.

> Mode of the Times and come to any Excellence in the Fable, except in the *Merry Wives of Windsor* and the *Tempest*.[441]

In the second essay, "Remarks on the Plays of Shakespeare," Gildon did not change his opinion: in the conclusion, firstly, he claimed to have demonstrated both the Bard's qualities and defects to the admirers of the acknowledged greatest poetic genius of modern times that England had; secondly, he confirmed his personal preference for the Classics. Their principles, in fact, are the only defense against the lush natural beauty of Shakespeare, whose genius shines despite his lack of art and classical limitations:

> Besides, if I have shown you all that was any way beautiful in him I have also been so just to the Art as often to point out his Errors in that particular. And having gone over this celebrated Author with so much Care, an Author asserted by the Number of his Admirers ... to be the greatest Genius of the modern Times, especially of this Nation, I find myself confirm'd in the Opinion I have long had of the Antients in the Drama, I mean in Tragedy. For, having been so long conversant with the Confusions of want of Art in this Poet (tho' supported with all the Advantages of a great Genius) the Beauty of Order, Uniformity, and Harmony of Design appears infinitely more Charming, and that is only to be found in the Greek Poets.[442]

In a piece appearing in n. 70 of *The Censor* dated April 2, 1717, Lewis Theobald wrote in defense of *Julius Caesar*, declaring that pseudo-Aristotelian classifications are not suited for judging Shakespeare because his genius is above any rule:

> As to particular Irregularities it is not to be expected that a Genius like Shakespeare's should be judg'd by the Laws of Aristotle and the other Prescribers of the Stage. It will be sufficient to fix a Character of Excellence to his Performances if there are in them a Number of beautiful Incidents, true and exquisite Turns of Nature and Passion, fine and delicate Sentiments, uncommon Images, and great Boldness of Expression.[443]

In the following decade, Alexander Pope followed the same line of thought as Theobald, whom he more or less paraphrased. In the preface to his 1725 edition of the Shakespeare canon, he wrote "to judge therefore

---

441 Ibid., xxxiii.

442 Gildon, "Remarks on the Plays of Shakespeare," 424.

443 Theobald, *The Censor*.

Shakespeare by Aristotle's rules is like trying a man by the Laws of one Country who acted under those of another."[444] He also defends the Bard against his adversaries by putting the blame essentially on everybody else except Shakespeare: the low style and inconsistencies were there to please the theater audience's low and gross tastes, the corruption of texts were there because of the players' interventions or faulty memory that changed the original text during the process of transmission from manuscript to print.

Pope's eulogy was quite remarkable. Even if there were some defects, Shakespeare "is justly and universally elevated above all other dramatic writers"; he is more original than Homer; his poetry is pure inspiration; "he is not so much an imitator, as an instrument, of nature."[445] His greatest qualities probably lie in the depiction of the human characters: "his characters are so much nature herself,"[446] as remembered by Harold Bloom in *The Invention of the Human*, at the end of the twentieth century, almost three hundred years later.

In the following year, Theobald presented his *Shakespeare Restored*, a book that included the first systematic examination of the Shakespearean text, beginning with his criticism of the errors in the edition edited by Pope. Previously, the Bard had been variously defended (in a more-or-less uncritical way) against the accusations of his detractors by laying blame on Shakespeare's time, society, and the actors who were cast in his plays. Another category may be added: that of the *editor*, who, thanks to Theobald, assumed real critical weight:

> The Design of this Work [*Shakespeare Restored*] was an honest Endeavour to restore Shakespeare from the Corruptions that have taken Place in all his Editions, and to this End I gave it as my Opinion that an Editor of Him ought to be a Critick upon him too.[447]

Some years later, in 1733, in the preface to his edition of the Canon, he paid tribute to the Bard, his variety, genius, and creative ardor in a passage with clear idolatrous overtones:

444 Pope, preface to *The Works of Shakespeare, Collated and Corrected,* iii.

445 Ibid., ii.

446 Ibid.

447 Theobald, appendix to *Shakespeare Restored,* 133.

> No Age, perhaps, can produce an Author more various from himself, than Shakespeare has been universally acknowledg'd to be. The Diversity in Stile, and other Parts of Composition, so obvious in him, is as variously accounted for. His Education, we find, was at best but begun, and he started early into Science from his force of Genius, unequally assisted by acquir'd Improvements. His Fire, Spirit, and Exuberance of Imagination gave an impetuosity to his Pen; his Ideas flow'd from him in a stream rapid, but not ever over-bearing its Shores. The Ease and Sweetness of his Temper might not a little contribute to his Facility in Writing, as his Employment as a Player gave him an Advantage and Habit of fancying himself the very Character he meant to delineate.[448]

The opening paragraphs set off identifying Shakespeare with a source of light that illuminates the mind of those who meet him "a glare of light suddenly breaks upon you: and a thousand beauties of genius and character … diffuse and throw themselves out to the mind,"[449] and, a little later, "in how many points of light must we be oblig'd to gaze at this great poet!"[450] Among the various laudatory epithets employed, the Bard was recurrently called "Genius," but he was also the "British Homer."[451]

One of his major attributes was imagination, a strong, powerful rich flowing vein that sometimes, when the blaze was too powerful, led him to commit some errors, especially when writing histories.[452] Nevertheless, its exuberance, heat and abundance, was such a great gift that such a small flaws can easily be pardoned. Even in the works unworthy of him, Theobald asserted that it was possible to "recognize the *divine* composer."[453] A little later, when discussing the role of the Shakespearean critic, he stated that "his genuine text is *religiously* adher'd to,"[454] thus using rhetoric related to the sacred, which heightened the Bard and his work to a superhuman condition.

448 Theobald, preface to *The Works of Shakespeare,* xxv.
449 Ibid., i.
450 Ibid., ii.
451 Ibid., xxv.
452 Ibid., xxx.
453 Ibid., xxxiv.
454 Ibid., xl.

3.8 Bardolatry and Barbarous Language[455]

In the second decade of the eighteenth century, the historicist perspective in the area of languages had not yet been established. Thus, the language of the preceding age was judged without consideration of the chronological gap. Anthony Cooper stated that:

> The British Muses … lisp as in their Cradles; and their stammering Tongues, which nothing beside their Youth and Rawness can excuse, have hitherto spoken in wretched Pun and Quibble. Our Dramatick Shakespeare, our Fletcher, Johnson, and our Epick Milton preserve this Style.[456]

Along the same lines, Elijah Fenton adds a good dose of bardolatry:

> Shakespeare the Genius of our Isle, whose Mind –
> The universal Mirror of Mankind –
> Express'd all Images, enrich'd the Stage
> But stoop'd too low to please a barb'rous Age.
> When his Immortal Bays began to grow
> Rude was the Language, and the Humour Low.
> He, like the God of Day, was always bright,
> But Rolling in its Course, his Orb of Light
> Was sully'd and obscur'd, tho' soaring high,
> With Spots contracted from the nether Sky.
> But whither is th' advent'rous Muse betray'd?
> Forgive her Rashness, venerable Shade!
> May Spring with Purple Flow'rs perfume thy Urn,
> And Avon with Greens thy Grave adorn.
> Be all thy Faults, whatever Faults there be,
> Imputed to the Times, and not to Thee. (vv. 29–45)[457]

455 Earl of Shaftesbury (Anthony Ashley Cooper), *Characteristicks of Men, Manners, Opinions, Times* (London, 1710); Elijah Fenton, *An Epistle to Mr. Southerne, From Kent, January 28* (London, 1711); Joseph Addison, *Spectator* No. 39, April 14, 1711; No. 419, July 1, 1712; No. 592, September 10, 1714.

456 Earl of Shaftesbury, *Characteristicks of Men,* 217.

457 Fenton, *An Epistle.*

Addison also believed Shakespearean language to be defective:

> I must in the next place observe that when our Thoughts are great and just they are often obscured by the sounding Phrases, hard Metaphors, and forced Expressions in which they are cloathed. Shakespeare is often very Faulty in this Particular.[458]

His negative appraisal of Shakespearean language did not prevent him from being eulogistic towards the Bard on other occasions. Addison thus displayed an attitude of ambiguous alternation, which characterized others such as Dryden and Gildon.

Shakespeare's genius was best expressed when his fantasy and imagination freely create fantastical characters:

> Amongst the English Shakespeare has incomparably excelled all others. That noble Extravagance of Fancy, which he had in so great Perfection, thoroughly qualified him to touch this weak superstitious Part of his Reader's Imagination, and made him capable of succeeding where he had nothing to support him besides the Strength of his own Genius.[459]

Shakespeare's innate genius expresses a beauty that goes beyond neo-Classical rules, as has already been seen earlier:

> In the next Place, our Criticks do not seem sensible that there is more Beauty in the Works of a great Genius who is ignorant of the Rules of Art than in those of a little Genius who knows and observes them... Our inimitable Shakespeare is a Stumbling-block to the whole Tribe of these rigid Criticks. Who would not rather read one of his Plays, where there is not a single Rule of the Stage observed, than any Production of a modern Critick, where there is not one of them violated? Shakespeare was indeed born with all the Seeds of Poetry, and may be compared to the Stone in Pyrrhus's Ring, which, as Pliny tells us, had the Figure of Apollo and the Nine Muses in the Veins of it, produced by the spontaneous Hand of Nature without any Help from Art.[460]

---

458 Addison, *Spectator*, No. 39, April 14, 1711.

459 Addison, *Spectator*, No. 419, July 1, 1712.

460 Addison, *Spectator*, No. 592, September 10, 1714.

3.9 Voices before the Censorship Law[461]

In the first half of the eighteenth century Shakespeare continued to be idolized on many fronts. He was praised as a sublime poet in 1712 by Leonard Welsted in *Remarks on Longinus* ("There are numberless Instances of this kind of Sublime to be produced from our Poets: Shakespeare and Milton every where abound with them");[462] and in 1729 as the father of English theater in the preface to *Sophocles' Tragedies, Translated from the Greek* by George Adams:

> But to come to the Writers of our own Nation, the divine Shakespeare was the first who began this Art among us, and indeed who ended it too, for he has gain'd so much Praise in it that he hath scarce left any for those who come after him. And he is so much the more to be admir'd because he perform'd what he did without the Help of Learning; nor indeed did he need it, he could look within himself and there find all the Images of Nature perfectly painted.[463]

And by William Levin in *Universal Spectator,* No. 131, of April 10, 1731:

> Shakespeare and Jonson were the two first Writers who gave any Lustre to the Dramatick Performances of our Nation; and tho' we have since them had abundance of Authors in that Way yet I believe I shall hardly be contradicted in saying that there have been very few who can with any Justice be call'd their Equals, and not so much as one who can be said to have excell'd them.[464]

Or by John Dennis, whose idolatry does not display any cones of shadow. In 1711, in *An Essay upon the Genius and Writings of Shakespeare*, Dennis states that:

---

461 Leonard Welsted, *Remarks on Longinus* (London, 1712); George Adams, *Sophocles' Tragedies, Translated from the Greek* (London, 1729); William Levin, *Universal Spectator*, No. 131, April 10, 1731; John Dennis, *An Essay upon the Genius and Writings of Shakespeare* (London, 1711), and *Original Letters* (London, 1721); David Mallet, *Of Verbal Criticism* (London, 1733); George Stubbs, *Some Remarks on the Tragedy of Hamlet* (London, 1736).

462 Welsted, *Remarks on Longinus,* 110.

463 Adams, preface to *Sophocles' Tragedies,* n.p.

464 Levin, *Universal Spectator*, No. 131, April 10, 1731 n.p.

> Shakespeare was one of the greatest Geniuses that the World e'er saw for the Tragick Stage. Tho' he lay under greater Disadvantages than any of his Successors, yet had he greater and more genuine Beauties than the best and the greatest of them. And what makes the brightest Glory of his Character, those Beauties were entirely his own, and owing to the force of his own Nature; whereas his Faults were owing to his Education and to the Age that he liv'd in. One may say of him as they did of Homer, that he had none to imitate, and is himself inimitable. His Imaginations were often as just as they were bold and strong.[465]

Some years later, in 1719 (though printed two years later), in one of the *Original Letters,* we can read:

> Shakespeare is very justly celebrated for the Truth and Justness of his Characters, for the Beauty of his Sentiments, for the Simplicity and Dignity of his Dialogue, and for his moving the Passions powerfully by the meer force of Nature.[466]

Finally, in the fourth decade of the eighteenth century, there was still evidence of praise for the Bard as a natural genius who was above neo-Classical rules and as father of English theater. This praise is manifest in David Mallet's *Of Verbal Criticism* (1733):

> Pride of his own, and wonder of his age,
> Who first created, and yet rules, the stage,
> Bold to design, all-powerful to express,
> Shakespeare each passion drew in every dress:
> Great above rule, and imitating none;
> Rich without borrowing, Nature was his own. (vv. 47–52)

In 1736, George Stubbs, in *Some Remarks on the Tragedy of Hamlet*, completed his review of epitexts contributing to the construction of Shakespearean bardolatry by employing words and language that were not innovative in according high praise to the Bard of Avon:

> I am going to do what to some may appear extravagant, but by those of a true taste in Works of Genius will be approv'd of. I intend to examine one of the Pieces of the greatest Tragick Writer that ever liv'd ... He had (beyond Dispute) a most unbounded Genius, very little regulated by Art. His particular Excellency consists in the Variety and Singularity of his Characters, and in the constant Conformity of each Character to itself from its very first setting our in the Play quite to the End.

465 Dennis, *An Essay,* 1.
466 Dennis, *Original Letters,* 71.

> And still further, no Poet ever came up to him in the Nobleness and Sublimity of Thought so frequent in his Tragedies, and all express'd with the most Energick Comprehensiveness of Diction.[467]

3.10 Concluding Remarks

The above analysis of the varied panorama of epitexts closes the present study's overview of the construction of bardolatry, which begins with Shakespearean adaptations of the Restoration period, a subject that started to be addressed starting at the end of the sixteenth century and for whom I have brought forward the most important examples.

Emphasizing a trend already visible in the previous two sections devoted to the peritext, the epitexts cited in this chapter clearly display idolatrous overtones. These are countered by voices of opposition to Shakespeare, thereby creating a concrete vision of polyphony and contrast of the Bard. It has been shown how the treatises by Rymer and Collier ignited a lively cultural and literary debate with supporters on both sides. Shakespeare's detractors, however, did not prevail, for the Bard was increasingly constructed as a national poet who clashed with neo-Classical rules originating overseas, winning the struggle.

This category of epitexts, like the peritexts discussed in the preceding chapter, presents again core concepts associated with the sacred and religion. These notions define Shakespeare as divine poet, father of the English language, elevating him to status of absolute icon of culture within an unhistorical, eternal, and absolute dimension whose apex is occupied by an entity now transcending the material reality and imperfections of his creations.

467 Stubbs, *Some Remarks,* 8.

4 Conclusion

The year 1737 represents an end and a beginning. Indeed, it is not only the year of theater censorship laws, but also the year in which David Garrick arrived in London, and, in just a few years, established a new acting style. The new *star* of the stage is found responding to and moving in a new theatrical environment, which is now rigidly prescribed.

Perhaps partly as a result of the various and violent satirical and controversial attacks against him, Robert Walpole passed the Theatrical Licensing Act on June 21. From that day onwards, every play had to pass the strictures of censorship wielded by Lord Chamberlain, who approved, banished or imposed changes that he deemed appropriate before the play could be staged. An effect of the Licensing Act was that theaters were no longer the main place for cultural debate; thus, new ideas were no longer introduced on the stage, but on the printed page. Henry Fielding and Henry Brooke, for example, had to change their channel of communication with the public, turning their energies from theater to novel, and thus contributing to the transition from the performance of the recited word to the reading of the printed word, which, as was demonstrated earlier, characterized bardolatry in the early eighteenth century.

Jean Marsden underlines how the process of canonization of the Bard, the first literary saint of England, "the increasing idolization of Shakespeare and his works," witnessed a movement from public to private, from theater to salon, and how the emphasis shifted to personal interpretation of the printed page.[468] Starting from the performances of the great actors of the early Restoration, the focus moved to Shakespeare's language, this being recognizable in various adaptations of the early eighteenth century. This stance was then resumed and more systematically treated in the Canon editions from 1709, and by mid-century Shakespeare's works were widely recognizable as printed text, and attitudes towards them were

468 Marsden, *The Re-Imagined Text,* 6.

influenced by a process of canonization in which the words themselves were sanctified.[469]

In the second half of the eighteenth century, this trend persisted and even intensified: "the later eighteenth century saw Shakespeare as magician, as nature, and above all as divinity."[470] The seeds of this idolatry and sacralization were planted more than a century before, long before John Cook or the *Northern Nuntio* compared the Bard to the Holy Scriptures. Shakespeare now became the Author, his text a Sacred Object, and his Canon a secular Bible.[471]

The Shakespearean adaptations of the Restoration are a relevant link in the process, guaranteeing continuity in the sanctification of the Bard. The peritexts of these plays display the typical spirit of the age: the bardolatry with which these texts are infused. That they sometime appear to have a slightly ventriloquistic or contradictory voice is due to the fact that the cult of Shakespeare was still under construction. They begin with praise for the man, creator, genius, poet, and criticism for his word and work, but they conclude with a complete eulogy for Shakespeare and his language, including also what they first criticized. It is a polyphonic voice that moves both from the stage and the actors, and from the pages of the essays of playwrights, critics, and editors.

Sonia Massai's observations regarding the rise of the Shakespearean editor and the changes that this figure contributes to the concepts of text and textual authorship are in part also true for the figure of the adapter, who is similar (at that time) in some ways to the editor. The passage below describes a situation that also occurs, albeit rarely, in the vast landscape of Shakespearean adaptations, which have never known a *folio* edition because of the variety of authors who have created an *alteration* of a Bard's play between 1660 and 1737:

> The unprecedented appearance of the name of the editor alongside the name of the author on the title page of a printed collection of English plays signaled the rise of a self-conscious proprietary stance towards the dramatic text.[472]

469 Ibid., 75.

470 Ibid., 127.

471 Ibid.

472 Sonia Massai, *Shakespeare and the Rise of the Editor* (Cambridge: Cambridge University Press, 2007), 1.

This is similar to what happened to the first edition of the Shakespeare canon of 1709:

> Whereas seventeenth-century readers had been encouraged to buy *Mr. William Shakespeare Comedies, Histories, & Tragedies. Published according to the True Originall Copies* in the four Folio Editions of 1623, 1632, 1663–4, and 1685, readers willing to invest in the new collected edition of Shakespeare's works in 1709 were duly informed that what they were purchasing was Nicholas Rowe's "Shakespeare"[473]

In other words, even the readers and buyers of adapted Shakespearean texts were occasionally made aware of the fact that the new text was an *alteration*, which sometimes differed significantly from its source.

When Massai states that "the conscious editorial manipulation of Shakespeare's dramatic texts had started well before Nicholas Rowe's edition,"[474] it is difficult not to think of the action of the adapters in the Restoration.

The aim of the present analysis of the paratexts of the Shakespearean adaptations between 1660 and 1737 is to highlight the relevance of these elements in the creation and positioning of Shakespeare at the center of English culture, as well as to examine their multiple voices of bardolatry. Such an investigation has demonstrated the significant role of adaptations of the Restoration period, given that in more than one case they are the means through which English society and culture recover what had been taken from them during the puritan regime of the Commonwealth.

Theatrically speaking, in the Restoration the adaptations are only a part of the total phenomenon of bardolatry, as they coexisted with their dramatic sources. Also, chronologically speaking, adaptations are expressions of a provisional significance because their force, along with number and afterlife, decrease as time passes;[475] nevertheless, despite these limitations, Shakespearean adaptations are a phenomenon highly characteristic of the Restoration.

In the end, however, the voices of the adaptations merged to create a common discourse of praise with great power and relevance in the global

473 Ibid.

474 Ibid., 2.

475 With their endurance lasting for over a century, Cibber's *Richard III* and Tate's *King Lear* are in fact the exceptions.

movement of the *grand récit* of bardolatry. This was based not only on the Shakespearean texts of *quartos* and *folios*, or the large amount of epitexts composed by external sources. The construction and placement of the Bard in the center of English culture also passed through the adaptations of the Restoration and their rich paratexts, which added a key tile in the great mosaic of Shakespearean bardolatry.

Appendix

The following tables give the most important information for each adaptation. The first set of information consists of the title of the original Shakespearean play, the name of the adaptation, and the name of the adapter; the second set deals with the adaptation's first stage representation, identifying its date, place, company and main actors; the third set contains information pertaining to the first printed edition, recording date, place, and printer; the last set provides an act-by-act summary of the adaptation's plot. When dates are uncertain, they appear in square brackets. The last set of tables will help to highlight the similarities and differences emerging from the comparison of the plot of the adaptation and Shakespeare's original (not provided here) – something that has been done only for the most successful adaptations.

The information in the first and third sets derives principally from the adaptation's paratext. The main texts used for collecting information for the second set are the first three volumes of *London Stage*, and, for plays after 1700, Charles Beecher Hogan's study titled *Shakespeare in the Theatre*.[476] The original spelling and abbreviations of seventeen and eighteenth centuries have been retained. The present study has also drawn upon George C. D. Odell's *Shakespeare from Betterton to Irving*,[477] and John Genest's *Some Account of the English Stage*.[478] The plot is obviously resumed directly from the play itself.

The layout, with the first sets of information on one page facing the plot on the other, is aimed at conveying all the information at a glance.

476 Charles Beecher Hogan, *Shakespeare in the Theatre*, 2 vols. (Oxford: Clarendon Press, 1952–7).

477 George C. D. Odell, *Shakespeare from Betterton to Irving*, 2 vols. (New York: Charles Scribner's Sons, 1920).

478 John Genest, *Some Account of the English Stage*, 10 vols. (Bath: H. E. Carrington, 1832).

1. *All for Love*

GENERAL INFORMATION
ADAPTOR'S NAME: Dryden, John
ADAPTED PLAY: *All for Love, or The World Well Lost*
SHAKESPEARE'S PLAY: *Antony and Cleopatra*

FIRST STAGED
DATE: [December 12, 1677][479]
PLACE: Drury Lane
MAIN ACTORS

Men
Marc Anthony, Mr. Hart
Ventidius, his general, Mr. Mohun
Dollabella, his friend, Mr. Clarke
Alexas, the Queens Eunuch, Mr. Goodman
Serapion, Priest of Isis, Mr. Griffin
Another priest, servants to Anthony, Mr. Coysh

Women
Cleopatra, Queen of Egypt, Mrs. Boutell
Octavia, Anthony's wife, Mrs. Corey

FIRST PRINTED
DATE: 1678
PLACE: London

OTHER INFORMATION
In the SAVOY: Printed by Tho. Newcomb, for Henry Herringman, at the Blew Anchor in the Lower Walk of the New-Exchange.

479 In *London Stage* the above is the "first certainly known performance … probably not the premiere."

1. *All for Love*

PLOT

Act 1

In Alexandria, Egypt, after the battle of Actium, Ventidius meets the defeated Anthony in despair, and comforts him; by giving him the support of Roman soldiers, Ventidius convinces Anthony to return to the battlefield to face Octavian once again.

Act 2

Cleopatra learns of Anthony's decision, and sends Alexas to request a meeting before his departure. Ventidius opposes to this, but Anthony accepts the Queen's request, and meets Cleopatra.

Act 3

Antonio meets Cleopatra. Ventidius lets Antonio meet with Dolabella first, then with his wife Octavia and their two young daughters, with whom he temporarily makes peace. Octavia meets Cleopatra in a harsh verbal confrontation in which they both make accusations against each other.

Act 4

Dolabella meets Cleopatra on the orders of Anthony, who charges him with telling the Queen his decision to leave and to say goodbye. Ventidius and Octavia observe the meeting, and report to Anthony about Cleopatra's inconstancy, which is then confirmed by Alexas. Dolabella re-enters, and is accused of treason by Anthony.

Act 5

Cleopatra receives news of Anthony's defeat in the second battle against Octavian. Alexas tells Anthony the false news of Cleopatra's suicide. Upon hearing this, Anthony asks Ventidius to kill him, but the latter disobeys and commits suicide. Anthony attempts to kill himself, but he only manages to hurt himself. Cleopatra arrives and finds Anthony dying. Anthony dies, and Cleopatra decides to follow him, killing herself by means of an asp bite.

2. *Love in a Forest*

GENERAL INFORMATION

ADAPTOR'S NAME: Johnson, Charles
ADAPTATION TITLE: *Love in a Forest*
SHAKESPEARE'S PLAY*: As You Like It; A Midsummer Night's Dream*[480]

FIRST STAGED

DATE: January 9, 1723
PLACE: Drury Lane
MAIN ACTORS[481]

Men

Frederick, the usurping Duke, Mr. Williams
Alberto, the banished Duke, Mr. Booth
Jacques, friend to Alberto, Mr. Cibber
Amiens, friend to Alberto, Mr. Cory
Oliver, one of three brothers, Mr. Thurmond
Orlando, one of three brothers, Mr. Thurmond
Roberto, one of three brothers, Mr. Roberts
Adam, an old servant to Orlando, Mr. Mills
Le-Beu, Mr. Theo. Cibber
Charles, Master of the Duke's Academy, Mr. W. Mills

Women

Rosalind, Mrs. Booth
Cælia, Mrs. Thurmond
Hymen, Miss Linder
Play within the play of Pyramus and Thisby
Pyramus, Mr. Penkethman
Thisby, Mr. Miller
Wall, Mr. Norris
Lion, Mr. Wilson
Moonshine, Mr. Ray

FIRST PRINTED

DATE: 1723
PLACE: London

OTHER INFORMATION

Printed for W. Chetwood at Cato's-Head in Russel-street, Covent-Garden; and Tho. Edlin, at the Prince's-Arms, over-against Exeter-Exchange in the Strand.

480 From this play the adapter used only the part of the mock play *Pyramus and Thisby.*
481 The cast list is missing; the list provided here was taken from the 1723 printed edition.

2. *Love in a Forest*

PLOT

Act 1

Oliver and Orlando, two of Sir Rowland's three children, fight. Duke Albert lives in the Forest of Arden following his banishment by Duke Frederick, who had usurped his power. Oliver convinces Charles, Frederick's fencing master, to charge Orlando with treason only to challenge him to a duel; Oliver wrongly believes that Charles will easily defeat Orlando. Rosalind, Albert's daughter, remains at court because she is a friend of Celia, Frederick's daughter. Rosalind and Celia watch the duel between Charles and Orlando. Rosalind falls in love with Orlando, who defeats Charles and claims to be Sir Rowland's son. Frederick banishes Rosalind, because she is Albert's daughter, and thus he no longer trusts her. Celia flees the court with her. Both women go to the Forest of Arden in search of Albert. To incur fewer risks, they disguise themselves as men: Rosalind becomes Ganymede, and Celia becomes Aliena.

Act 2

Adam tells Orlando that Charles wants to murder him and to set fire to his home in the woods. Adam becomes Orlando's servant. Frederick banishes Orlando too. Albert praises rural life. Rosalind and Celia cross the forest disguised as men, and encounter a shepherd. Orlando arrives at Albert's banquet. Preparations for the staging of Pyramus and Thisby.

Act 3

In the forest, Orlando writes rough messages of love to Rosalind; Celia and Rosalind find them. Jacques encounters Celia and Rosalind, to whom Jacques admits his misogyny. Orlando encounters Celia and Rosalind, declaring them to be the poet who is hanging love poems on trees. Rosalind allows Orlando to court her. Jacques and Celia meet, and Jacques falls in love with her.

Act 4

Jacques asks Rosalind to plead with Celia for her love, but Rosalind refuses to do this. There are amorous encounters between Rosalind and Orlando. Robert, Orlando and Oliver's brother, tell Rosalind and Celia about the fight between the lioness and Orlando, who is wounded. Robert gives them news of Oliver's death. Charles is dead, too, because he opposed the Duke by defending Orlando from Oliver's false accusations. Rosalind announces her marriage to Orlando, and Orlando that of Jacques to Celia.

Act 5

Representation of the scene with Pyramus and Thisby; at the end of this, Rosalind and Celia arrive with Hymen, the divine protector of marriage. Robert informs them that a religious man converted Frederick as he was going to murder his brother, and that now he is a pious and religious man. The assets that he had previously seized from the exiled nobles in the forest will be returned to their rightful owners.

3. *The Ingratitude of a Common-Wealth*

GENERAL INFORMATION
ADAPTOR'S NAME: Tate, Nahum
ADAPTATION TITLE: *The Ingratitude of a Common-Wealth, or The Fall of Caius Martius Coriolanus*
SHAKESPEARE'S PLAY: *Corialanus*

FIRST STAGED
DATE: [December 1681][482]
PLACE: Drury Lane
MAIN ACTORS: –

FIRST PRINTED
DATE: 1682
PLACE: London

OTHER INFORMATION
Printed by T.M. for Joseph Hindmarsh, at the Black-Bull in Cornhill.

482 In *London Stage*: "the date of the first performance is not known," though, in *Term Catalogue*, it is believed that there was "a premiere in December."

3. *The Ingratitude of a Common-Wealth*

PLOT

Act 1
The plebeians are angry because of the high price of grain, and they want the head of Caius Martius, later called Coriolanus; Menenius tells the fable of the arm and belly, and the rioters are placated; Caius Martius takes his place among the ranks of the army to fight against Corioles. The tribunes intend to set the people once again against Caius Martius. Volumnia and Virgilia, respectively mother and wife of Caius Martius, speak about the valor of Caius Martius, who risks his life in war until the arrival of Valeria, a frivolous woman of the world. Aufidius and Caius Martius clash on the battlefield: Caius Martius returns to Rome a hero.

Act 2
Caius Martius enters Rome triumphantly; despite this, his enemies, Brutus and Sicinius, tribunes for the plebeians, speak against Caius Martius, who in their view is too proud and aristocratic. To receive support for becoming consul, as required by ancient custom, Caius Martius walks through the streets of Rome displaying his wounds from war and requesting the vote of ordinary citizens. Caius Martius receives their support, but the two tribunes set the crowd against Caius Martius, and consequently the senate no longer supports the post of consul.

Act 3
When Caius Martius does not receive support for the post of consul from the tribunes, plebeians and patricians come up against each other. Dialogue between Valeria and Volumnia. Volumnia convinces Caius Martius to speak to the plebeians to calm them, but he is unable to suppress his scorn for the lower social class, and is thus banished from Rome.

Act 4
Caius Martius goes to Corioles, and strikes an alliance with Aufidius against Rome. The plebeians are frightened and now say that they banished Caius Martius without really wanting to. Cominius attempts to deal with Caius Martius, who is now leading an assault on Rome, but is not successful; Volumnia, Virgilia and her son implore Caius Martius to halt his march on Rome, and they convince him.

Act 5
Aufidius regrets having placed his trust in Caius Martius, and so Nigridius encourages him to gain revenge; Menenius, Virgilia and her son go to Corioles to speak to Aufidius, who sets them up. Caius Martius brings the peace treaty agreed with Rome to the senate of Corioles, but there he is accused of betrayal by Aufidius. Aufidius fights and injures Caius Martius in the senate. The armies of Aufidius and Caius Martius are about to engage in battle in the city. Aufidius intends to rape Virgilia in front of Caius Martius, but he dies before being able to do so. Virgilia, injured and blind, dies by a self-inflicted wound to prevent herself from being dishonored by Aufidius. Meanwhile, there is news that Nigridius has killed Menenius and tortured Caius Martius' son. Volumnia kills Nigridius. In the final hecatomb, Caius Martius and his son also die.

4. *The Invader of His Country*

GENERAL INFORMATION
ADAPTOR'S NAME: Dennis, John
ADAPTATION TITLE: *The Invader of His Country, or The Fatal Resentment*
SHAKESPEARE'S PLAY: *Coriolanus*

FIRST STAGED
DATE: November 11, 1719
PLACE: Drury Lane
MAIN ACTORS[483]

Men
Caius Martius Coriolanus, Mr. Booth
Aufidius, Mr. Mills
Menenius, Mr. Corey
Cominius, Mr. Thurmond
Sicinius, a tribune of the people, Mr. W. Wilks
Brutus, a tribune of the people, Mr. Walker
Lucius Cluentius, Mr. Boman, Sen.
Titus Largius, Mr. Williams; Ædile, Mr. Oates
First citizen of Coriolanus' party, Mr. Bickerstaff
Second citizen of Coriolanus' party, Mr. Penkethman
Third citizen of Coriolanus' party, Mr. Johnson
Fourth citizen of Coriolanus' party, Mr. Miller
First citizen of Sempronius' party, Mr. Norris
Second Citizen of Sempronius' party, Mr. Cross
First servant to Aufidius, Mr. Penkethman
Second servant to Aufidius, Mr. Norris
Third servant to Aufidius, Mr. Miller

Women
Volumnia, Mother to Coriolanus, Mrs. Porter
Virgilia, Wife to Coriolanus, Mrs. Thurmond

FIRST PRINTED
DATE: 1720
PLACE: London

OTHER INFORMATION
Printed for J. Pemberton in Fleet-street, and J. Watts near Lincolns-Inn-Fields: And Sold by J. Brotherton and W. Meadows in Cornhill; T. Jauncy and A. Dodd without Temple-Bar; W. Lewis in Covent-Garden, and J. Graves at St. James's.

483 In *London Stage*, the "cast [is] not listed"; the list comes from the 1720 printed edition.

4. *The Invader of His Country*

PLOT

Act 1

A battle between Rome and Corioles ensues, and is not going well for the Romans; Cominius regrets going to battle. Caius Martius, leads a victorious offensive, even fighting against Aufidius, and is given the name Coriolanus for his courage. Returning from battle, Caius Martius expresses his aristocratic ideas on the concept of power.

Act 2

Caius Martius returns to the city, where his mother Volumnia, his wife Virgilia and senator Menenius greet him; on the contrary, Brutus and Sicinius view Caius Martius from the negative perspective of the people. Caius Martius is reluctant to wear the gown of humility and to walk among the people displaying his wounds, although it is required of him by ancient custom if he wishes support as consul. There is competition between Sempronius and Caius Martius for the consul position in the senate. Caius Martius tries to gain the people's support. The two tribunes turn the people's support against Caius Martius.

Act 3

Brutus and Sicinius tell Caius Martius that the people no longer wish to support him as consul; moreover he is accused of betrayal; the two tribunes want to condemn Caius Martius to death. Menenius intervenes and commutes the death penalty in a ban from Rome. Caius Martius bids farewell to his wife and leaves the city.

Act 4

Caius Martius goes to Antium where Aufidius is reunited with the aristocracy of the Volsces, and is debating whether he should immediately attack Rome. Caius Martius strikes an alliance with Aufidius. The servants of the Volsces discuss the possibilities for social advancement that the war to Rome would provide for them. Aufidius and Caius Martius march on Rome: when the news reaches the city, panic strikes, and the people intend to kill the two tribunes who advised them to kill and banish Caius Martius.

Act 5

Marching on Rome, Caius Martius meets his mother, Volumnia, and his wife, Virgilia, the two women make him change his mind. Caius Martius meets Aufidius, who criticizes him for having accepted peace with Rome: the two men fight, Aufidius is defeated and dies. Caius Martius commits suicide. Volumnia and Virgilia weep because of his death.

5. *The Injured Princess*

GENERAL INFORMATION
ADAPTOR'S NAME: D'Urfey, Thomas
ADAPTATION TITLE: *The Injured Princess, or the Fatal Wager*
SHAKESPEARE'S PLAY: *Cymbeline*

FIRST STAGED
DATE: [March 1682][484]
PLACE: Drury Lane
MAIN ACTORS: –

FIRST PRINTED
DATE: 1682
PLACE: London

OTHER INFORMATION
Printed for R. Bentley and M. Magnes in Russel-Street in Covent-Garden, near the Piazza.

484 In *London Stage*: "there is no indication as to when the first performance occurred"; the date reported is the one suggested by the *Term Catalogue*.

5. *The Injured Princess*

PLOT

Act 1

Banished by King Cymbeline, Ursace is forced to leave Innogen, and he gives her a bracelet as a token of his love. Cymbeline and the Queen would like Innogen to marry Cloten. Shattilion wagers a bet with Ursace that Innogen will give in to his advances.

Act 2

Pisanio attests to the King his loyalty to Ursace, thus angering the King. The Queen receives poison from a doctor to carry out her evil plans, but, instead, the doctor gives her a false poison, which only creates a temporary numbness of the senses. Shattilion tries to convince Innogen that Ursace has been unfaithful to her, but she does not believe him; he thus changes his strategy, and says that it was Ursace's idea so as to test her love for him; finally, he asks her to watch a chest of precious objects in her bedroom. Shattilion plans to hide in this chest. At night, Shattilion gets out of the chest, carefully observes Innogen and the bedroom, and then steals her bracelet. Cloten courts Innogen, but with so success.

Act 3

Shattilion tells Ursace that he enjoyed his wife. Belarius, Arviragus, and Palladour discuss virtue. Pisanio, who is in the woods with Innogen, does not murder her, as he was ordered to by Ursace, but sets her free.

Act 4

The Queen accuses Clarina of betrayal, and Cloten plans to have her raped before sentencing her. The Roman army disembarks in Great Britain. Belarius and Palladour encounter Innogen in the woods. Following Cloten's orders, Iachimo tries to rape Clarina; Pisanio arrives and saves her; then Pisanio murders Iachimo. Iachimo had injured Pisanio, so Cloten takes advantage of the situation: rips out his eyes and take his clothes. Arviragus murders Cloten, who is wearing Pisanio's clothes, and cuts off his head. Innogen, disguised as a man, becomes the Roman general's page.

Act 5

Battle between the Roman and British armies. Belarius, Arviragus and Palladour rescue Cymbeline. Ursace and Shattilion meet and engage in combat; Shattilion confesses, declaring Innogen's chastity and fidelity. Upon hearing this, Ursace is stricken with guilt. The play ends with recognitions and revelations: Innogen reveals herself to Ursace, Pisanio relates the facts of Cloten and Iachimo in the woods with Innogen, Belarius exposes the noble origins of Palladour and Arviragus, who are the King's sons.

6. *Hamlet*

GENERAL INFORMATION
ADAPTOR'S NAME: Davenant, William
ADAPTATION TITLE: *Hamlet*
SHAKESPEARE'S PLAY: *Hamlet*

FIRST STAGED
DATE: August 31, 1668
PLACE: Lincoln's Inn Fields
MAIN ACTORS: –

FIRST PRINTED
DATE: 1676
PLACE: London

OTHER INFORMATION
Printed by Andr. Clark, for J. Martyn, and H. Herringman, at the Bell in St. Paul's Church-Yard, and at the Blue Anchor in the lower Walk of the New Exchange

6. *Hamlet*

PLOT

Act 1
Marcellus, Bernardo, and Horatio see the ghost of the late old king; Claudius, the new king, officially validates his marriage to Queen Gertrude. Claudius and Gertrude give Laertes permission to leave Elsinore while they invite Hamlet to stay. Horatio tells Hamlet about the appearance of his father's ghost. Laertes and Polonius urge Ophelia to be chaste and modest when she is with Hamlet. Hamlet meets his father's ghost, who tells him that his brother had murdered him, and asks him to seek revenge. Hamlet compels Horatio to remain silent regarding the appearance of the ghost.

Act 2
Polonius gives Reynaldo instructions on obtaining news about Laertes, who is currently in Paris; Polonius and Ophelia discuss Hamlet's strange behavior. The King and Queen send Rosencrantz and Guildenstern to spy on Hamlet. The ambassadors Voltimand and Cornelius are sent on a mission ordered by the King and Queen in order to obtain news of Fortinbras; Polonius speaks to the King and Queen about Hamlet, whom he believes to be mad for the love of Ophelia. Polonius and Hamlet meet in the lobby, where Hamlet pretends to be mad. Hamlet meets Rosencrantz and Guildenstern, and learns that they are the King's spies. The actors arrive at Elsinore.

Act 3
Rosencrantz and Guildenstern tell the King that they failed their mission. Hamlet distances Ophelia, telling her "get thee to a nunnery." Hamlet prepares the *Gonzago play* with the actors. Staging of dumb show and the *Gonzago play*. The King interrupts the play. The King prepares to send Hamlet to England. Hamlet has the opportunity to kill the King while he is in prayer, but he does not. Closet scene: Hamlet kills Polonius and harshly chastises his mother for having married the King's brother.

Act 4
Hamlet tells the King where Polonius' body is; Hamlet is sent to England, where the King has planned for his murder. Fortinbras and his army advance towards Elsinore. Rejected by Hamlet, Ophelia goes mad. Laertes returns to Elsinore, and, leading the rioters, asks about his father while the crowd would like him to become king. During the confrontation between Claudius and Laertes, a letter from Hamlet arrives, announcing Hamlet's return from England. The King brings Laertes to his side, and hatches the plan for a sword duel between Hamlet and Laertes in which he will dip the sword's tip in poison and, as a backup, poison the victory cup in case Hamlet wins. Gertrude announces the news that Ophelia has committed suicide by drowning.

Act 5
Two gravediggers dig a grave for Ophelia's burial; Horatio and Hamlet meet them; the Prince speaks with one of the gravediggers. Ophelia's funeral takes place, and the King, Queen, and Laertes are present. There is an argument between Hamlet and Laertes. Later, Hamlet is told by a courtier about the bet made by the King regarding the duel with Laertes; Hamlet agrees to fight. During the duel, which Osric attends, Gertrude drinks from the poisonous cup and dies; Hamlet kills Laertes and the King too, and then dies from the wounds inflicted on him from the poisoned sword during the duel. Fortinbras enters, and orders a solemn funeral for the Prince.

7. *King Henry IV*

GENERAL INFORMATION
ADAPTOR'S NAME: Betterton, Thomas
ADAPTATION TITLE: *King Henry IV with the Humours of Sir John Falstaffe*
SHAKESPEARE'S PLAY: *1 Henry IV*

FIRST STAGED
DATE: January 9, 1700
PLACE: Lincoln's Inn Fields
MAIN ACTORS

Men
King Henry IV, Mr. Berry
Prince Henry, Prince of Wales, Mr. Scudemore
John Earl of Lancaster, Prince John, Second Son to King Henry, Mr. Bayly
Northumberland, Henry Percy, Mr. Boman
Harry Percy, surnamed Hotspur, his son, Mr. Verbruggen
Westmerland, Earl of Westmoreland, Mr. Pack
Worcester, Thomas Percy, Mr. Freeman
Mortimer, Edmund Mortimer, Owen Glendower, Mr. Hodgson
Dowglas, Archibald, Mr. Arnold
Sir Walter Blunt, Mr. Trout
Sir Richard Vernon, Mr. Harris
Sir John Falstaff, The Prince's Companion, Mr. Betterton
Bardolph, The Prince's Companion, Mr. Bright
Francis the Drawer, Mr. Bowen

Women
Katherine Percy, Lady Percy, Hotspur's Wife, Mrs. Boman

FIRST PRINTED
DATE: 1700
PLACE: London

OTHER INFORMATION
Printed for R. W. and Sold by John Deeve at Bernards-Inn-Gate in Holborn.

7. *King Henry IV*

PLOT

Act 1

The King speaks about Henry (Harry) Percy Hotspur's success on the battlefield, and about his son's debauchery. Mortimer Glendower is critical towards the King, and has already virtually sided against the sovereign. Hal and Falstaff are absorbed in a life of debauchery; Poins and Hal agree to play a trick on Falstaff by stealing the loot that Falstaff himself intends to steal. Hal announces that the time will come when he will abandon Falstaff and the dissolute life. Hotspur refuses to hand over the prisoners from the battle to the King, rebelling against his authority.

Act 2

To the detriment of the travelers, Falstaff carries out the robbery that he had planned. Hal and Poins rob Falstaff and his companions. Lady Percy tries to keep her husband Henry Percy Hotspur from going to war. Hal and Poins are at an inn, and then Falstaff enters with his companions and tells his version of the stolen loot. As in a kind of play-within-the-play, Falstaff pretends to be the King and speaks to Hal. The sheriff enters searching for the bandits who robbed the travelers, and Falstaff hides.

Act 3

Hotspur, Mortimer, and Worcester meet in order to plan the revolt. The King and his son Hal prepare for the clash against the rebels. Hal and Falstaff, at the inn, speaking about the money stolen by Falstaff.

Act 4

Harry Percy Hotspur prepares to confront Prince Hal. Falstaff is preparing for battle as a fearful fighter; earlier he was bribing men who were fit for enlistment in exchange of a false declaration of unfit condition for military service so that he could avoid the enlistment. The rebels speak with Blunt, the King's messenger.

Act 5

Through Worcester, the King makes amends with the rioters, but Worcester purposely does not update Hotspur with the news. Battle of Shrewsbury. Douglas murders Blunt, mistaking him for the King. Hal chastises Falstaff for his lack of warlike spirit. Hal murders Hotspur; Falstaff feigns his death. The battle is won, the rebels are captured and imprisoned (including Westmerland, Worcester and Vernon), but Glendower and March still need to be fought.

8. *The Sequel of Henry the Fourth*

GENERAL INFORMATION
ADAPTOR'S NAME: Betteron, Thomas
ADAPTATION TITLE: *The Sequel of Henry the Fourth, With the Humours of Sir John Falstaffe, and Justice Shallow*
SHAKESPEARE'S PLAY: *2 Henry IV*

FIRST STAGED
DATE: [1704][485]
PLACE: Lincoln's Inn Fields
MAIN ACTORS: –

FIRST PRINTED
DATE: [1720]
PLACE: London

OTHER INFORMATION
Printed for W. Chetwood, at Cato's Head in Russel-street, Covent-garden; and T. Jauncey, at the Angle without Temple-Bar.

485 The date is documented in Hogan's *Shakespeare in the Theatre*.

8. *The Sequel of Henry the Fourth*

PLOT

Act 1

Falstaff describes the Battle of Shrewsbury, but soon there will be another battle against Northumberland. Hastings and the Archbishop of York prepare their forces as they await Northumberland. The hostess asks the judge that Falstaff pay his debts to her; Falstaff promises to marry her at the end of the war.

Act 2

News arrives to Hal that Falstaff is in a relationship with the prostitute Moll Tearsheet. Hal decides to look for Falstaff. Scene with Moll, Pistol, Bardolph, the hostess, and Falstaff. Hal criticizes Falstaff for his dissolute life.

Act 3

Shallow, Silence, Davy, Bardolph, and Falstaff do roll call for the enlistment of fools. The Archbishop of York, Mowbray, and Hastings are in the Forest of Gualtree when they receive news that Northumberland has gone to Scotland, and will not take part in the battle. Lancaster and Westmoreland meet with the rebels and agree to peace. The rebel army disperses and the leaders Hastings, York, and Mowbray are arrested and charged with treason. Falstaff plans to return to Shallow.

Act 4

The King is with Clarence and Gloucester when he is reached by the news that Northumberland and Bardolph were defeated. The King does not feel well, and faints. With the dying King in his bed, Harry imagines being king, seizes the crown and leaves; the King awakes, summons his son, and has a serious conversation with the Prince about power and responsibility. Falstaff and his companions receive news of the King's death. Harry meets his old friends from his dissolute life.

Act 5

Harry rejects his friends from the dissolute life. Harry deals with the issue of the Salic law, which stipulates preparations for war against France. Cambridge, Marsham, and Northumberland are arrested and charged with treason.

9. *King Henry the Fifth*

GENERAL INFORMATION
ADAPTOR'S NAME: Hill, Aaron
ADAPTATION TITLE: *King Henry the Fifth, or The Conquest of France, by the English*
SHAKESPEARE'S PLAY: *Henry V*

FIRST STAGED
DATE: December 5, 1723
PLACE: Drury Lane
MAIN ACTORS[486]

Men
King Henry, Mr. Booth
Dauphin, Lewis, Mr. Wilks
King of France, Charles VI, Mr. Thurmond
Duke of Exeter, Mr. Mills
Duke of York, Mr. Cory
Lord Scroop, Mr. Williams
Duke of Bourbon, Mr. Bridgwater
Duke of Orleans, Mr. Watson
Earl of Cambridge, Mr. Mills Jun.
Sir Thomas Grey, Mr. Oates
French Officer, Mr. Roberts

Women
Princess Catherine, Mrs. Oldfield
Harriet, Mrs. Thurmond
Charlot, Mrs. Campbell

FIRST PRINTED
DATE: 1723
PLACE: London

OTHER INFORMATION
Printed for W. Chetwood in the Passage to the Theatre-Royal in Drury-Lane, and J. Watts at the Printing-Office in Wild-Court near Lincoln's-Inn-Fields.

486 In *London Stage*: "cast [is] not listed." The list was taken from the 1723 printed edition.

9. *King Henry the Fifth*

PLOT

Act 1

At Harfleur, the Duke of Cambridge and other English nobles discuss the war with France and also discuss Henry V's maturity. The King seeks his advisors' opinion on the Salic law and the validity of his claim to the French throne; his advisors assure him that he is correct. French ambassadors arrive with a message from the French Dauphin, who invites the King to quit and sends him tennis balls to mock him. The conspirators Cambridge, Scroop, and Grey are preparing to assassinate Henry V. Harriet expresses her hatred for Henry V.

Act 2

In the French field, the King, his son the Dauphin, and the Duke of Orleans meet in council. The Dauphin criticizes France for its inadequate and poor warlike courage. Harriet meets with the Dauphin. Princess Catherine and her companion Charlot discuss matters of love. The Princess meets with the Dauphin, and comes to the realization that she is only a pawn in the political game of chess between the two sovereigns. The Princess loses heart over her role, and Harriet tells her of Henry V's seductive qualities.

Act 3

The Dauphin urges Catherine to refuse her marriage to Henry V. The two kings meet, and the Princess has conflicting feelings for Henry V: first hatred, then love. The two kings decide to fight each other, and this saddens the Princess. The Princess decides to reveal the plot ordered by English conspirators to assassinate Henry V.

Act 4

The Princess summons Charlot to warn Henry V about the conspiracy, and asks that he meet with her at Agincourt. Harriet, who is one of the conspirators, is captured. Henry V comforts her by affirming his love for her; she confesses to having wished his death, and commits suicide. Harriet had with her the letters containing evidence of the conspiracy by Cambridge and the other conspirators. Henry V summons the conspirators, and has them arrested. The Princess arrives at Agincourt. The battle is now imminent; the Dauphin advances, leading the French army.

Act 5

At nightfall, the French are attempting a sortie. Henry arrives on the French battlefield, and reflects upon the possible outcomes of the forthcoming battle and on the good of his country. The English win the battle. Sung recitative by the Genius of England. France's Dauphin admits defeat.

10. *Henry the Sixth, The First Part*

GENERAL INFORMATION
ADAPTOR'S NAME: Crowne, John
ADAPTATION TITLE: *Henry the Sixth, The First Part With the Murder of Humphrey Duke of Gloucester*
SHAKESPEARE'S PLAY: *2 Henry VI*

FIRST STAGED
DATE: [April 1681][487]
PLACE: Dorset Garden
MAIN ACTORS[488]

Men
King Henry VI, Mr. Jos. Williams
Humphrey Duke of Glocester, Lord Protector of the Kingdom, and uncle to the King, being brother to King Henry V, Mr. Batterton
Cardinal, Winchester, a bastard son of John of Gaunt, and so uncle to Duke Humphrey, Mr. Harris
Richard Plantagenet, heir of the house of York, pretender to the crown, Mr. D. Williams
Duke of Suffolk, a lover of the Queen, Mr. Smith

Women
Queen Margaret, wife of King Henry VI, in love with the Duke of Suffolk, La. Slingsby
Elianor, Duchess of Glocester, wife to the Lord Protector, Mrs. Batterton

FIRST PRINTED
DATE: 1681
PLACE: London

OTHER INFORMATION
Printed for R. Bentley, and M. Magnes, in Russel-Street, in Covent-Garden.

---

487 In *London Stage*: "The date of the first production is not known." The date is determined by a copy purchased by Narcissus Luttrell; the copy is currently owned by the Ohio State University Library.

488 The list comes from the 1681 printed edition.

10. *Henry the Sixth, The First Part*

PLOT

Act 1

Glocester, Lord Protector, meets with other nobles to discuss the current delicate political situation. Right from the start, the Cardinal presents himself as his opponent as well as a worthy villain; during the meeting, those present discuss the issue of the French provinces donated to the King of France as the dowry for Henry's wife. The nobles harshly criticize this decision because they conquered this territory during the war. The Cardinal aims to become Lord Protector, a position currently held by Glocester. Glocester and his wife, Elianor, discuss their loyalty to the King: she detests the Queen, and would like her husband to be king, while he instead affirms his loyalty to Henry. Some citizens submit petitions to the Queen and her lover Suffolk; the petitions were originally formulated for the Lord Protector, and question the legitimacy of the current King. The Queen laments the King's excessive religious devotion and, thus, his shortcomings as a companion and husband. The Queen detests Elianor, and, together with Humes, weaves a plot to try Elianor for sorcery, the first step towards also eliminating Somerset, Buckingham and York.

Act 2

The King and Queen meet with other nobles and the Cardinal, and, during the meeting, some call for the resignation of the Lord Protector. Elianor and the Queen are in open conflict, and the Cardinal plans to take advantage of this to eliminate Glocester. A struggle for power between York and Suffolk ensues. There is a return to the issue of the royal legitimacy: two citizens are questioned on Richard of York's legitimacy as ruler; a gunsmith and his helper, accuser and accused, argue over who is lying and will fight in a duel to establish who is right. The Cardinal states his intentions to assume the role of Lord Protector. Elianor and Humes witness a menacing evocation predicting the future; York and Buckingham burst on the scene and arrest them. The King, Queen, and Cardinal witness the friars of St. Albans stage a false miracle in which a blind and lame man claims to have been healed by the saint, but the man is exposed by Glocester and the other nobles. The King and Cardinal are notified of Elianor's spiritualist act. Suffolk and the Queen go to enjoy the spectacle of Elianor's fall. The Queen reaffirms her love for Suffolk.

Act 3

Salisbury and Warwick recognize Richard of York as the legitimate King of England, and plan for Glocester's downfall. The King condemns Elianor to exile on the Island of Man as the Queen welcomes the sentence imposed on her adversary. Glocester resigns from his post as Lord Protector. After the duel with his helper, the gunsmith is brought before the King. Suffolk and the Queen renew their vows of love. Glocester and Elianor do penance through the streets of the city.

Act 4

Suffolk, the Queen, and York try to convince the King that Glocester is a traitor, but to no effect because the King does not believe them; Glocester is arrested for treason anyway. Suffolk, the Queen, and York decide that Glocester must be murdered rather than put on trial, which could see the accused be acquitted of the charge against him. The Duke's three assassins discuss religion and charity, and when the Cardinal arrives they express doubts about the Church's infallibility. The assassins strangle Glocester as he is praying, and then position him in such a way so as to make it appear a natural death. The King is deeply saddened by Glocester's death; Warwick accuses Suffolk and the Cardinal of the death of Glocester. At Salisbury's suggestion, the King condemns Suffolk. The Cardinal feels remorse for Glocester's death, sees his ghost, faints, and goes mad. The assassins, the King, Salisbury, and Warwick witness the Cardinal's delirium. Pirates kill Suffolk, and this deeply saddens the Queen. Jack Cade and York march on London.

Act 5
[Not present].

11. *Humfrey Duke of Gloucester*

GENERAL INFORMATION
ADAPTOR'S NAME: Philips, Ambrose
ADAPTATION TITLE: *Humfrey Duke of Gloucester*
SHAKESPEARE'S PLAY: *2 Henry VI*

FIRST STAGED
DATE: February 15, 1723
PLACE: Drury Lane
MAIN ACTORS[489]

Men
Humfrey, Duke of Gloucester, uncle to the King, and Lord Protector of the Realm, Mr. Booth
His friends:
Richard Plantagenet, Duke of York, Mr. Mills
Richard Nevill, Earl of Salisbury, Mr. Thurmond
Richard Nevill, Earl of Warwick, son to the Earl of Salisbury, Mr. Williams
Henry Beaufort, Cardinal, and Bishop of Winchester, uncle to the Duke of Gloucester, and great-uncle to the King, Mr. Cibber
Of his, and the Queen's faction:
William de la Pole, Duke of Suffolk, Mr. Watson
Humfrey Stafford, Duke of Buckingham, Mr. Mills Jr.

Women
Margaret, Daughter to Reiner, Duke of Anjou, Queen to King Henry the Sixth, secretly in love with the Duke of Suffolk, Mrs. Oldfield
Eleanor, Duchess of Gloucester, Wife to Duke Humfrey, Mrs. Porter

FIRST PRINTED
DATE: 1723
PLACE: London

OTHER INFORMATION
Printed: And Sold by J. Roberts near the Oxford-Arms in Warwick-Lane.

489 In *London Stage*: "cast [is] not listed"; the list comes from the 1723 printed edition.

11. *Humfrey Duke of Gloucester*

PLOT

Act 1

York and Salisbury plan Lord Protector Gloucester's downfall by using his wife Eleanor. Cardinal Beaufort, together with Warwick, plans to use the same strategy. Queen Margaret, Suffolk and Beaufort discuss ways to bring about Gloucester's downfall. Eleanor is tried for witchcraft, found guilty, and exiled to the Isle of Man. Gloucester and Eleanor discuss their personal situation and that of the kingdom. Impulsive in character, Gloucester rebels against his current situation, and cannot accept the affronts against him by his enemies.

Act 2

Beaufort and Suffolk plan Gloucester's elimination. Suffolk, Beaufort, and Gloucester argue. York, Warwick, and Gloucester argue.

Act 3

Beaufort, Buckingham and the Queen plan to ensure that Parliament remove Gloucester from the post of Lord Protector. The Queen has Gloucester arrested for treason. Warwick is against Beaufort.

Act 4

York argues with Beaufort. The Queen, Suffolk, and Beaufort unite against Gloucester. Salisbury and York support Gloucester. The crowd revolts against the unjust imprisonment of Gloucester. Warwick placates the crowd pending the convening of Parliament the next day, when York, Warwick, and Gloucester plan to present a detailed discourse against Beaufort and his allies. Gloucester dreams that he is killed by Beaufort. Beaufort hires two killers to suffocate Gloucester.

Act 5

Dialogue between the Queen, Suffolk, and Beaufort. The Queen has a dream in which she sees the past and the future (Gloucester's death and her rise to the throne of York). Warwick and Eleanor find Gloucester dead. Parliament receives news of Gloucester's death; the Queen and Beaufort maintain their innocence. York, as well as Warwick and then Salisbury, accuse Beaufort of Gloucester's murder. The hired killers have already confessed to the crime. Banished, Suffolk escapes and abandons the Queen, who criticizes him for this. Salisbury and York stand against the Queen. Warwick, Eleanor, and Salisbury witness Beaufort's death in his delirium.

12. *The Misery of Civil War*

GENERAL INFORMATION
ADAPTOR'S NAME: Crowne, John
ADAPTATION TITLE: *The Misery of Civil War*
SHAKESPEARE'S PLAY: *2 Henry VI; 3 Henry VI*

FIRST STAGED
DATE: [February 1680][490]
PLACE: Dorset Garden
MAIN ACTORS

Men
King Henry VI, Joseph Williams
Richard Plantagenet, David Williams
Edward, Smith
George, Duke of Clarence, Bowman
Richard, Gillow
Earl of Warwick, Batterton
Old Lord Clifford, Percival
Young Clifford, Wiltshire

Women
Queen Margaret, Mrs. Leigh (Mrs. Mary Lee)
Lady Grey, Mrs Batterton
Lady Eleanor Butler, Mrs. Currer

FIRST PRINTED
DATE: 1680
PLACE: London

OTHER INFORMATION
Printed for R. Bentley, and M. Magnes, in Russel-Street in Covent-Garden.

490 In *London Stage*: "the date of the first production is not known": the date is assumed from a copy purchased by Narcissus Luttrell, currently owned by the Ohio State University Library.

12. *The Misery of Civil War*

PLOT

Act 1

After returning to London, Jack Cade proclaims himself Lord Mortimer, and the insanity of his government is displayed with indiscriminate hangings. With a shoemaker and a butcher-executioner, he enacts a tyrannical and carnivalesque law. Jack Cade meets Clifford Senior, the King's emissary, and when Clifford Junior arrives unexpectedly, tempers rise and the two sides fight against each other. Clifford Junior murders Jack Cade. King Henry VI Lancaster arrests Plantagenet, the Duke of York, charging him with treason. York Plantagenet believes he is the legitimate King of England. Warwick supports York. The King and York agree to battle in an open field.

Act 2

York Plantagenet murders Clifford Senior, and for this Clifford Junior vows revenge against the Yorks. York Plantagenet and his family win the battle. York Plantagenet congratulates Warwick for a well fought battle. Lady Grey laments her husband's death; Warwick falls in love with her, and openly courts her; however, she refuses him. There is a private and intimate meeting between Elianor Butler and Edward. In Parliament the Yorks draw their swords, and, to win the Crown, an armed battle ensues between the two sides. The King agrees to proclaim York his successor; Clifford Junior strongly disagrees. The Queen harshly criticizes the King for his decision.

Act 3

The army loyal to the Queen divides the forces of the Yorks. Clifford Junior murders the young Rutland York. The battle turns in favor of the Lancasters. Clifford Junior fights against York Plantagenet and defeats him; the Queen brings the news that the young Rutland has been killed. Clifford Junior and the Queen kill York Plantagenet. Edward convinces Lady Elianor to search for a private place in the countryside where they can live and love each other. Some soldiers force farmers to give them their savings, and attempt to rape their daughters. Thus: "The Scene is drawn, and there appears Houses and Towns burning, Men and Women hang'd upon Trees, and Children on the tops of Pikes." Warwick is tempted to support the King.

Act 4

The Queen, the Prince and Clifford Junior argue with the King, who has now ceded the Crown. Henry reflects upon the weight of the Crown. Scenes condemning war: a son has killed his father, and a father has killed his son. The King's army has been defeated; the King flees to Scotland, and the Queen to France. Clifford Junior dies. Edward is proclaimed King. Warwick will go to France to ask the King for his daughter's hand in marriage. Dialogue between Lady Grey and Warwick: he still resolutely courts her, and she still refuses him. Lady Grey asks for mercy for the orphaned children, and her beauty fascinates King Edward. He courts her and promises to marry her, while Warwick has already left for France. Richard concocts his bloody plans to take the Crown. Henry is captured and brought to London. At Edward and Lady Grey's marriage ceremony, Lady

Elianor Butler criticizes the King. Warwick bursts into scene armed against King Edward and Lady Grey, and takes them as prisoners.

Act 5

King Henry, his wife, and Warwick are in power again. The marriage ceremony of the Prince is interrupted by the news that Edward and Richard York are marching on London with an army. Edward and Lady Elianor go to battle (Lady Elianor is disguised as a man), and when she is defeated, she reveals her true identity to Edward before dying from her battle wounds. Edward and Warwick fight; Warwick is defeated and dies. Richard and Edward fight against the Prince and the Queen: Richard and Edward kill the Prince in front of the Queen, and then take her as prisoner. Richard also plans to kill Henry, who is imprisoned in the tower of London. Henry sleeps in the tower, and dreams of the ghost of Richard II, who is a good spirit. A song extols the pious Henry VI, who is about to be assassinated. Henry awakens, and is killed by Richard, who is, however, acting against the will of King Edward. Edward arrives at the tower of London to meet Henry, and finds him dead. Edward criticizes Richard for his act, and reflects upon the destructiveness of civil war.

13. *King Henry VI*

GENERAL INFORMATION
ADAPTOR'S NAME: Cibber, Teophilus
ADAPTATION TITLE: *King Henry VI An Historical Tragedy of the Civil Wars between the Houses of York and Lancaster in the Reign of King Henry The Sixth*
SHAKESPEARE'S PLAY*2 Henry VI; 3 Henry VI*

FIRST STAGED
DATE: July 5, 1723
PLACE: Drury Lane
MAIN ACTORS[491]

Men
King Henry, Mr. Roberts
Prince Edward, Mr. Cibber Junior
Old Clifford, Lord Clifford, Mr. Boman
Young Clifford, Mr. Wilks Junior
York Plantagenet, Mr. Savage
Edward, Mr. Oates
George, Mr. Parlour
Richard, Mr. Wilson
Warwick, Earl of Warwick, Mr. Bridgwater

Women
Queen Margaret, Mrs. Campbell
Lady Grey, Mrs. Seal
Lady Elizabeth, Mrs. Davison
Lady Anne, Mrs. Brett

FIRST PRINTED
DATE: [1723]
PLACE: London

OTHER INFORMATION[492]
Printed for J. Walthoe, Jun. in Cornhill; W. Chetwood, in Russel-Street, Covent-Garden; and J. Stagg, in Westminster-Hall: and sold by J. Roberts, in Warwick-Lane.

491 In *London Stage*: "Cast [is] not listed. Cast not listed in edition of 1723"; the list comes from the 1724 printed edition.

492 In *Shakespeare in the Theatre*, Hogan documents a 1724 edition printed by W. Chetwood.

13. *King Henry VI*

PLOT

Act 1

King, Queen, Clifford Senior, and Clifford Junior learn of Jack Cade's death. From Ireland, York is marching against the King. Clifford Senior meets and asks York why he is leading an armed march, York replies that he is marching against Somerset, who, in his view, should be imprisoned for treason. Somerset is, instead, free and wants York arrested. York proclaims himself King of England, and is supported by Warwick. During battle, York kills Clifford Senior, Richard kills Somerset, and Clifford Junior vows revenge against the York family. The Battle of St Albans sees the triumph of the Yorks.

Act 2

Lancasters and Yorks confront each other in Parliament. Henry agrees to cede the Crown to the York family at his death. Clifford Junior is indignant and leaves to inform the Queen. Along with the Prince, the Queen harshly criticizes Henry for his decision to cede the Crown. During battle, Clifford Junior murders the young Rutland York. There is a duel between Clifford Junior and York, who is defeated. The Queen tells York that Rutland was killed, and so Clifford Junior decides to kill York.

Act 3

Richard and Edward learn of York's death. A new battle ensues: Henry reflects on the misfortunes brought upon by civil war. The Yorks are triumphant in the battle; Clifford Junior fights against Richard, and dies from his wounds. The Yorks plan for the Coronation in London while Warwick goes to France on a diplomatic mission in search of a bride for Edward. But Edward falls in love when he meets Lady Grey. Henry is imprisoned and sent to the Tower of London. Richard begins to concoct his bloody rise to the throne.

Act 4

Warwick argues with Edward. To Edward, a messenger relays the negative opinions of his opponents regarding his marriage. Warwick and Henry are now allies, and speak to the Queen about the legitimacy of his power. Warwick and Edward come into conflict with each other; Edward is imprisoned and handed over to the Archbishop of York. Warwick is now deployed to protect the King, who has once again taken over in London.

Act 5

Edward eludes his tenuous watch over the Archbishop of York, and flees to France, where he organizes an army of soldiers of mixed nationality with whom he returns to England to fight against Henry. On the eve of the battle, George Clarence changes alliances and returns to the Yorks. Henry's prince son bids farewell to his new bride. The Queen addresses the army before the battle. Following the battle, Henry is imprisoned, and brought to the tower of London. Edward kills Warwick, and the Queen and Prince are taken as prisoners. George and Richard murder the Prince in front of the Queen. Richard heads towards the tower of London to kill Henry.

14. *The History of King Lear*

GENERAL INFORMATION
ADAPTOR'S NAME: Tate, Nahum
ADAPTATION TITLE: *The History of King Lear*
SHAKESPEARE'S PLAY: *King Lear*

FIRST STAGED
DATE: [March 1681][493]
PLACE: Dorset Garden
MAIN ACTORS

Men
King Lear, Mr. Betterton
Gloster, Earl of Gloucester, Mr. Gillo
Kent, Earl of Kent, Mr. Wiltshire
Edgar, Mr. Smith
Bastard, Edmund, Mr. Jo. Williams
Cornwall, Duke of Cornwall, Mr. Norris
Albany, Duke of Albany, Mr. Bowman
Gentleman Usher, Mr. Jevon

Women
Gonerill, Mrs. Shadwell
Regan, Lady Slingsby
Cordelia, Mrs. Barry

FIRST PRINTED
DATE: 1681
PLACE: London

OTHER INFORMATION
Printed for E. Flesher, and are to be sold by R. Bentley, and M. Magnes in Russel-street near Covent-Garden.

493 In *London Stage*: "The date of the first performance is not known"; the date is determined in *Term Catalogue*.

14. *The History of King Lear*

PLOT

Act 1

Edmund begins to concoct a plan to discredit Edgar in the eyes of his father, Gloucester. Edgar and Cordelia are in a relationship, but Lear plans to end it because he wishes to marry his daughter to Burgundy. Lear plans to divide his kingdom into three parts for his three daughters and their respective husbands. The couples are as follows: Goneril and Albany, Regan and Cornwall, and Cordelia and Burgundy. Cordelia, however, refuses to be part of her father's "love contest" oratory. Lear's choleric temperament is displayed when he disowns Cordelia after hearing her words. Kent's attempts to defend Cordelia and to reason with Lear are in vain; he is, in fact, banished from the kingdom. Because Cordelia has no dowry, Burgundy refuses her. Discouraged by Burgundy's behavior, Cordelia becomes suspicious of Edgar's love for her, and wishes to test the constancy of his love. Edmund writes a false letter, and makes Gloucester believe that Edgar wants to kill him, thus pitting father against son. Kent, who is now disguised, becomes Lear's servant. Goneril and Lear argue.

Act 2

Edmund injures himself and lies to his father, telling him that it is Edgar who injured him. A fight ensues between Kent and one of Regan's servants; Cornwall and Regan thus place Kent in shackles. Confident of Cordelia's love, Edgar goes into hiding. Lear is infuriated when he sees Kent in shackles. Regan and Lear argue, then Goneril arrives and the two sisters unite against their father.

Act 3

Lear and Kent are on the heath, in a storm. Edmund boasts of his power, and the two sisters each send him a love letter. The two daughters are now queens, and impose heavy taxation on the people, who are unhappy and speak of rebellion and restoration of the old king. Gloucester orders Edmund to deliver important letters, but Edmund plans to disobey him so as to have him sentenced. In hiding with the page Arant, Cordelia, together with Gloucester, plans to support Lear, even though her actions go against her sisters' orders. Lear and Kent are still on the heath during the storm; here, they encounter Edgar and then Gloucester. Two criminals on the heath assault Cordelia, but Edgar puts them to flight. Edgar and Cordelia both reveal their true identities. Thanks to Edmund, Cornwall and Regan learn of Gloucester's betrayal; they arrest him and torture him by ripping out his eyes; a servant speaks against such a barbarous act and injures Cornwall.

Act 4

In a cave, Regan and Edmund have a clandestine love affair. Regan then realizes that Goneril is also in a relationship with Edmund. Gloucester leads a revolt against the tyrannical queen. Wearing Tom's clothes, Edgar encounters the blind Gloucester, and goes to Dover with him. Cordelia and Kent meet with Gloucester and Edgar. Goneril learns of Cornwall's death from the wounds inflicted on him by the outspoken servant. Widowed, Regan makes Edmund the general of her army. Edgar pretends to bring Gloucester to a cliff. When Gloucester jumps, Edgar pretends to be somebody else, and saves him. Lear arrives wearing a crown of flowers. Edgar murders Goneril's servant because he was carrying a letter for Edmund with instructions to kill her husband Albany. Lear is cured, regains consciousness, rejoins Cordelia and makes amends with her.

Act 5

Edmund has enjoyed the widow Regan, and plans to do the same with Goneril after the imminent battle against Lear; Kent commands this army, Edgar serves it, and Gloucester charges it up. During the battle Lear's army is defeated, and Lear and Cordelia are imprisoned. Albany plans to murder them, unlike Edmund and Goneril who want them alive. In disguise, Kent accuses Edmund of betrayal, and proposes a challenge to prove it. Kent and Cordelia comfort Lear. Now Goneril plans to have one of his army officials secretly kill the two prisoners. A duel ensues between Edgar and Edmund, who is defeated; Edgar gives Albany the letter that accuses Edmund. The two sisters, who have both poisoned themselves at the banquet to celebrate their triumph in battle, lock horns over Edmund's love. Some soldiers enter the prison to kill Lear and Cordelia: Lear acts quickly and kills two of the soldiers, and then Edgar and Albany arrive to save Lear and Cordelia. Meanwhile, Albany has defeated the army led by Edmund, who is guilty of treason, and so he returns a part of the kingdom to Lear, who, in turn, gives it to Cordelia, who will thus become Queen. Edmund dies from his wounds in the duel with Edgar, and the two sisters from the poison. Edgar and Cordelia will soon be married; Lear, Kent and Gloucester retire to private life. Edgar proclaims that his love for Cordelia is greater than that for the Crown, and that Cordelia's example demonstrates that truth and virtue always prevail in the end.

15. *Macbeth*

GENERAL INFORMATION
ADAPTOR'S NAME: Davenant, William
ADAPTATION TITLE: *Macbeth*
SHAKESPEARE'S PLAY: *Macbeth*

FIRST STAGED
DATE: November 5, 1664
PLACE: Lincoln's Inn Fields
MAIN ACTORS[494]

Men
King of Scotland, Duncan, Mr. Lee
Malcolm, his son, Prince of Cumberland, Mr. Norris
Donalbain, Mr. Cademan
Lenox, Mr. Medbourn
Macbeth, Mr. Batterton
Banquo, Mr. Smith
Macduff, Mr. Harris
Ghost of Banquo, Mr. Sanford

Women
Macbeth's Wife, Lady Macbeth, Mrs. Batterton
Macduff's Wife, Lady Macduff, Mrs. Long

FIRST PRINTED
DATE: 1674
PLACE: London

OTHER INFORMATION
Printed for P. Chetwin, and are to be sold by most booksellers.

494 In *London Stage*: "cast [is] not known"; the cast is determined from the 1673 *quarto*.

15. *Macbeth*

PLOT

Act 1

Opening scene with the three witches. Seyton and Macduff tell the King of Macbeth and Banquo's victory against the rebels. Thanks to stage machinery, the witches are able to simulate flying; they encounter Macbeth and Banquo, and predict their future. Macduff tells Macbeth that he has become the lord of Cawdor. The King congratulates Macbeth and Banquo for their courage in battle. The King will go to Inverness as Macbeth's guest. In a dialogue between Lady Macbeth and Lady Macduff, Lady Macduff expresses her feelings of pure love for her husband, and speaks against the transiency of glory. Lady Macbeth reads the letter from her husband, and begins to think of killing the King. The King and his retinue arrive at Macbeth's castle in Inverness. Macbeth is hesitant to kill the King; his wife goads him into murdering him, and they decide to take action in the middle of the night.

Act 2

At nightfall, Macbeth and Banquo speak of the witches they met earlier. In a dialogue between Lady Macbeth and Macbeth, Macbeth is not yet entirely convinced that he wants to murder the King, while Lady Macbeth pushes him to do it. Macduff arrives, and finds the King murdered. Macbeth accuses the King's guards of the murder, and has them killed. The King's sons separate, and leave Inverness; because of this, they are suspected of having killed the King. Macbeth prepares for his coronation. Lady Macduff and her children meet with Macduff on a heath. The witches gather around them: they dance, sing and make predictions about Macbeth and Macduff.

Act 3

Now King, Macbeth hires three assassins to murder Banquo and his son Fleance. In a dialogue between Macduff and Lady Macduff, Lady Macduff urges her husband not to give in to the ambition of power, and not to become a murderer like Macbeth who is a usurper. The assassins kill Banquo, but Fleance manages to escape. At a banquet, an assassin reports to Macbeth the success of the homicide, but Macbeth is not satisfied. Macbeth sees Banquo's ghost, and the banquet guests are confused by Macbeth's odd behavior. In a dialogue between Macduff and Lady Macduff: with Banquo dead, the couple fears to lose their lives. The witches and Hecate appear together on stage in a scene with sung recitatives and machinery, enabling them to fly.

Act 4

More scenes with music and sung recitatives, with the supernatural characters: one with the three witches, another with Hecate and three other witches. Macbeth consults the three witches; then Banquo's ghost and the ghosts of eight kings parade in front of him. Macduff takes refuge in England, leaving his children and wife in Scotland. Lady Macduff fears for her life. In the forest of Birnam, Malcolm and Macduff discuss Macbeth, his accession to the throne, and his administration of power. The murdered King's ghost haunts

Lady Macbeth. Macduff learns that Macbeth ordered the death of his three children and wife; he thus decides to take the field against Macbeth.

Act 5
Lady Macbeth's sleepwalking scene. The rebel forces take position around the castle of Dunsinane, where Macbeth is currently located. Lady Macbeth dies. The forest of Birnam "moves" towards Macbeth's castle. During the battle that ensues, Macbeth kills Lennox, Macduff kills Macbeth; Macbeth dies and regrets having been tempted by ambition, the greatest vice in the world. Malcolm becomes King, and his virtue shines more brightly next to the vice of Macbeth the tyrant.

16. *The Law Against Lovers*

GENERAL INFORMATION
ADAPTOR'S NAME: Davenant, William
ADAPTATION TITLE: *The Law Against Lovers*
SHAKESPEARE'S PLAY: *Measure for Measure*, *Much Ado About Nothing*

FIRST STAGED
DATE: February 15, 1662
PLACE: Lincoln's Inn Fields
MAIN ACTORS[495]

Men
–

Women
Viola, Moll Davies

FIRST PRINTED
DATE: 1673
PLACE: London

OTHER INFORMATION
Printed by T. N. for Henry Herringman, at the Sign of the Blew Anchor in the Lower Walk of the New Exchange.

495 Of the performance held on February 18, 1662.

16. *The Law Against Lovers*

PLOT

Act 1

In Turin, the Duke hands power over to Angelo. Beatrice awaits Angelo's brother Benedick's return from war. Viola is a young coquette. Benedick returns to the city, and encounters Escalus and Lucius; the latter tells him about the reinstatement of the law against lovers. There is argument between Beatrice and Benedick. Claudio is arrested, and will be beheaded in three days time; he is married to Beatrice, although it is not official, and Juliet is pregnant. Claudio asks Isabella to go to Angelo to ask for his pardon. Dialogue between the Duke and Friar Thomas sees the Duke reveal his true intentions to Friar Thomas – that is, to give power to Angelo, to enforce the laws, and, meanwhile, to remain disguised as a monk. Lucius and Balthazar go to Isabella to inform her of her brother Claudio's situation; they ask her to see Angelo to try to convince him to pardon Claudio.

Act 2

Benedick tries in vain to convince Angelo to reconsider Claudio's sentence. There is dialogue between Benedick and Escalus, then with Beatrice. There is widespread discontent among the many damaged by the law against lovers. The mayor announces Isabella's arrival to Angelo. Isabella begs Angelo to not execute Claudio, but she only manages to fix another meeting with him on the following day. The disguised Duke meets with Juliet to ensure that her feelings for Claudio are genuine.

Act 3

Dialogue between Isabella and Angelo: Angelo tells Isabella that he wants her in exchange for Claudio's life, and gives her a day to make a decision. Viola performs a sung recitative. Lucius and Balthazar try to make Beatrice fall in love with Benedick. In dialogue between Isabella and Claudio, Isabella tells Claudio about the proposal she refused from Angelo. The Duke, who is still in disguise, tells Isabella to wait until the Duke arrives before she accuses Angelo. Benedick and Beatrice prepare a false document with a seal for Claudio's pardon, and then Benedick goes to Escalus.

Act 4

Dance performed by Beatrice, Benedick, and Viola. Isabella and Juliet discuss the nature of love; Isabella still refuses to give up her honor in exchange for her brother's life. Argument between Benedick and Beatrice. Benedick does not agree with his brother's way of governing, and prepares to oppose him forcefully. In prison, the condemned Bernardino attempts to postpone his death sentence. Claudio and the madman plan Juliet's escape from prison in which she should pretend to be a page. The mayor's wife offers Claudio an escape, but he rejects her because of his love for Juliet. Encounter between Isabella and Angelo: Angelo reveals that he has feigned everything – that is, that he did not intend to take Isabella's honor, nor Claudio's life; he, instead, wanted to test Isabella's constancy and chastity, and would now like to marry her; Isabella, however, still refuses him.

Act 5

Lucius, Beatrice, and Benedick sing a song about Angelo and his way of administering justice. Benedick leads a group of rioters, and plans to attack the prison to free Claudio and Juliet. There is a clash between the mayor and Angelo's soldiers on one side and Benedick's on the other. Balthazar tells of the clash between militias: Benedick is wounded, the mayor displays a decapitated head (leading people to believe that it is Claudio's) to put an end to the rioters' siege, the Duke reveals himself, and arrests both Benedick and Angelo. Beatrice asks the Duke to release Benedick. The mayor goes to Angelo and gives him false news at the Duke's behest: that Claudio was beheaded, and that before dying he was married to Juliet, who, however, has all her assets confiscated by state law. Angelo is moved by this, and decides to give her all his possessions. Meanwhile, the Duke prepares for Angelo's possessions to go to Isabella to compensate her for the offence by Angelo against her. Claudio and Juliet are alive and free thanks to the Duke's plan realized by the mayor, who believes he has executed Bernardino in place of Claudio. The Duke pardons both Angelo and Benedick; Bernardino is alive because nobody has executed him, and the head that everyone believed to be Claudio's belonged, instead, to a prisoner who died of natural causes in prison. Bernardine, a lazy man and a drunkard, has been pardoned and promises to change his life. Lucius is also pardoned despite the fact that he showed the Duke disrespect when he was disguised as a monk. The Duke announces the triple marriages of Isabella and Angelo, Beatrice and Benedick, and Claudio and Juliet. The Duke also proclaims an amnesty, ordering that the prison be open and that the prisoners set free, so that this day, when it is recounted in the future, will be a poetic dream with a moral lesson.

17. *Measure for Measure*

GENERAL INFORMATION
ADAPTOR'S NAME: Gildon, Charles
ADAPTATION TITLE: *Measure for Measure, or Beauty the Best Advocate*
SHAKESPEARE'S PLAY: *Measure for Measure*

FIRST STAGED
DATE: [February 1700][496]
PLACE: Lincoln's Inn Fields
MAIN ACTORS

Men
The Duke of Savoy, Vincentio, Mr. Arnold
Angelo, his deputy, privately married to Mariana, Mr. Betterton
Escalus, Chief Minister under Angelo, Mr. Berry
Claudio, a young nobleman, of an ancient family, but decayed fortune, one that behaved himself well in the war, privately married to Julietta, Mr. Verbrugen
Lucio, a courtier, Mr. Baile
Balthasar, a courtier, Mr. Pack
Provost, Mr. Freeman

Women
Isabella, sister to Claudio, a young votary, design'd, for want of fortune, to a nunnery, Mrs. Bracegirdle
Juliet, a lady of considerable fortune, but left in the hands of a covetous uncle, who is a hypocrite, and will give consent to none, that he may not part with it, Mrs. Bowman
Mariana, a lady of no fortune, secretly married to Angelo, Mrs. Prince

FIRST PRINTED
DATE: 1700
PLACE: London

OTHER INFORMATION
Printed for D. Brown, at the Black Swan without Temple-Bar, and R. Parker at the Unicorn Under the Royal-Exchange in Cornhill.

496 In *London Stage*: "The date of the first production is not known"; the date is determined according to evidence contained in the play's prologue.

17. *Measure for Measure*

PLOT

Act 1

In Turin, Lucio and Balthazar discuss the new law against lovers, which Angelo has reinstated and for which Claudio and Juliet have been sentenced (they married privately without witnesses, and so by law their marriage is invalid). First encounter between Angelo and Isabella: Isabella pleads with Angelo to pardon Claudio, but he only offers to postpone the execution by one day. First entertainment: a play-within-a-play with Dido and Aeneas, which Angelo and other characters attend. While watching the play, Angelo falls in love with Isabella.

Act 2

Second encounter between Angelo and Isabella: Angelo offers to set Claudio free if he can have her, she refuses him, but they however agree to meet a third time at the third entertainment. Second entertainment: the continuation of the story of Dido and Aeneas. Meanwhile in prison, the Duke, disguised as a monk, speaks with Friar Thomas about his decision to give power to Angelo, his willingness to help Mariana, Angelo's wife, and to free Claudio. The Duke speaks to Claudio, who confirms his secret wedding with Juliet; he also tells him that Angelo's right-hand man, Pedro, is planning to murder Claudio and to take possession of Juliet's dowry. The Duke speaks to Juliet, and is confident that Juliet's love for Claudio is genuine.

Act 3

Still disguised, the Duke suggests that Claudio prepare for his death. In a dialogue between Isabella and Claudio, Isabella tells Claudio about Angelo's offer. In a dialogue between the Duke and Isabella, the Duke tells Isabella about Angelo's past behavior with Mariana, and orders her to arrange a further meeting with Angelo when they meet again. Angelo and Isabella attend the third entertainment, a continuation of the story of Dido and Aeneas.

Act 4

The third encounter between Angelo and Isabella: Angelo gives Isabella diamonds, and fixes a fourth meeting with her in the royal cave. In a three-way dialogue between Mariana, the Duke, and Isabella: Mariana will go to the clandestine meeting with Angelo in place of Isabella. Claudio receives confirmation of his imminent death from the mayor; Claudio meets with Juliet, and they both affirm their love for each other. In a dialogue between Isabella and the Duke: the Duke tells her that Claudio was executed (though, in reality, this is not true), and orders that she and Mariana confront Angelo the next day to ask for justice in the presence of the Duke, who by then will have returned to Turin.

Act 5

The Duke returns to the city, and Isabella and Mariana ask him for justice. Mariana reveals her true identity, and Angelo confesses to what occurred between the two of them in the past. Mariana relates the meeting in the royal cave with Angelo. The Duke condemns Angelo to death, and reveals that Claudio and Juliet are alive and free. The fourth entertainment is a saraband.

18. *The Jew of Venice*

GENERAL INFORMATION
ADAPTOR'S NAME: Granville, George
ADAPTATION TITLE: *The Jew of Venice*
SHAKESPEARE'S PLAY: *The Merchant of Venice*

FIRST STAGED
DATE: [January 1701];[497] [May 1701][498]
PLACE: Lincoln's Inn Fields
MAIN ACTORS[499]

Men
Bassanio, gentleman of Venice, and friend, Mr. Betterton
Antonio, gentleman of Venice, and friend, Mr. Verbruggen
Gratiano, companion to Bassanio and Antonio, Mr. Booth
Lorenzo, in love with Jessica, Mr. Baily
Shylock, the Jew, Mr. Dogget
Duke of Venice, Mr. Harris

Women
Portia, a rich heiress, Mrs. Bracegirdle
Nerissa, her friend, Mrs. Bowman
Jessica, daughter to the Jew, Mrs. Porter

FIRST PRINTED
DATE: 1701
PLACE: London

OTHER INFORMATION
Printed for BER. LINTOTT at the Post-House in the Middle Temple-Gate, Fleetstreet.

497 In *London Stage*: "Date of premiere [is] unknown."
498 Date proposed by Hogan in *Shakespeare in the Theatre*.
499 In *London Stage*: "Cast [is] not listed"; the cast is determined according to the 1701 edition.

18. *The Jew of Venice*

PLOT

Act 1

The comedy's opening echoes *A Midsummer Night's Dream*, outlining the ties of the close friendship between Antonio and Bassanio. Bassanio asks Antonio for a loan so that he may court Portia of Belmonte. Portia complains to Nerissa about the destiny that her dying father has decreed for her: she is to marry the man who will choose the right chest; her suitors are a Frenchman, an Englishman and a Dutchman, none of whom is pleasing to the young heiress. Bassanio goes to the Jew Shylock to ask for a loan, and then Antonio arrives as well; Bassanio and Shylock sign a pact agreeing to a pound of Antonio's flesh if he cannot repay the loan. Shylock professes to detest Christians, especially Antonio.

Act 2

Shylock leaves home; there, Jessica awaits her Christian fiancé Lorenzo to run away with him. A banquet with Shylock, Antonio, Bassanio, and Gratiano takes place before a play within a play in the form of the entertainment of the mask of Peleus and Teti. Bassanio goes to Belmonte.

Act 3

Bassanio arrives in Belmonte, chooses the right chest, and, thus, also unites the couple Gratiano and Nerissa. Lorenzo arrives with a letter announcing the shipwreck of all Antonio's ships, and thus announces his ruin. Portia offers to pay the debt agreed to with Shylock. In shackles, Antonio is brought to prison to await the sentence. Shylock reciprocates the hatred that Christians hold for Jews, and vows that he will have his one pound of flesh.

Act 4

At the trial, Shylock demands his one pound of flesh, rejecting the ducats offered to him by third parties as means of settlement. The intervention by Portia and Nerissa in disguise, reverses the outcome of the trial, and condemns Shylock. During the trial, which sometimes echoes *Othello*, Bassanio draws his sword to defend Antonio before the turn of events which sees blame transferred from Antonio to Shylock. The Duke offers to pardon Shylock, but half of his goods are allocated to Antonio and the other half to the State of Venice. Antonio forgoes his half to Shylock's daughter at his death so that the Jew has enough to live on. Portia and Nerissa, still disguised, ask for Bassanio and Gratiano's rings which they gave to them.

Act 5

Portia and Nerissa argue over the rings that Bassanio and Gratiano unjustly gave away. A letter announces that Antonio's ships have reached their destination, and that his fortunes are now saved. The comedy ends with Bassanio's reflection on love, and on the obligations and gratitude that love requires to prosper.

19. *The Comical Gallant*

GENERAL INFORMATION
ADAPTOR'S NAME: Dennis, John
ADAPTATION TITLE: *The Comical Gallant, or The Amours of Sir John Falstaffe*
SHAKESPEARE'S PLAY: *The Merry Wives of Windsor*

FIRST STAGED
DATE: [April 1702];[500] [May 1702][501]
PLACE: Drury Lane
MAIN ACTORS: –

FIRST PRINTED
DATE: 1702
PLACE: London

OTHER INFORMATION
Printed, and Sold by A. Baldwin, near the Oxford Arms in Warwicklane

500 Date proposed by Hogan in *Shakespeare in the Theatre*.
501 In *London Stage*: "Date of premiere [is] unknown."

19. *The Comical Gallant*

PLOT

Act 1

Fenton and the innkeeper introduce the stories of the various couples in the comedy. Dialogue between Fenton and Ann Page: Ann promises her hand in marriage to Fenton, but Sir Hugh, a Welsh priest, has already proposed marriage to Ann's parents. Fenton has convinced Falstaff that both Mrs. Page and Mrs. Ford have fallen in love with him, and plans to reap the rewards of this situation. Falstaff plans to court both women, also because they are wealthy. Dr. Caius, a French doctor, also plans to court Ann Page. After reading a love letter written by Falstaff, Mrs. Page and Mrs. Ford decide to make a fool of him. Pistol and Nym warn Mr. Ford and Mr. Page of Falstaff's intentions. Sir Hugh and Dr. Caius discuss love. While Mr. Page is not worried, Mr. Ford is tormented by the possibility of his wife's infidelity; Mr. Ford plans to go to the innkeeper in disguise in order to discover what he can about Falstaff's plans for seducing the two women.

Act 2

Dr. Caius prepares to approach Sir Hugh to ask Ann Page's hand in marriage. Disguised, Mr. Ford encounters Falstaff at the inn. Mrs. Page and Mrs. Ford tell Falstaff that they would like to meet him secretly. Mr. Ford, still disguised, and Falstaff speak about Mrs. Ford, and about the ways in which Falstaff will win her heart. Dr. Caius, Slender, and the innkeeper discuss love.

Act 3

With the innkeeper's help, Mrs. Ford meets with Falstaff, and makes a fool of him. The soldier Dingboy, who is Mrs. Page disguised as a man, bursts onto the scene, and interrupts the "amorous encounter" between Falstaff and Mrs. Ford, courting Mrs. Ford, while Falstaff hides behind a screen. Falstaff comes out and argues with Dingboy/Mrs. Page. Dingboy fires a shot with his gun, and wounds Falstaff. Mr. Ford suddenly arrives because he is suspicious of his wife; Falstaff is hidden in the laundry basket, and forced to leave the house secretly. Dingboy/Mrs. Page is exposed.

Act 4

Mr. Ford argues with the innkeeper, who tells him that Falstaff was in his house with his wife; Mr. Ford holds him responsible for what happened. Mr. Ford, disguised, speaks to Falstaff about his adventures at the Ford residence: how he got out and how he was then thrown into the Thames. Mr. Ford speaks with the innkeeper, who tells him that Falstaff has arranged another meeting at midnight in the woods at the hunter's oak tree. He also learns that Fenton organized the first meeting between Falstaff and Mrs. Ford and Mrs. Page so that he could distract them from their intentions to marry Ann Page to Dr. Caius. The meeting at the oak tree will be in disguise, so Fenton wants to take advantage of this to confuse all the others and to win Ann Page's heart. His plan is also to direct Slender to another person. In a dialogue between Slender and Ann Page, Ann Page pretends to agree to a night-time meeting at the oak tree.

Act 5

Those who are meeting in the woods at midnight are getting prepared. Falstaff is disguised as a hunter, and Mr. Ford as Falstaff to test his wife's fidelity. There is singing and dancing in the woods. Mr. Ford is beaten in Falstaff's place, but he is happy about this because he learns that his wife is faithful. Thanks to the previous plan, Fenton, who is with Ann Page, fools Slender and Dr. Caius. Fenton and Ann Page do not yet marry because they are awaiting Mr. Page's consent. Mr. Page marries them, although he reminds them of the dangers of a marriage agreed upon in secret and its possible negative outcomes.

20. *The Fairy Queen*

GENERAL INFORMATION
ADAPTOR'S NAME: Anonymous[502]
ADAPTATION TITLE: *The Fairy Queen*
SHAKESPEARE'S PLAY: *A Midsummer Night's Dream*

FIRST STAGED
DATE: [May 2, 1692][503]
PLACE: Dorset Garden
MAIN ACTORS: –

FIRST PRINTED
DATE: 1692
PLACE: London

OTHER INFORMATION
Printed for Jacob Tonson, at the Judges-Head, in Chancery-Lane.

502 In *London Stage* the play is attributed to Elkanah Settle.

503 In *London Stage*: "The date of the first performance is stated in Luttrell, *A Brief Relation*, II, 435, April 28, 1692."

20. *The Fairy Queen*

PLOT

Act 1

Egeo brings his daughter Ermia to the Duke in his palace; Demetrio and Lisandro are also present; Egeo accuses Lisandro of seducing his daughter with magic. If Ermia does not change her mind, she will have to live in a cloister. Lisandro and Ermia agree to meet late at night in the woods so they can escape together; they share their plan with Elena, who decides that she will go to the meeting as well. The group of actors representing "the lamentable comedy … of Pyramus and Thisbe" for Ermia's wedding meets to discuss who will play who in the cast.

Act 2

A fairy and Puck/Robin Goodfellow tell the story of how Oberon and Titiana are arguing over Titiana's new beautiful Indian servant. Oberon and Titiana compete for the servant, but Titiana refuses to surrender; Oberon, thus, wants revenge, and sends Robin to seek a magical flower of love. Demetrio and Elena meet in the woods; Demetrio confirms that he does not love Elena. Robin returns to Oberon with the magic flower, and Oberon orders Robin to pour the flower's juice into Titiana's eyes while she sleeps so that when she awakens she will fall in love with the first person she sees. Titiana makes a cave appear in which there is an entertainment with songs and dance of operatic recitatives interpreted by elves and fairies. Ermia and Lisandro fall asleep in the woods; Robin arrives and pours the magic juice in Lisandro's eyes.

Act 3

Lisandro awakens, sees Elena, and falls in love with her; Elena believes he is feigning love for her. The actors rehearse the play of Pyramus and Thisbe in the woods, under the eyes of Robin, who interrupts them and scares them away during the epilogue. One of the actors, Bottom, returns wearing a mask of a mule, and Titiana falls in love with him. Dialogue between Oberon and Robin: Robin did right with Titiana, but not with Lisandro as he was supposed to act on Demetrio. The enamored Titiana organizes an operatic recitation with songs and dance for Bottom.

Act 4

Oberon orders Robin to pour the magic juice in Demetrio's eyes while he sleeps. Lisandro courts Elena, who rejects him because she believes he is only pretending to love her; Demetrio awakens, falls in love with Elena, and courts her, but she also refuses him. Ermia arrives and the scene becomes more complicated: Elena accuses Ermia of pretending, while Ermia understands that Lisandro now truly loves Elena; Demetrio and Lisandro on one hand, Elena and Ermia on another, run in the woods to confront one another. Oberon accuses Robin of having intentionally poured the magic juice in the eyes of the wrong people; he will now have to resolve the situation by undoing the effects from Lisandro's eyes. Robin puts all four to asleep. Oberon undoes the magic from Titiana's eyes after he had her give up the Indian servant; Titiana loves Oberon again. Oberon orders a recitative with song and dance to celebrate the dawn of the new day.

Act 5

Before the Duke and Egeo, the couples recompose: Demetrio and Elena, Lisandro and Ermia. Bottom tells the other actors what occurred with Titiana, believing it to be a dream. Oberon and Titiana participate in the entertainment with the song of the goddess Juno. The play ends with a great recitative operatic scene with features strongly reminiscent of exoticism: scenography, Chinese songs and dances present Hymen, the goddess of marriage. In the final metatheatrical dialogue, Oberon and Titiana comment upon the various figures constituting the typical theater audience of the Restoration.

21. *The Universal Passion*

GENERAL INFORMATION
ADAPTOR'S NAME: Miller, James
ADAPTATION TITLE: *The Universal Passion*
SHAKESPEARE'S PLAY: *Much Ado About Nothing*

FIRST STAGED
DATE: February 28, 1737
PLACE: Drury Lane
MAIN ACTORS[504]

Men
Gratiano, Duke of Genoa, Mr. Millward
Bellario, a young Venetian Lord, Mr. Mills
Protheus, a nobleman of Genoa, Mr. Quin
Joculo, a court jester, Mr. [T.] Cibber
Byron, bastard brother to the Duke, Mr. Berry
Gremio, his favorite, Mr. Winstone
Lucentius, tutor to Bellario, Mr. Shephard
Porco, constable of the watch, Mr. Harper
Asino, constable of the watch, Mr. Mechlin

Women
Lucilia, daughter to the Duke, Mrs. Butler
Liberia, niece to the Duke, Mrs. Clive
Delia, attendant on Lucilia, Mrs. Pritchard

FIRST PRINTED
DATE: 1737
PLACE: London

OTHER INFORMATION
Printed for J. Watts at the Printing-Office in Wild Court, near Lincoln's-Inn Fields.

504 In *London Stage*: "Cast [is] not listed"; the cast is determined from the 1737 edition.

21. *The Universal Passion*

PLOT

Act 1

In Genoa, Bellario and Lucentius are in a forest: Bellario is in love with Lucilia, a chaste and proud woman. In a dialogue between Bellario and Joculo the fool, Bellario asks Joculo if he has spoken to Lucilia about his love for her, and Joculo tells him that he has not; so they speak instead about courtly life. In a three-way dialogue between Lucilia, Liberia and Delia, Lucilia praises rural life. In a dialogue between Lucilia and Joculo, Joculo confesses his love for her. Gratiano, Lucilia's father, Bellario and Lucentius arrive, and speak with the three women. There will be a competition between Lucilia's suitors; Lucilia, however, does not intend to marry any of them; Bellario will also take part in this competition, but only for reasons of glory and honor, because according to him "love's a bauble, and fit only to be disputed by beardless boys." Departing in a haughty manner, Bellario attracts Lucilia's attention; Lucilia thus decides to change her mind. Gratiano receives a letter that announces the imminent arrival of Protheus, whom Liberia begins to mock. Argument between Protheus and Liberia. First aria of a sung recitative. In a dialogue between Byron and his servant Gremio, we learn that Byron is Gratiano's evil brother, and he plans to break the marriage between Bellario and Lucilia.

Act 2

Lucilia and Delia discuss matters of love. In a three-way dialogue between Bellario, Lucentius, and Joculo, Bellario confesses his love for Lucilia, even though she did not even notice him at the competition. In a dialogue between Protheus and Bellario, Protheus admits he is misogynist. In a dialogue between Lucilia and Joculo, Joculo makes Lucilia jealous of Bellario. In a dialogue between Lucilia and Bellario, Bellario lies and tells Lucilia that he is in love with Liberia. In a dialogue between Joculo and Delia, Delia says that she is in love with Gremio. In a dialogue between Lucilia and Liberia, Lucilia asks Liberia to reject Bellario because she wants him to fall in love with her instead. Sung recitative.

Act 3

In a dialogue between Lucilia and Joculo, Joculo tells Lucilia how Bellario saved Gratiano from two outlaws. Gratiano announces to Lucilia his decision to marry her to Bellario, and tells her that Bellario's behavior towards her was false and that, in reality, he loves her. Gratiano, Joculo, Bellario, and Lucilia hope to convince Liberia to marry Protheus. Byron and Gremio confess that they were behind the outlaws who assaulted Gratiano. Gremio plans to use his influence on Delia, Lucilia's servant, for his criminal plan, which will entail telling Byron to tell Bellario that Lucilia also pays favors to her servants, and that he can prove it that same night; that night, Bellario will instead see and hear Gremio speaking amorously with Delia. Gratiano, Joculo, Bellario, and Lucilia, once again, turn to discuss how they can convince Liberia to marry Protheus. There is argument between Liberia and Protheus. Sung recitative. In a dialogue between Joculo and Liberia, Joculo tells Liberia that Protheus hates her, and this leads her to love him. Sung recitative.

Act 4

In a three-way dialogue between Bellario, Byron, and Lucentius, Byron tells Bellario that Lucilia is unfaithful. There is comical dialogue between the guards Porco, Asino, and two other sentinels. Gremio is captured by the guards and confesses his criminal plan hatched with Byron. In a three-way dialogue between Lucilia, Delia, and Liberia, Lucilia prepares for her marriage. Sung recitative. In a three-way dialogue between Asino, Porco, and Gratiano, Asino and Porco cannot manage to tell Gratiano about Gremio's arrest. At church, Bellario renounces Lucilia, who faints from the sorrow and is believed to be dead until she comes to life again. Protheus suggests that Lucilia pretend to be dead to see the reaction of Bellario and the other men of court.

Act 5

In a dialogue between Protheus and Liberia, Liberia asks Protheus to murder Bellario because she believes that he unjustly hurt Lucilia. Porco and Asino bring Gremio to Bellario to confess his criminal plan. Gratiano reveals that he has a niece like Lucilia, who is now the only heiress of his wealth and fortune, and that he would like Bellario to marry her; Bellario accepts but only because he believes that refusing would have cost him his life. In a dialogue between Joculo and Delia, Delia is saddened by the fact that she unwittingly played a role in Gremio's criminal plan. Bellario marries Lucilia, and Protheus Liberia. Sung recitative. Having escaped, Byron is captured. The comedy closes with Protheus singing about the joys of marriage and the primacy of love among all other human sentiments.

22. *The History of Richard II*

GENERAL INFORMATION
ADAPTOR'S NAME: Tate, Nahum
ADAPTATION TITLE: *The History of Richard II* (*The Sicilian Usurper*)
SHAKESPEARE'S PLAY: *Richard II*

FIRST STAGED
DATE: [December 1680][505]
PLACE: Drury Lane
MAIN ACTORS: –

FIRST PRINTED
DATE: 1681
PLACE: London

OTHER INFORMATION
Printed for Richard Tonson, and Jacob Tonson, at Grays-Inn Gate, and at the Judges-Head in Chancery-Lane near Fleet-Street.

505 In *London Stage*: "The date of the premiere is not certain"; the date is determined from the evidence in the dedication, and from the decree documented in Nicholl's *Restoration Drama*. Based on this information, it can be surmised that the date of the first performance was November 11, 1680 (or January 18, 1681).

22. *The History of Richard II*

PLOT

Act 1

John of Gaunt's son, Henry (Harry) Herford Bullingbrook argues with Norfolk. In a dialogue between Thomas Mowbray and Bullingbrook, Bullingbrook accuses Mowbray of betrayal and of Gloucester's murder; they both agree to a duel to reveal the truth. The Duchess of Gloucester, York, and Gaunt discuss politics. The duel between Bullingbrook and Mowray is about to begin when the King interrupts the formal occasion and banishes the two rivals: Bullingbrook for ten years, and Mowbray for life. In the meanwhile, news arrives that Ireland is up in arms.

Act 2

By Gaunt on his deathbed, York cautions the King about the current situation of the English court, which has been reduced to luxury, pomp, and diversion. The King proclaims York Lord Governor of England. Gaunt dies, and the King temporarily acquires the income of the banished Bullingbrook. Some nobles unite with Bullingbrook, who returns to England at the head of an army.

Act 3

Bullingbrook arrives in England, and York goes to oppose him. Some low-class characters discuss politics. Bullingbrook encounters a crowd of people, and speaks with them about politics. King Richard, Carlisle, and Aumerle, York's son, speak about the traitor Bullingbrook. The Duchess of York and the Queen discuss the political situation. Some nobles have aligned themselves with Bullingbrook. The King and Queen discuss politics. First meeting between Richard and Bullingbrook.

Act 4

Bullingbrook summons Parliament to force Richard to abdicate. Moving dialogue between King and Queen before Bullingbrook's coronation. Bullingbrook's coronation; Carlisle argues with Bullingbrook. Scene of Richard's abdication: tears and shattered mirror. Richard is brought to the prison of the tower of London.

Act 5

Because of a medal around Aumerle's neck, York discovers Oxford's plot to murder Bullingbrook. The King and Queen reflect upon their unfortunate fate. Bullingbrook orders that the couple be separated: the King must be transferred to Pomfret, and the Queen sent into exile to France. Aumerle, York, and his wife the Duchess go to Bullingbrook to explain their version of the conspiracy: Aumerle admits fault, the Duchess requests forgiveness on behalf of her son, and York condemns his actions. Richard is in prison at Pomfret: after he manages to kill four hired killers, he is murdered by Exton, who acts on his own initiative. Meanwhile, Bullingbrook has ruined Oxford's plot by killing the conspirators. Exton delivers Richard's head to Bullingbrook, who regrets the bloodshed because he did not order Richard's murder.

23. *The Tragedy of King Richard II*

GENERAL INFORMATION
ADAPTOR'S NAME: Theobald, Lewis
ADAPTATION TITLE: *The Tragedy of King Richard II*
SHAKESPEARE'S PLAY: *Richard II*

FIRST STAGED
DATE: December 10, 1719
PLACE: Lincoln's Inn Fields
MAIN ACTORS[506]

Men
King Richard II, Mr. Ryan
Duke of York, Edmund of Langley, Mr. Boheme
Duke of Aumerle, Mr. Smith
Lord Salisbury, Earl of Salisbury, Mr. Egleton
Bishop of Carlisle, Mr. C. Bullock
Bolingbroke, Henry Bolingbroke, Mr. Leigh
Earl of Northumberland, Mr. Ogden
Lord Ross, Mr. Diggs
Lord Willoughby, Mr. Coker

Women
Queen, Mrs. Bullock
Lady Piercy, Mrs. Spiller

FIRST PRINTED
DATE: 1720
PLACE: London

OTHER INFORMATION
Printed for G. Strahan at the Golden Ball in Cornhill, W. Mears without Temple Bar, T. Meiohan in Drury Lane, B. Barker in Westminster Hall, and-Sold by J. Morphew near Stationers Hall.

506 In *London Stage*: "Cast [is] not listed;" the cast is determined from the 1720 edition.

23. *The Tragedy of King Richard II*

PLOT

Act 1

In front of the Tower of London, York, loyal to the King, reflects on the current administrative and political situation: on one hand, money is missing from the state's coffers, while on the other, the war in Ireland has left Scotland without garrisons, and rebels have thus had an easy life and are preparing to head south. York's son Aumerle, young and impetuous, plans to challenge Bolingbroke to a duel. Aumerle is in love with Lady Piercy. In a dialogue between the King, Carlisle, Aumerle, and York we learn that Wiltshire, Bagot and Bushy have aligned themselves with Bolingbroke. The King and Queen discuss the current difficult political situation.

Act 2

Aumerle and Lady Piercy are in the Tower of London: the two lovers argue, and then Aumerle discovers a letter from Northumberland, Lady Piercy's father, who has sided with Bolingbroke, and has ordered her to leave him. Bolingbroke and York confront each other in front of the Tower of London. Dressed as Bolingbroke's ambassador, Northumberland speaks to the King. In a dialogue between Bolingbroke and the King, Bolingbroke confirms that, after his exile, the King was ill advised when he took his income, his territory, his title of nobility, and his rights as successor. These are the reasons that pushed him to return to England in arms. The King decides to abdicate in favor of Bolingbroke.

Act 3

Carlisle and Salisbury describe the triumphant welcome that Bolingbroke was given when he arrived in London. Intimate dialogue between King and Queen. In Parliament, Aumerle is accused of betrayal against Bolingbroke; Richard's deposition is debated, an unprecedented act in history. Carlisle's oration in favor of Richard. Richard enters Parliament, and abdicates: he weeps and shatters a mirror. Aumerle makes an attempt on Bolingbroke's life.

Act 4

Salisbury and Aumerle begin to plan Oxford's attempt on Bolingbroke's life; during the meeting between Aumerle and Lady Piercy, Northumberland finds a lost parchment, and in it reads of Oxford's plot. Dialogue between the King, Queen, and York about the current political situation. Intimate dialogue between King and Queen. Northumberland warns Bolingbroke about Oxford's conspiracy. The main conspirators are Aumerle, Suffolk, Exeter, and Salisbury, who will now be punished. Bolingbroke warns York of the conspiracy ordered by his son, Aumerle; York begs Bolingbroke to spare his son's life, but his plea falls on deaf ears.

Act 5

The conspirators are captured, and await their execution. In a dialogue between Northumberland and Lady Piercy, Northumberland sentences Aumerle to death, and Lady Piercy is in despair. Bolingbroke shows mercy towards Carlisle, being a man of the Church, on the condition that he withdraws from politics. Aumerle and Salisbury prepare to die with dignity. Before the Queen, Northumberland informs that the King must be transferred from the Tower of London to Pomfret, but the King refuses to be separated from his wife. Swords are drawn, Richard kills two guards, but Exton then kills him. At the same time, word arrives that Lady Piercy has died; she committed suicide not long after she learned that Aumerle was sentenced to death. York dies of grief for the loss of his son Aumerle. Bolingbroke bitterly concludes with an admonition that a kingdom founded on the blood-shed of a king can only be cursed, thus anticipating future events.

24. *The Tragical History of Richard III*

GENERAL INFORMATION

ADAPTOR'S NAME: Cibber, Colley
ADAPTATION TITLE: *The Tragical History of Richard III*
SHAKESPEARE'S PLAY: *Richard III*

FIRST STAGED
DATE[507]: [December 1699][508]
PLACE: Drury Lane
MAIN ACTORS

Men
King Henry VI, *designed for* Mr. Wilks
Richard Duke of Gloucester, afterwards King of England, Mr. Cibber
Duke of Buckingham, Mr. Powel
Lord Stanley, Mr. Mills
Duke of Norfolk, Mr. Simpson
Ratcliff, Sir Richard Ratcliff, Mr. Kent
Catesby, Sir William Catesby, Mr. Thomas
Henry Earl of Richmond, afterwards King of England, Mr. Evans
Oxford, Earl of Oxford, Mr. Fairbank

Women
Edward Prince of Wales, the young son of Edward IV, Mrs. Allison
Richard Duke of York, the young son of Edward IV, Miss Chock
Elizabeth, relict of Edward IV, Mrs. Knight
Ann, Lady Anne, relict of Edward Prince of Wales, son to Henry VI, afterwards married to Richard III, Mrs. Rogers
Cicely, Duchess of York, Duchess of York, mother to Richard III, Mrs. Powel

FIRST PRINTED
DATE: [1700]
PLACE: London

OTHER INFORMATION
For B. Lintott at the Middle Temple-Gate, in Elect-Street, and A. Bettesworth at the Red-Lyon on London-Bridge.

---

507 In *London Stage*: "Late December [1699]."
508 In *London Stage*: "The date of the premiere is not known"; the date is determined based on the evidence in the play's dedication from *Term Catalogue* and the *Flying Post* dated March 16, 1699–1700.

24. *The Tragical History of King Richard III*

PLOT

Act 1

Edward York triumphs in the battle of Tewkesbury and is King of England. Henry VI is imprisoned in the tower of London, and Tressel brings him news of the battle: the Queen has been imprisoned and Richard and Clarence stabbed Prince Edward in the back in cold blood. Richard, who, from the beginning, appears as a ruthless villain, goes to the Tower, meets Henry VI and murders him; indeed, he is already considering other imminent murders necessary for his accession to the throne.

Act 2

Henry's body is shown in St. Paul's Cathedral: Henry's grieving widow Lady Ann follows the casket, and is courted and won over by Richard. Edward York dies, thus making Richard Lord Protector. While the York family and its female members grieve Edward's death, Richard continues to plan his accession to the throne.

Act 3

Richard arrives in London with the young Prince Edward York, heir to the throne, and the brother Duke of York. The mayor welcomes them, while Richard already has in mind how to murder them in the Tower, where Clarence York died. Richard plans to get rid of Lady Ann and to marry Elizabeth. Richard is offered the throne, but he hesitates, pretending to be a pious man absorbed in the spiritual life; at his summoning, in fact, he arrives with an ecclesiastical book and in the company of two men of the Church. After feigning disinterest he ends up accepting the throne.

Act 4

The two York brothers, heirs to the throne, are imprisoned in the tower and fear for their lives. Rivers, Grey, and Vaughan are killed at Pomfret. Richard orders that the two York brothers be separated from their mother, the Queen. Richard plans to kill the two York brothers. Buckingham, who was allied with Richard, is now his opponent. In the Tower, two killers hired by Richard strangle the two York brothers to death. The Queen Mother and the Duchess of York confront Richard and accuse him of all the recent deaths. Richard states that he did what he had to do to marry Elizabeth York. Richmond and Buckingham side against Richard. Fearing betrayal, Richard takes Lord Stanley's son hostage; Lord Stanley is to lead the royal army. Bad weather decimates Buckingham's army, and he is captured; Richard orders that Buckingham be beheaded, using the famous "Off with his head. So much for Buckingham." Richard arrives at Milford.

Act 5

At Bosworth, Richmond and Richard prepare for battle. Stanley goes to Richmond in disguise to assure him that he has his support. At night, Richard dreams of the ghosts of his victims: Henry VI, the two young Yorks, and Lady Ann. During the battle, Stanley does not fight alongside Richard. Richard and Richmond, who are on foot, both seek a horse and exclaim "A horse! A horse! My Kingdom for a horse!" They argue, and Richmond kills Richard. Richmond, the future king, will marry Lady Elizabeth, thus uniting the York and Lancaster families, the two families who fought as pretenders to the throne who thus far had been rivals.

25. *The History and Fall of Caius Marius*

GENERAL INFORMATION
ADAPTOR'S NAME: Otway, Thomas
ADAPTATION TITLE: *The History and Fall of Caius Marius*
SHAKESPEARE'S PLAY: *Romeo and Juliet*

FIRST STAGED
DATE: [October 1679][509]
PLACE: Dorset Garden
MAIN ACTORS

Men
Caius Marius, Mr. Betterton
Sylla, Mr. Williams
Marius junior, Mr. Smith
Granius, Mr. Percivale
Metellus, Mr. Gillow
Quintus Pompeius, Mr. Williams
Cinna, Mr. Jevon
Sulpitius, Mr. Underhill

Women
Lavinia, Mrs. Barry
Nurse, Mr. Boakes

FIRST PRINTED
DATE: 1680
PLACE: London

OTHER INFORMATION
Printed for Tho. Flesher, at the Angel and Crown in St. Paul's Churchyard.

509 In *London Stage*: "The date of the premiere is not known"; the date is determined on the evidence in the play's prologue and from *Term Catalogue*.

25. *The History and Fall of Caius Marius*

PLOT

Act 1

The setting is in Ancient Rome, during the time of Marius and Sylla. Metellus and Cinna discuss the current uncertain and corrupt political situation in Rome and the inconsistent pleb; they accuse Marius Senior, whom they hate, for everything that is bad; finally they resolve to support Sylla. To please her father, Metellus' daughter Lavinia is forced to marry Sylla instead of Marius's son. Marius Senior and Marius Junior speak of the current political situation in Rome and of Lavinia, whom Marius Junior loves. Sulpitius has killed a member of Metellus' family, and speaks to Marius Junior about the Queen Mab.

Act 2

Metellus proposes that Lavinia marry Sylla, but she refuses, and argues with her father; the nurse, however, seems to support Lavinia's decision. There is a balcony scene with Marius Junior and Lavinia. At the forum, Sulpitius addresses the crowd in favour of Marius Senior, so that he can be elected consul, while Metellus speaks against Marius Senior; Sulpitius kills Pompeius Junior. This murder triggers a civil war, and Marius Senior vows that he will free all slaves who side with him against Sylla.

Act 3

Sylla is at the doors of Rome with an army; the city's citizens side with the elder Marius. Sulpitius and Marius Junior speak with Lavinia's nurse: the nurse organizes a meeting between the two lovers, who will meet that evening. Marius Junior confesses to his father that he detests the Metellus family and that he has married Lavinia. The nurse announces Marius Junior's arrival to Lavinia. At the forum, Marius Senior and Sylla have an argument; they draw their swords, and both sides begin a battle; Marius Senior is imprisoned, and so too are Marius Junior and Sulpitius; they are all banished from Rome and sentenced to death.

Act 4

In the garden of Metellus' house, Lavinia and Marius Junior meet and vow their love for each other before they separate. Marius Junior is forced to leave the city; because of this, Lavinia escapes from home. Some of Sylla's soldiers clash with some of Marius Senior's halberdiers; meanwhile, Marius Senior has escaped Rome. In the woods, Marius Senior encounters his son, who then leaves in search of food for his famished father and then encounters Lavinia. Marius Senior accepts Lavinia as his son's wife; Marius Junior arrives and the three come together. Encounter with Marta, a Syrian prophetess who was banished from Rome because she prophesied Marius Senior's fortune. Sulpitius brings Cinna to Marius Senior, and they prepare to return to Rome. Lavinia is captured, returned to the Metellus house, and betrothed to Sylla; so as to avoid marrying him, she drinks a potion that will make her lose consciousness.

Act 5

At the doors of Rome, leading an army, Cinna and Marius Senior speak with the city ambassadors. Cinna and Marius Senior decide to march on Rome; the city is set on fire. At Metellus' home, Lavinia is unconscious and believed to be dead. Masters of the city, Marius Senior and Sulpitius, enter the forum. While in the cemetery, Marius Junior learns of Lavinia's death, and buys poison. Marius Junior mistakenly kills the priest who married him and Lavinia. Marius Junior, seeing Lavinia unconscious, believes she is dead and drinks the poison he just bought. Minutes before Marius Junior dies, Lavinia regains consciousness, and Marius Junior dies in her arms. Metellus is followed in the cemetery, and then killed there by Marius Senior's soldiers. In a dialogue between Marius Senior and Lavinia, Lavinia kills herself, having been left without a husband, and a father who was murdered in front of her at Marius Senior's command. From Capua, the news arrives that Sylla's army has left to march on Rome. The city is then once again overcome by riots, during which Sulpitius dies from wounds. The play closes with Sulpitius who speaks an epitaph for a man who lived a fool and died a thief.

26. *Sauny the Scot*

GENERAL INFORMATION
ADAPTOR'S NAME: Lacy, John
ADAPTATION TITLE: *Sauny the Scot*
SHAKESPEARE'S PLAY: *The Taming of the Shrew*

FIRST STAGED
DATE: [April 1667]
PLACE: Bridges[510]
MAIN ACTORS

Men
Sauny, Lacy

Women
–

FIRST PRINTED
DATE: 1698
PLACE: London

OTHER INFORMATION
Printed and Sold by E. Whitlock, near Stationers-Hall.

510 (First) Drury Lane.

26. *Sauny the Scot*

PLOT

Act 1

Winlove and his servant, Tranio, discuss the differences between rural and urban life. Beaufoy states that he does not wish to marry his youngest daughter Bianca to either of her admirers, Geraldo or Woodall, before his eldest daughter marry. Winlove falls in love with Bianca and decides to court her as her French teacher; to do so, he exchanges clothing with Tranio.

Act 2

Petruchio and his servant, Sauny, go to Petruchio's friend Geraldo. Petruchio is in the city in search of a wife; he is only interested in a future wife for her dowry, and so Geraldo recommends Margherita, who, however, is notorious for her impudence. The three suitors begin to compete for Bianca's affection. Margherita hits Bianca. Petruchio tells Beaufoy his wish to marry Margherita. Geraldo pretends to be a lute teacher to enter the Beaufoy residence, but Margherita hits him during their first music lesson. Verbal and physical clash between Petruchio and Margherita. Petruchio decides to marry her, even though Margherita does not want to. Beaufoy promises his daughter Bianca in marriage to Tranio (who is still wearing Winlove's clothes) if he can prove that his possessions are those he has declared; otherwise Bianca will marry Woodall. Tranio has to find somebody who can pretend to be Sir Lyonell, Winlove's father.

Act 3

Geraldo, disguised as a music teacher, and Winlove, as a French teacher, court Bianca, and reveal their true identity to her. Bianca prefers Winlove, so Geraldo decides to focus his efforts on a widow. Dressed very strangely, Petruchio enters to marry Margherita. Winlove and Tranio still have to find somebody who will pretend to be Sir Lyonell to ensure that Bianca be married to Winlove. Immediately after the marriage ceremony, Petruchio takes Margherita away. Winlove and Tranio hire Snatchpenny to pretend to be Sir Lyonell. Petruchio and Margherita arrive at home. Petruchio does not let Margherita eat or sleep, but, instead, gives her beer to drink and tobacco to smoke.

Act 4

At Petruchio's behest, Sauny does not give Margherita food. The dressmaker tries to make Margherita a dress for her sister Bianca's wedding, but he is treated poorly and chased away by Petruchio; so Margherita does not have a dress. Snatchpenny pretends to be Sir Lyonell, and assures Beaufoy of his promise of possessions for the young couple; thus Beaufoy gives consent to the marriage. Winlove prepares to marry Bianca. On their way to Bianca's wedding, Petruchio speaks blatant falsities, i.e. that the sun is really the moon, and the elderly traveler they just met is really a young woman and then asks her wife if she agrees or not with him; Margherita meekly agrees with her husband's false statements. The elderly traveler is, in reality, the real Sir Lyonell, and the three of them continue their journey together. Sir Lyonell is worried that his son is about to get married without his permission. When they arrive in the city, Sir Lyonell asks to speak with Winlove, but

Snatchpenny, who is pretending to be Sir Lyonell, prevents him from doing so. Winlove and Bianca get married secretly; Beaufoy and Sir Lyonell accept their children's decision.

Act 5
Margherita confides to Bianca that she plans to rebel against her despotic husband, Petruchio. Margherita tries to rebel against Petruchio, but she does not prevail. Margherita suffers for the fail and is not well. The doctor arrives to extract her a tooth, but he is unable to do so. Margherita appears to be dead and so Petruchio plans her funeral. Seeing that Petruchio is serious, Margherita is encouraged and promises to obey her husband. Petruchio, Winlove, and Geraldo place bets on Margherita's obedience; Petruchio wins. The comedy closes with a metatheatrical comment by Petruchio who says that he will not be surprised if after having seen the taming of the shrew, the public will immediately see the tamer tamed (*Tamer Tam'd*), a comedy that in the Restoration often followed the performances of the *Taming of the Shrew*.

27. *The Tempest*

GENERAL INFORMATION
ADAPTOR'S NAME: Davenant, William; Dryden, John
ADAPTATION TITLE: *The Tempest, or The Enchanted Island*
SHAKESPEARE'S PLAY: *The Tempest*

FIRST STAGED
DATE: November 7, 1667
PLACE: Lincoln's Inn Fields
MAIN ACTORS[511]

Men
Ferdinand, Harris
Stephano, Angel
Trincalo, Underhill

Women
Ariel, Mary Davies
Hyppolito, Mrs. Long

FIRST PRINTED
DATE: 1670
PLACE: London

OTHER INFORMATION
Printed by J. M. for Henry Herringman at the Blew Anchor in the Lower-walk of the New-Exchange.

511 In *London Stage*: "A possible cast."

27. *The Tempest*

PLOT

Act 1

Mustacho, Ventoso, Trincalo, and Stephano, together with Alonzo, Antonio, and Gonzalo, are on a sinking ship in the middle of a tempest; Ferdinando is separated from his father Alonzo. From an island, Prospero and Miranda see the sinking ship, which is under Prospero's control. He tells his two daughters the story about their arrival to the island and about the help they received from Gonzalo when they were distanced from Milan because of Antonio, Prospero's brother and usurper of the duchy. In a dialogue between Prospero and Ariel, Ariel reclaims his freedom, then the two speak about the siblings Sycorax and Caliban, the hideous children of a witch. Argument between Prospero and Caliban, who, against his will, is forced to obey Prospero's orders. Prospero's two daughters Dorinda and Miranda have never seen another man other than their father, and speak about the new "creatures" that have arrived on the island because of the sinking of the ship.

Act 2

Alonzo, Antonio, and Gonzalo reflect upon their present fate and their past faults. Spirits sing and stage a representation (in which pride, fraud, theft, and murder are on display) that accuses Alonzo and Antonio for their past crimes. Ariel sings a song in praise of Ferdinand. Stephano, Mustacho, and Ventoso drink, and discuss a parody of a political structure. Trincalo enters in a drunken state and singing, and reopens the discussion on the political structure. When Caliban arrives, he drinks, gets drunk, and becomes the sailors' servant. Prospero describes women to Hyppolito, who has never seen a woman before. Prospero warns Miranda and Dorinda to stay away from the area where Hyppolito stays. Dorinda and Hyppolito meet for the first time.

Act 3

Prospero speaks about Hyppolito to Miranda, who has not yet seen him, and to Dorinda, who has already met him. Dorinda wishes to see Hyppolito again, but Prospero is against this idea. Prospero speaks with Ariel, who updates him on the shipwreck survivors. Alonzo, Antonio, and Gonzalo praise the song by Ariel, who is invisible to them; then some spirits bring food and a prepared table magically appears. In a three-way dialogue between Trincalo, Caliban, and Sycorax, the main subject is a bottle of wine, which Ariel transforms into water; Stephano, Mustacho, and Ventoso discuss the political structure on the island with Trincalo; Trincalo marries Sycorax and presents himself as lord of the island. Ferdinand with the invisible Ariel: the echo scene, in part sung, that very much impressed Pepys. Prospero and Miranda encounter Ferdinand, who falls in love with her, but is rendered immobile by Prospero's magic. Prospero meets Hyppolito, and asks him about his encounter with Dorinda. When Hyppolito and Ferdinand meet, the contrast between a man of nature and a man of civilization is apparent; Hyppolito begins to believe that Prospero has thus far lied to him and deceived him.

Act 4
With Prospero's permission, Ferdinand and Miranda meet, and the courting begins. At the end of their encounter, Prospero forces Miranda to tell him what happened with Ferdinand. Hyppolito and Dorinda meet, and Prospero leaves their "love to grow in secret"; Ferdinand, however, told Hyppolito that there are more women in the world, and so Hyppolito now desires all of them. Hyppolito meets Ferdinand; they fight because Hyppolito also wishes to have the woman whom Ferdinand is courting. In a dialogue between Trincalo, Caliban, and Sycorax, Stephano, Ventoso, and Mustacho, the subject is still the bottle of wine, and then there are arguments about who gets to own the island. Hyppolito is defeated in a duel against Ferdinand, and believed to be dead; Prospero arrives, and summons Ariel who is ordered to call Alonzo, Gonzalo, and Antonio; in the meantime, Miranda and Dorinda also arrive. Alonzo, Gonzalo, and Antonio arrive; Alonzo and Ferdinand, father and son, are reunited. Prospero demands Ferdinand's life in exchange for Hyppolito's, and gives him one night to prepare for his death. Miranda and Dorinda fight over Ferdinand and Hyppolito. Acting as the chorus, Ariel recapitulates the facts of the story up to that moment.

Act 5
Miranda asks Prospero to show pity for Ferdinand, but he refuses. Ariel tells Prospero that Hyppolito is not dead, and that at night he sought medicine for him. The wounded Hyppolito is with Dorinda, who takes care of him; Hyppolito is reformed and gives up his polygamous ways for monogamy. When Miranda and Ferdinand arrive, all differences are worked out, and the couples are reunited. Prospero, Alonzo, Antonio, and Gonzalo make amends and prepare for the coming marriages. In the Prospero's presence, Ariel brings sailors and monsters, and everything is resolved. Ariel is freed, and calls her companion spirit Milcha.

28. *The Tempest*

GENERAL INFORMATION
ADAPTOR'S NAME: Davenant, William; Dryden, John; Shadwell, Thomas
ADAPTATION TITLE: *The Tempest, or The Enchanted Island*
SHAKESPEARE'S PLAY: *The Tempest*

FIRST STAGED
DATE: [April 30, 1674][512]
PLACE: Dorset Garden
MAIN ACTORS:[513] –

FIRST PRINTED
DATE: 1674
PLACE: London

OTHER INFORMATION
Printed T. N. for Henry Herringham, at the Blew Anchor in the Lower Walk of the New-Exchange.

512 In *London Stage*: "This date of performance is not a certainty"; the date is determined by the evidence in Spencer's *Shakespeare Improved* (94).

513 In *London Stage*: "Probably Underhill acted Trinculo."

28. *The Tempest*

PLOT[514]

Act 1

Extended paratextual indications describe a grandiose overture with an orchestra of 24 violins and elaborate scenes. Mustacho, Ventoso, Trincalo, and Stephano, together with Alonzo, Antonio, and Gonzalo, are on a sinking ship in the middle of a tempest; Ferdinando is separated from his father Alonzo. From an island, Prospero and Miranda see the sinking ship, which is under Prospero's control. He tells his two daughters the story about their arrival on the island and about the help they received from Gonzalo when they were exiled from Milan because of Antonio, Prospero's brother and usurper of the duchy. In a dialogue between Prospero and Ariel, Ariel reclaims his freedom, then the two speak about the siblings Sycorax and Caliban, the hideous children of a witch. **To execute an assignment given to him by Prospero, Ariel summons the help of another spirit, Milcha**. Argument between Prospero and Caliban, who, against his will, is forced to obey Prospero's orders. Prospero's two daughters Dorinda and Miranda have never seen another man other than their father, and speak about the new "creatures" that have arrived on the island because of the sinking of the ship.

Act 2

Stephano, Mustacho, and Ventoso drink, and discuss a parody of political structure. Trincalo arrives singing and in a drunken state; he returns to the issue of political structure. Caliban arrives, drinks, gets drunk, and becomes the sailors' servant. Prospero describes women to Hyppolito, who has never seen a woman before. Prospero warns Miranda and Dorinda to stay away from the area where Hyppolito is. Dorinda and Hyppolito meet for the first time.

Unlike the adaptation by Davenant and Dryden, the scene in which Alonzo, Antonio, and Gonzalo reflect upon their present fate and their past faults is placed at the end of the Act. Spirits sing and stage a representation (in which pride, fraud, theft, and murder are paraded) accusing Alonzo and Antonio for their past crimes. Ariel's song praising Ferdinand is omitted. ***It is replaced with an apparition of another singing spirit, Milcha. The dance of winds.***

Act 3

Ariel and Milcha, who are both invisible, fly and sing around Ferdinand: Ariel's song, Milcha's song. Prospero speaks about Hyppolito to Miranda, who has not yet seen him, and to Dorinda who has already met him. Dorinda wishes to see Hyppolito again, but Prospero is against this idea. Prospero speaks with Ariel, who updates him on the shipwreck survivors. **Alonzo, Antonio, and Gonzalo praise the songs they hear, sung by Ariel and Milcha, who are both invisible to them;** then some spirits bring food and

514 The plot is very similar to Davenant and Dryden's 1670 version. The scene omissions or changes have been noted in the body of the discourse in italics, while the additions have been indicated in bold type.

a prepared table magically appears. In a three-way dialogue between Trincalo, Calibano, and Sycorax, the main subject is a bottle of wine, which Ariel transforms into water; Stephano, Mustacho, and Ventoso discuss the political structure on the island with Trincalo; Trincalo marries Sycorax and presents himself as lord of the island. Ferdinand with the invisible Ariel: the echo scene, in part sung, that very much impressed Pepys. Prospero and Miranda encounter Ferdinand, who falls in love with her, but is rendered immobile by Prospero's magic. Prospero meets Hyppolito, and asks him about his encounter with Dorinda. When Hyppolito and Ferdinand meet, there is a contrast between a man of nature and a man of civilization; Hyppolito begins to believe that Prospero has thus far lied to him and deceived him.

Act 4

With Prospero's permission, Ferdinand and Miranda meet, and the courting begins. At the end of their encounter, Prospero forces Miranda to tell him what happened with Ferdinand. Hyppolito and Dorinda meet, and Prospero leaves their "love to grow in secret"; Ferdinand, however, told Hyppolito that there are more women in the world, and so Hyppolito now desires all of them. Hyppolito meets Ferdinand; they fight because Hyppolito also wishes to have the woman whom Ferdinand is courting. In a dialogue between Trincalo, Calibano and Sycorax, Stephano, Ventoso and Mustacho, the subject is still the bottle of wine, and then there are arguments about who gets to own the island. Hyppolito is defeated in a duel against Ferdinand, and believed to be dead; Prospero arrives, and summons Ariel who is ordered to call Alonzo, Gonzalo, and Antonio; in the meantime, Miranda and Dorinda also arrive. Alonzo, Gonzalo, and Antonio arrive; Alonzo and Ferdinand, father and son, are reunited. Prospero demands Ferdinand's life in exchange for Hyppolito's, and gives him one night to prepare for his death. Miranda and Dorinda fight over Ferdinand and Hyppolito. Acting as the chorus, Ariel recapitulates the facts of the story up to that moment.

Act 5

Miranda asks Prospero to show pity for Ferdinand, but he refuses. Ariel tells Prospero that Hyppolito is not dead, and that at night he sought medicine for him. The wounded Hyppolito is with Dorinda, who takes care of him; Hyppolito is reformed and gives up his polygamous ways for monogamy. When Miranda and Ferdinand arrive, all differences are worked out, and the couples are reunited. Prospero, Alonzo, Antonio, and Gonzalo make amends and prepare for the upcoming marriages. In Prospero's presence, Ariel brings sailors and monsters, and everything is resolved. *The part in which Ariel is freed, and calls her companion spirit Milcha, is omitted.* **It is replaced with great song and dance entertainment in honor of the two new couples: Neptune, Amphitrite, Oceanus, Teti, tritons, and nereids, and Aeolus too; Ariel dances and sings with other spirits, but without Milcha.**

29. *The History of Timon of Athens*

GENERAL INFORMATION
ADAPTOR'S NAME: Shadwell, Thomas
ADAPTATION TITLE: *The History of Timon of Athens The Man Hater*
SHAKESPEARE'S PLAY: *Timon of Athens*

FIRST STAGED
DATE: [January 1678][515]
PLACE: Dorset Garden
MAIN ACTORS

Men
Timon of Athens, Mr. Betterton
Alcibiades, an Athenian captain, Mr. Smith
Apemantus, a rigid philosopher, Mr. Harris
Nicias, senator of Athens, Mr. Sandford
Phæax, senator of Athens, Mr. Underhill
Ælius, senator of Athens, Mr. Leigh
Cleon, senator of Athens, Mr. Norris
Isander, senator of Athens, Mr. Percival
Isidore, senator of Athens, Mr. Gillo
Demetrius, Timon's steward, Mr. Medburne
Diphilus, servant to Timon, Mr. Bowman
Old man, old Athenian, Mr. Richards
Poet, Mr. Jevon

Women
Evandra, Mrs. Betterton
Melissa, Mrs. Shadwell
Chloe, Mrs. Gibbs
Thais, mistress to Alcibiades, Mrs. Seymor

FIRST PRINTED
DATE: 1678
PLACE: London

OTHER INFORMATION
Licensed, Feb. 18. 1677/8. Ro. L'Estrange.
LONDON, Printed by J. M. for Henry Herringman, at the Blue Anchor, in the Lower Walk of the New Exchange.

515 In *London Stage*: "The date of the premiere is not known"; the date is a hypothesis based on the play's license date, February 18, 1677–78.

29. *The History of Timon of Athens*

PLOT

Act 1

Demetrius, an honest and faithful servant to Timon, introduces his master as a rich man, but also as one who is squandering all his wealth. Demetrius and the poet discuss heroic poems. The merchant, jeweler, painter, and senator arrive: they are flattering parasites and profiteers who praise Timon for his generosity. Timon chooses to pay his debt to Lampridio to give him back his freedom, and to give a dowry to a servant who is about to be married. The philosopher Apemantus criticizes and ridicules society and Athenians, but Timon does not take his criticisms seriously. Dialogue between Timon and Nicias, the father of Melissa, Timon's bride to be. In a dialogue between Evandra and Timon, Timon says that he will marry Melissa, but Evandra, a sincere lover who has given herself to Timon, expresses her love and tries to convince Timon to not marry Melissa; feeling guilty, Timon distances himself from Evandra.

Act 2

In a dialogue between Melissa and Chloe, we learn that Melissa is a frivolous and venal woman who abandoned Alcibiades when he was robbed and stripped of all his possessions. Timon and Melissa vow their love to each other. Argument between Apemantus and the poet. Timon hosts a great banquet. Pastoral masquerade with nymphs, shepherds, Bacchus and Cupid. Evandra bids farewell to Timon. Demetrius wishes to warn his master that he is nearly bankrupt, but Timon dismisses him before he is able to say anything to him.

Act 3

Demetrius is finally able to speak to Timon about the state of his goods. Timon sends his servants to ask for loans from friends and the senate, but nobody offers to lend him anything. Apemantus criticizes the corrupt ways of Athenian society. In a dialogue between Melissa and Chloe, Melissa, who has learned of Timon's disgrace, plans to leave him; her opportunism becomes more evident when, soon after her decision to leave Timon, Alcibiades arrives disguised, revealing his identity to her, and she welcomes him with open arms. Timon discovers that nobody lent him anything; given the situation, some creditors try to obtain payment. Lampridio, who was granted bail thanks to Timon, shows disdain towards his benefactor now that he is destitute, and is ungrateful for the favor he received from him. Timon personally experiences the ingratitude of the people whom he believed to be his friends, and is emotionally very shaken up by this; he thus decides to spread the rumor that he is not, in fact, destitute, and that he will hold a great banquet. Melissa encounters Timon and refuses him, while Evandra affirms her love for him. At Timon's banquet, the host addresses those whom he believed his friends, revealing their true nature as parasites; accused of being ungrateful, they flee, frightened by Timon's behavior.

Act 4

Timon's invective against Athens. Alcibiades requests a pardon for Trasibulo, one of his soldiers. The Senate denies his request, but Alcibiades persists, with the result that the Senate becomes irritated and banishes him. In the woods and far away from civilization, Timon finds treasure while digging and sends proof of this to the city of Athens. Evandra goes to the woods in search of Timon; they meet and Evandra convinces him to stay with her. Argument between Apemantus and Timon. The musician and the poet encounter Timon in the woods, and see his treasure; Timon chases them away knowing now that they are only parasites and profiteers. Timon prepares his tomb. Melissa hears of the treasure, and goes to the woods in search of Timon; Melissa encounters Timon and Evandra; Timon, who now knows she is an egoist and opportunist, chases her away too.

Act 5

Timon prepares for his death. With the threat of Alcibiades' march on the city and Timon's discovery of treasure, ambassadors arrive from the city to offer Timon a public apology from the senate and invite him to return to the city; Timon, however, refuses. Alcibiades encounters Timon, who confirms his misanthropy. Alcibiades arrives at the doors of Athens, and the senators offer him unconditional surrender of the city so long as he does not use force. Timon dies serenely in the arms of Evandra, who, due to her sorrow, takes her life by stabbing herself. Alcibiades distances Melissa because he understands that she is a false and opportunistic woman. Alcibiades encounters Apemantus, who criticizes him harshly, but the general spares him his life. The senators, who have been imprisoned, admit their guilt, and are thus freed. Alcibiades proclaims the creation of a government of the people, and a messenger brings in news of Timon's and Evandra's death.

30. *Titus Andronicus*

GENERAL INFORMATION
ADAPTOR'S NAME: Ravenscroft, Edward
ADAPTATION TITLE: *Titus Andronicus, or The Rape of Lavinia*
SHAKESPEARE'S PLAY: *Titus Andronicus*

FIRST STAGED
DATE: [1678][516]
PLACE: Drury Lane
MAIN ACTORS: –

FIRST PRINTED
DATE: 1687
PLACE: London

OTHER INFORMATION
Licensed, Dec. 21. 1686. R. L. S.
LONDON, Printed by J. B. for J. Hindmarsh, at the Golden-B in Cornhill, over against the Royal-Exchange.

516 In *London Stage*: "The time of its first production is not known"; the play was licensed on December 21, 1686; but "If the preface is to be taken literally, the play may have appeared in the autumn of 1678."

30. *Titus Andronicus*

PLOT

Act 1

In Ancient Rome, Saturninus and Bassianus are at the Capitol both vying for the emperor's crown, which, instead, goes to Titus, a brave general who fought and defeated the Goths. Titus enters Rome triumphantly, though also in grief for the death of one of his sons; among the Goth prisoners, Queen Tamora asks for mercy for Alarbus' life, but Titus does not grant it. Funeral for Titus' son. Rome would like to name Titus as emperor, but Titus cedes the crown to Saturninus. Bassianus rapes Lavinia, the emperor's bride to be.

Act 2

In the chaos that follows, Titus murders Mutius, one of his sons, for having disobeyed him. Saturninus marries Tamora. Marcus and Lucius ask Titus to bury Mutius in the Andronicus mausoleum, and Titus grants them their wish. Tamora decides to feign friendship for Rome so that she may then get her revenge; Aaron reveals his true nature as a villain. Chiron and Demetrius, Tamora's two sons, fight over Lavinia; Aaron advises them, instead, to make amends and to rape the woman, because, since she is chaste, will never give herself to any of the competing Goths.

Act 3

Aaron buries some gold as part of a malicious plan against Bassianus, Lavinia, and the Andronici family. Tamora meets with Aaron, her lover; Bassianus and Lavinia see Tamora kiss Aaron, and this gives rise to an altercation. Chiron and Demetrius kill Bassianus; Lavinia attempts suicide, but she is impeded by Tamora's sons, who plan to rape her instead. Titus' sons Martius and Quintus are drawn to a false promise of love in the place where Bassianus' dead body was purposely left. Saturninus arrives, and, because of a false message, he accuses Martius and Quintus of Bassianus' death. Chiron and Demetrius rape Lavinia and then cut off her tongue and hands so that she is unable to reveal the names of the offenders. Marcus finds Lavinia mutilated and emotionally devastated.

Act 4

Titus pleads with the judges to revoke the sentence on his two sons, but he receives no reply. Marcus enters with the mutilated Lavinia, and Titus is profoundly saddened. Aaron enters with a false statement for Titus from the Roman senate; the statement maintains that if a member from the Andronici family cuts off a hand and sends it to the senate, the lives of Titus' sons will be spared. Lucius, Marcus, and Titus offer to sacrifice themselves but, in the end, Titus cuts off his hand. The young Juno and Lavinia enters; with an arrow in her mouth and with the help of her stumps, Lavinia writes the names of her rapists on the sand: Chiron and Demetrius; Titus vows revenge against Tamora's sons. Marcus returns to Titus with the heads of Martius and Quintus, whose execution was not stayed. Lavinia reveals that Chiron and Demetrius also committed Bassanio's murder. To save Lucius from possible retaliations, Titus decides to send him away from Rome, since the revenge that the Andronicus family will have on the Goths is about to begin.

Act 5

A nurse enters with Tamora and Aaron's son; Aaron argues with Chiron and Demetrius because they want to kill the newborn. Aaron murders the nurse. The nurse's husband finds his dead wife, and vows revenge on Aaron. Titus disseminates word of a rebellion against the emperor, and with Marcus he leads a popular revolt. Titus, who seems to have lost his senses from all the grief he has endured, vows revenge on Saturninus and Tamora. Tamora who is disguised as Revenge, speaks with Titus, and proposes that he organize a banquet. Juno scatters gold coins on the ground, and, taking advantage of their greed, lures Tamora's sons into a trap in the Andronici's garden. Lucius leads an army at the gates of Rome. Tamora's sons are captured and imprisoned in the Andronici garden, and will then be immediately murdered by Titus. The nurse's husband reveals Aaron and Tamora's secret to the Andronici family. The Andronicis, Saturninus, and Tamora are at the banquet. Following the example of Virginius, Titus kills Lavinia. Aaron is brought into the banquet hall on a torture machine, and then Chiron and Demetrius are shown decapitated; their tongue, heart, and blood were used in preparation for the banquet. The bloodbath begins: Titus strikes Tamora, Saturninus strikes and kills Titus, Lucius strikes and kills Saturninus. Aaron confesses everything he and the Goths have done. Tamora hits and kills Aaron's son. Aaron dies on the torture machine when it is put on fire. With a sad heart, Lucius, who has been named emperor of Rome, orders solemn funerals for Titus and Lavinia.

31. *Troilus and Cressida*

GENERAL INFORMATION
ADAPTOR'S NAME: Dryden, John
ADAPTATION TITLE: *Troilus and Cressida, or Truth Found Too Love*
SHAKESPEARE'S PLAY: *Troilus and Cressida*

FIRST STAGED
DATE: [April 1679][517]
PLACE: Dorset Garden
MAIN ACTORS:

Men
Hector, Mr. Smith
Troilus, Mr. Betterton
Priam, Mr. Percivall
Æneas, Mr. Joseph Williams
Pandarus, Mr. Leigh
Calchas, Mr. Percivall
Agamemnon, Mr. Gillo
Ulysses, Mr. Harris
Achilles, Mr. David Williams
Ajax, Mr. Bright
Nestor, Mr. Norris
Diomedes, Mr. Crosby
Patroclus, Mr. Boman
Menelaus, Mr. Richards
Thersites, Mr. Underhill

Women
Cressida, Mrs. Mary Lee
Andromache, Mrs. Betterton

FIRST PRINTED
DATE: 1679
PLACE: London

OTHER INFORMATION
Printed for Abel Swall at the Unicorn at the West-end of S. Pauls. and Jacob Tonson at the Judges Head in Chancery lane near Fleet Street.

517 In *London Stage*: "The date of the first performance is uncertain"; the date is a hypothesis based on the play's entry in the *Stationer's Register* dated April 14, 1679.

31. *Troilus and Cressida*

PLOT

Act 1
After nine years of siege at Troy, the Achaeans assemble: their army is fragmented in small groups of soldiers who do not obey the military hierarchy, a fact that has its roots in the bad example of Achilles. Troilus speaks with Pandarus of Cressida, the woman he loves. Pandarus speaks highly of Troilus to Cressida. Æneas, Antenor, and Hector parade in front of Pandarus and Cressida; then Paris and Helenus; and finally Troilus. During a monologue, Cressida admits that she too is in love with Troilus, but does not want anybody to know this.

Act 2
Priam, Hector, Æneas, and Troilus discuss the offer by the Achaeans, who have asked for Helen to be returned in order to put an end to the hostility. Andromache informs her husband, Hector, that their son, Astyanax, although quite young still, wishes to fight against the Achaeans. Despite pleas against his decision, Hector sends a challenge for a one-on-one duel with the champion of the Achaeans. Pandarus praises Troilus to Cressida, and then Cressida to Troilus. Ulysses plans to send Ajax to fight Troilus instead of Achilles to quash Troilus' pride. Thersites' invectives against the Achaeans, in particular, hit Ulysses, Nestor, and Ajax. Ajax strikes Thersites and stops when Achilles and Patroclus arrive. There is argument between Ajax and Achilles.

Act 3
Thersites utters invectives in the presence of Achilles and Patroclus. Achilles refuses to fight. According to Ulysses' plan, Ajax will challenge Hector. Troilus encounters Cressida, and woos her in the presence of the consenting Pandarus. In a three-way dialogue between Æneas, Diomedes, and Hector they discuss a prelude to the exchange of prisoners, Cressida for Antenor. Dialogue between Troilus and Cressida, without the presence of Pandarus. There is sung recitative. Hector goes to Pandarus' home to seek Troilus, to whom he relays the decision to execute an exchange of prisoners. Confrontation between the two men, who first argue, but then compose themselves: during their conversation they discuss issues of love, brotherhood, and friendship.

Act 4
Pandarus tells Cressida that she will be exchanged for Antenor; Cressida bids farewell to Troilus: they both vow their love and fidelity to each other. The Achaean leaders are indignant when they greet Achilles in order to quell his pride, and they succeed. Ajax fights Hector, but the duel is interrupted because of the blood ties between them. There is argument between Achilles and Hector. A banquet is held in the evening. Thersites utters invectives. Calchas orders Cressida to feign love for Diomedes; this episode takes place under the eyes of Troilus, though Calchas is not aware of this. The Trojan prince feels anger and sorrow after Pandarus tells of how Cressida was kindly welcomed in the Achaean field. Thersites makes sarcastic remarks about the

harsh argument between Diomedes and Troilus that nearly ended in bloodshed; the two postpone their argument to the following day.

Act 5

Andromache begs Hector not to go to the battlefield because of a foreboding dream she had, and she convinces him; but when Troilus arrives, he changes his mind. In the battlefield, Patroclus leads the Myrmidons, and is killed by Hector. The Trojans are at an advantage. Thersites leads Troilus to Cressida. In Calchas' tent, Diomedes and Troilus argue over Cressida, who is believed to be false and adulterous. Cressida stabs herself to death because of the false accusation. In the clash that follows, Troilus kills Diomedes, but then Achilles arrives and kills Troilus. In the final scene, the Achaeans are victorious; they have also killed Hector, but there is no glory in the victory, for, as Ajax observes, both Troy and Hector "fell by multitudes oppress't." The final moral of the tragedy is that conflict is dangerous and that all subjects must show obedience to their king.

32. *Love Betray'd*

GENERAL INFORMATION
ADAPTOR'S NAME: Burnaby, William
ADAPTATION TITLE: *Love Betray'd, or The Agreeable Disappointment*
SHAKESPEARE'S PLAY: *Twelfth Night*

FIRST STAGED
DATE: [February 1703][518]
PLACE: Lincoln's Inn Fields
MAIN ACTORS[519]

Men
Moreno, Mr. Verbrugen
Drances, Mr. Powell
Sebastian, Mr. Booth
Taquilet, Mr. Dogget
Rodoregue, Mr. Fieldhouse
Pedro, Mr. Pack

Women
Villaretta, Mrs. Bracegirdle
Cæsario, Mrs. Prince
Dromia, Mrs. Leigh
Laura, Mrs. Lawson

FIRST PRINTED
DATE: 1703
PLACE: London

OTHER INFORMATION
Printed for D. Brown at the Black-Swan without Temple-Bar, F. Coggan in the Inner-Temple-Lane, Fleet-Street, W. Davis at the Black-Bull, and G. Strahan at the Golden-Ball against the Exchange in Cornhill.

518 In *London Stage*: "Date of premiere [is] unknown."
519 In *London Stage*: "Cast [is] not listed"; the cast is determined from the 1703 edition.

32. *Love Betray'd*

PLOT

Act 1

In Venice, Villaretta speaks to Emilia about the letter of courtship that she received from Antonio, which she intends to reject; the two women also speak of love, lovers, and marriage. Duke Moreno courts Villaretta, but she too rejects him. Drances discusses marriage with Moreno, thus presenting a male perspective on the subject. Viola disguises herself as Cæsario so that she can be closer to Moreno, the man she loves. Cæsario and Laura discuss love. Except for a mole on her arm, Viola is identical to her twin brother Sebastian. Viola/Cæsario serves Moreno so that she may be close to the man he loves, but Moreno loves Villaretta, who, however, does not reciprocate his love.

Act 2

Cæsario sings a recitative for Moreno. Moreno confesses his love pains to Cæsario. Moreno sends Cæsario to Villaretta with a love letter. Cæsario goes to Villaretta, who then falls in love with Cæsario. In a three-way dialogue between Rodoregue, Sebastian, and Pedro, Sebastian says that he is in search of his sister. Villaretta passes close to them, and Pedro decides to woo her. Wanting to see him again, Villaretta sends a servant to Cæsario to give him a ring, pretending that he had forgotten it.

Act 3

Dialogue between Emilia, Dromia, and Drances; after this, Emilia and Dromia hide to spy on Drances and Taquilet, who meet and discuss love in a comical manner. In the second encounter between Cæsario and Villaretta, Villaretta intimately approaches Cæsario, who is frightened and runs off; Emilia consoles Villaretta. Drances is about to lead a duel between Taquilet and Cæsario, whom neither of the two wishes to fight. Taquilet withdraws before even fighting, and so Drances steps forward; Cæsario then withdraws, and, finally, Rodoregue, who believes him to be Sebastian, arrives and defends Cæsario. Rodoregue is arrested for betrayal. In a dialogue between Cæsario and the servant, Laura, Cæsario decides to disguise as a doctor.

Act 4

Villaretta and Emilia discuss love. Cæsario pretends to be a doctor, and goes to visit Villaretta. Sebastian and Pedro are on the Rialto Bridge when one of Villaretta's servants confuses Sebastian for Cæsario, and so invites him to his master's home. Drances and Taquilet fight against Sebastian and Pedro, because the first two believed that Sebastian was Cæsario; the fighting is interrupted when Villaretta arrives, and she invites Sebastian into her home, because she believes he is Cæsario. Pedro tries to seduce Emilia, but his advances are rejected. In a dialogue between Moreno and Cæsario, Cæsario tries to discourage Moreno from courting Villaretta, and asks for forgiveness for Rodoregue, the Duke's enemy, who was arrested earlier. Sebastian and Pedro discuss Villaretta and her wealth. Villaretta express her will to marry Sebastian.

Act 5

The Duke's guards capture Rodoregue, on the run. Cæsario asks that Rodoregue be pardoned, while Rodoregue believes that Cæsario is Sebastian. Villaretta refuses Moreno's love because she is in love with Cæsario. Moreno, thus, attempts to stab Cæsario, but then Laura reveals Cæsario's true identity. Believing that Cæsario is Sebastian, Villaretta announces that she has married him, and calls the priest to testify that she has been married. When Sebastian arrives, confusion increases when Moreno exclaims "One Face! One Voice! One Habit! And Two Persons!" Final revelations: Cæsario shows Sebastian the mole on her arm, and he recognizes her as his sister Viola. The story concludes with a double marriage: one between Sebastian and Villaretta, another between Moreno and Viola; the Duke has the last word and praises love that is faithful, genuine, and pure.

Bibliography

Primary Texts

Adams, George. *Sophocles' Tragedies, Translated from the Greek*. London, 1729.

Addison, Joseph. *Spectator,* April 14, 1711; July 1, 1712; September 10, 1714.

Animadversions on Mr. Congreve's Late Answer to Mr. Collier. London, 1698.

Anstruther, William. *Essays, Moral and Divine*. London, 1701.

Antitheatrical Tracts 1702–1704. London, 1702–1704.

Aristotle. *Poetics*. Edited by Leonardo Tarán and Dimitri Gutas. Leiden: Brill, 2012.

Baker, Richard. *Theatrum Redivivum or the Theatre Vindicated*. London, 1662.

Beaumont, Francis, and John Fletcher. *Comedies and Tragedies, Never Printed Before, and now Published by the Authours Originall Copies*. London, 1647.

Comedies and Tragedies Written by Francis Beaumont and John Fletcher Gentlemen. London, 1711.

Bedford, Arthur. *A Second Advertisement Concerning the Profaneness of the Play-House*. London, 1705.

A Serious Remonstrance in Behalf of the Christian Religion. London, 1719.

A Sermon Preached in the Parish-Council of St. Butolph's Aldgate. London, 1730.

Serious Reflections on the Scandalous Abuse and Effects of the Stage. London, 1705.

The Evil and Danger of Stage-Plays. London, 1706.

Betterton, Thomas. *King Henry IV. With the Humours of Sir John Falstaff. A Tragi-Comedy*. London, 1700.

The Sequel of Henry the Fourth: With the Homours of Sir John Falstaffe, and Justice Shallow. London, [1719?].

Burnaby, William. *Love Betray'd; or, The Agreeable Disappointment. A Comedy*. London, 1703.
Carlyle, Thomas. *On Heroes, Hero-Worship, and the Heroic in History*. London: J. M. Dent & Co., [1900?].
Cavendish, Margaret. *CCXI Sociable Letters*. London, 1664.
Cibber, Colley. *The Tragical History of King Richard III*. London, 1700.
Cicero. *Cicero*. Vol. 28. Cambridge, MA: Harvard University Press, 1968.
Chettle, Henry. *Kind-Harts Dreame*. London, 1593.
Cockeram, Henry. *The English Dictionarie: or, an Interpreter of Hard English Words*. London, 1623.
Collier, Jeremy. *A Defence of the Short View of the Immorality and Profaneness of the English Stage*. London, 1699.
A Second Defence of the Short View of the Immorality and Profaneness of the English Stage. London, 1700.
A Short View of the Immorality and Profaneness of the English Stage. London, 1698. *Collier Tracts, 1698*. London, 1698.
Collier Tracts, 1703–1708. London, 1703–1708.
Commonwealth Tracts 1625–1650. London, 1625–1650.
The Conduct of the Stage Considered. London, 1721.
Congreve, William. *Amendments of Mr. Collier's False and Imperfect Citations*. London, 1698.
Cook, John. *King Charls his Case; or, an Appeal to all Rational Men, Concerning his Tryal*. London, 1649.
Crowne, John. *Henry the Sixth, The First Part. With the Murder of Humphrey Duke of Gloucester*. London, 1681. Wing C7388.
The Misery of Civil War. A Tragedy. London, 1680. Wing C7395.
The Dancing Devils, Or, The Roaring Dragon. London, 1724.
Davenant, William. *Macbeth, a Tragedy. With All the Alterations, Amendments, Additions, and New Songs*. London, 1674. Wing S2932.
The Law Against Lovers. London, 1673.
The Tragedy of Hamlet Prince of Denmark. London, 1676. Wing S2951.
Davenant, William, and John Dryden. *The Tempest, or the Enchanted Island. A Comedy*. London, 1670. Wing S2944.
Davenant, William, John Dryden, and Thomas Shadwell. *The Tempest, or the Enchanted Island. A Comedy*. London, 1674. Wing S2945.

Defoe, Daniel. “The True-Born Englishman.” *The Works of Daniel Defoe*. New York: Thomas Y. Crowell & Company, 1904.
Dennis, John. *The Advancement and Reformation of Modern Poetry*. London, 1701.
The Comical Gallant: or the Amours of Sir John Falstaffe. A Comedy. London, 1702.
The Impartial Critick. London, 1693.
The Invader of His Country: or, The Fatal Resentment. A Tragedy. London, 1720.
The Stage Defended. London, 1726.
The Usefulness of the Stage. London, 1698.
Downes, John. *Roscius Anglicanus, Or An Historical Review of the Stage*. London, 1708.
Drake, James. *The Antient and Modern Stages Survey'd*. London, 1699.
Dryden, John. *All for Love: or, The World Well Lost. A Tragedy, As It Is Acted at the Theatre-Royal; and Written in Imitation of Shakespeare's Stile*. London, 1678. Wing D2229.
An Essay of Dramatick Poesie. London, 1668.
Examen Poeticum. London, 1693.
(tr.), *The Satyrs of Decimus Junius Juvenalis, and of Aulius Persius Flaccus*. 1693. London, [1726]
Troilus and Cressida, or, Truth Found Too Late. London, 1679. Wing D2390.
Durfey, Thomas. *The Injured Princess, or the Fatal Wager*. London, 1682.
Evelyn, John. *Memoirs and Diary*. Ed. William Bray. 2 vols. London, 1819.
The Fairy-Queen: an Opera. London, 1692.
Farquhar, George. *Works*. 2 vols. London, 1711.
Fenton, Elijah. *An Epistle to Mr. Southerne, From Kent, January 28*. London, 1711.
Field, John. *A Godly Exhortation*. London, 1583.
Filmer, Edward. *A Defence of Plays*. London, 1707.
Flecknoe, Richard. “A Short Discourse of the English Stage.” *Love's Kingdom, A Pastoral Trage-Comedy, With a Short Treatise of the English Stage*. London, 1664.
Fletcher, John. *The Faithful Shepherdess*. In *Beaumont and Fletcher*. London, 1887.

Fuller, Thomas. *The Histories of the Worthies of England*. Warwickshire, 1662.

G. I. *A Refutation of the Apology for Actors*. London, 1615.

[Gildon, Charles?]. *A Comparison Between the Two Stages*. London, 1702.

Gildon, Charles. *Measure for Measure, or Beauty the Best Advocate*. London, 1700. Wing S2936.

Miscellaneous Letters and Essays. London, 1615.

Remarks on Mr. Rowe's Tragedy of the Lady Jane Gray, and All His Other Plays. London, 1715.

Gosson, Stephen. *The Ephemerides of Philao*. London, 1579.

Playes Confuted in Five Actions. London, 1582.

The School of Abuse. London, 1579.

Gould, Robert. "The Play-House. A Satyr." *Works*. London, 1709.

Granville, George. *The Jew of Venice. A Comedy*. London, 1701.

Heidegger, John James. *Heyddeger's Letter to the Bishop of London*. London, 1724.

Heywood, Thomas. *An Apology for Actors*. London, 1612.

Hill, Aaron. *King Henry the Fifth. Or The Conquest of France By the English. A Tragedy*. London, 1723.

Johnson, Charles. *Love in a Forest. A Comedy*. London, 1723.

Johnson, Samuel. *The Works of Samuel Johnson*. 14 vols. London, 1788.

Jonson, Ben. *The New Inn*. Ed. George B. Tennant. New York: Henry Holt and Company, 1908.

The Works of Beniamin Jonson. London, 1616.

Lacy, John. *Sauny the Scott: or the Taming of the Shrew: a Comedy*. London, 1698. Wing L146.

Langbaine, Gerard. *The Lives and Characters of the English Dramatick Poets*. London, 1691.

Momus Triumphans, Or, The Plagiaries of the English Stage. London, 1688.

Law, William. *The Absolute Unlawfulness of the Stage-Entertainment Fully Demonstrated*. London, 1726.

*A Letter to My Lord******* on the Present Diversions of the Town*. London, 1725.

Levin, William. *Universal Spectator,* April 10, 1731.

Lodge, Thomas. *A Reply to Gosson's School of Abuse*. London, 1579.

Lyly, John. *Galatea; Midas*, edited by George Hunter and David Bevington. Manchester: Manchester University Press, 2000.
Mallet, David. *Of Verbal Criticism*. London, 1733.
Meres, Francis. *Palladis Tamia, Wits Treasury*. London, 1598.
Miller, James. *The Universal Passion. A Comedy*. London, 1737.
Milton, John. *L'Allegro*. Oxford: Clarendon P, 1893.
Milton's Poems. London, 1645.
Mr. William Prynn His Defence of Stage-Plays. London, 1649.
Munday, Anthony. *A Second and Third Blast of Retrait from Plaies and Theatres*. London, 1580.
Nashe, Thomas. "Lenten Stuffe," in *Works*, edited by Ronald B. McKerrow. 3 vols. Oxford: Blackwell, 1958.
Preface to *Menaphon,* by Robert Greene. London, 1589.
Northbrooke, John. *A Treatise wherein dicing, dauncing, vaine playes or enterluds with other idle pastimes &c commonly vsed on the Sabbath day, ar reproued by the authoritie of the word of God and auntient writers*. London, 1577.
Northern Nuntio. York, 8 August 1643.
Oldmixon, John. *Reflections on the Stage*. London, 1699.
O., Mrs. S. *Law Outlaw'd*. London, 1726.
Otway, Thomas. *The History and Fall of Caius Marius. A Tragedy*. London, 1680. Wing O549.
Pepys, Samuel. *Diary*. 2 vols. London, 1825.
Diary and Correspondence of Samuel Pepys, Esq., F.R.S., Deciphered from his MS by Rev. Mynors Bright. London, 1875–7.
The Diary of Samuel Pepys. Henry B. Weatley, ed. 8 vols. London: G. Bell & Sons, 1913.
Philips, Ambrose. *Humfrey Duke of Gloucester, a Tragedy*. London, 1723.
Prynne, William. *Histriomastix*. London, 1633.
The Vindication of William Prynne. London, 1649.
Rainoldes, John, William Gager, and Alberico Gentili. *Th'overthrow of Stage-Plays*. London, 1599.
Ralph, James. *The Touch-Stone*. London, 1728.
Rankins, William. *A Mirrour of Monsters*. London, 1587.
Ravenscroft, Edward. *Titus Andronicus, or the Rape of Lavinia*. London, 1687. Wing S2949.

R., C. *The Danger of Masquerades and Raree-Shows*. London, 1718.
Ridpath, George. *The Stage Condemn'd*. London, 1698.
Rowe, John. *Tragi-Comoedia*. London, 1653.
Rymer, Thomas. *A Short View of Tragedy*. London, 1693.
The Tragedies of the Last Age Consider'd and Examin'd. London, 1677.
Settle, Elkanah. *A Defence of Dramatick Poetry*. London, 1698.
A Farther Defence of Dramatick Poetry. London, 1698.
Sidney, Philip. *Sydney's Apologie for Poetrie*. Ed. Churton J. Collins. Oxford: Clarendon Press, 1955. First published 1907.
Shadwell, Thomas. *The History of Timon of Athens, the Man-Hater*. London, 1678. Wing S2846.
Shaftesbury, Earl of. *Characteristicks of Men, Manners, Opinions, Times*. London, 1714. First published 1710.
Shakespeare, William. *Shakespeare's Comedies, Histories, & Tragedies. Published according to the True Originall Copies*. London, 1623.
Shakespeare's Poems. London, 1640.
The Works of Shakespear. Alexander Pope, ed. London, 1725.
The Works of Shakespeare. Lewis Theobald, ed. London, 1733.
The Works of William Shakespeare. Nicholas Rowe, ed. London, 1709.
The Stage Acquitted. London, 1699.
Steele, Richard. *The Tatler*, September 20, 1709.
Stubbs, George. *Some Remarks on the Tragedy of Hamlet*. London, 1736.
Stubbs, Phillip. *The Anatomy of Abuses*. London, 1583.
Tate, Nahum. *The History of King Lear*. London, 1681. Wing S2918.
The Ingratitude of a Common-Wealth: Or, the Fall of Caius Martius Coriolanus. London, 1682. Wing T190.
The Loyal General. London, 1680.
Terrent, Thomas. *Jonsonus Virbius*. London, 1638.
Theobald, Lewis. *The Tragedy of King Richard II; Alter'd from Shakespear*. London, 1720.
Treatise of Daunces. London, 1581.
Vanbrugh, John. *A Short Vindication of the Relapse and the Provok'd Wife*. London, 1698.
Visits from the Shades. London, 1704.
Welsted, Leonard. *Remarks on Longinus*. London, 1712.

W., P. *A Seasonable Apology for M. H-g-r*. London, 1724.
Wright, James. *Historia Histrionica, An Historical Account of the English-Stage*. London, 1699.

Secondary Texts

Anzi, Anna. *Storia del teatro inglese dalle origini al 1660*. Turin: Einaudi, 1997.
Bakhtin, Mikhail. *The Dialogic Imagination: Four Essays*. Translated by Caryl Emerson and Michael Holquist. Austin: University of Texas Press, 1987. First published 1981. Originally published as *Voprosy literatury i estetiki* (Moscow: Khudozhestvennaia literatura, 1975).
Bate, Jonathan. *The Genius of Shakespeare*. London: Picador, 1997.
Soul of the Age: The Life, Mind and World of William Shakespeare. London: Viking, 2008.
Battisti, Susanna. *Metamorfosi del teatro*. Bari: Adriatica, 2005.
Bertinetti, Paolo. *Storia del teatro inglese dalla Restaurazione all'Ottocento*. Turin: Einaudi, 2006. First published 1997.
Bjork, Lennart A., "The 'Inconsistencies' of Dryden's Criticism of Shakespeare." *Anglia* 91 (1973): 219–40.
Bloom, Harold. *Shakespeare: The Invention of the Human*. New York: Riverhead Books, 1998.
The Western Canon. London: Harcourt Brace, 1994.
Boitani, Piero. *Il genio dei migliorare un'invenzione*. Bologna: Il Mulino, 1999.
Ri-Scritture. Bologna: Il Mulino, 1997.
Boswell, Eleonore. *The Restoration Court Stage*. Cambridge, MA: Harvard University Press, 1932.
Branam, George Curtis. *Eighteenth-Century Adaptations of Shakespearean Tragedy*. Berkeley, Los Angeles: University of California Press, 1956.
Bruster, Douglas and Robert Weimann, *Prologues to Shakespeare's Theatre: Performance and Liminality in Early Modern Drama*. London: Routledge, 2004.
Cardwell, Sarah. *Adaptation Revisited: Television and the Classic Novel*. Manchester: Manchester University Press, 2002.

Cioni, Fernando "Textual Liaisons: Rewriting and Adaptation in Christopher Hampton's *Les Liaisons Dangereuses*." The European Legacy 4, no. 4 (1999): 77–93.

Clark, Sandra, ed. *Shakespeare Made Fit*. London: Dent, 1997.

Cohn, Ruby. *Modern Shakespeare Offshoots*. Princeton, NJ: Princeton University Press, 1976.

Danchin, Pierre, ed. *Prologues and Epilogues of the Eighteenth Century: A Complete Edition*. 4 vols. Nancy: Presses Universitaires de Nancy, 1990.

ed. *The Prologues and Epilogues of the Restoration 1660–1700: A Complete Edition.* 3 vols. Nancy: Publications de l'Université de Nancy II, 1981–8.

The Prologues and Epilogues of the Restoration (1660–1700): A Tentative Check-List. Nancy: Publications de l'Université de Nancy II, 1978.

Deelman, Christian. *The Great Shakespeare Jubilee*. London: Michael Joseph, 1964.

Dobson, Michael. *The Making of the National Poet*. Oxford: Clarendon Press, 2001. First published 1992.

Douglas, Mary. *Implicit Meanings: Essays in Anthropology*. London: Routledge & Kegan Paul, 1975.

In the Active Voice. London: Routledge & Kegan Paul, 1982.

Purity and Danger: An Analysis of Concepts of Pollution and Taboo. London, New York: Routledge, 1966 [2006].

Risk and Blame: Essays in Cultural Theory. London: Routledge, 1992.

Thinking in Circles. New Haven (CT): Yale UP, 2007.

Thought Styles: Critical Essays on Good Taste. London: Sage, 1996.

Douglas, Mary and Baron Isherwood. *The World of Goods*. London: Allen Lane, 1979.

Douglas, Mary and Aaron Wildavsky. *Risk and Culture*. Berkeley: University of California Press, 1982.

Eagleton, Terry. *Literary Theory*, 2nd ed. Oxford: Blackwell, 1996.

Ehrenzweig, Anton. *The Psycho-Analysis of Artistic Vision and Hearing: An Introduction to a Theory of Unconscious Perception*. London: Routledge & Kegan Paul, 1953.

Elam, Keir, ed. *La grande festa del linguaggio. Shakespeare e la lingua inglese*. Bologna: Il Mulino, 1986.

The Semiotics of Theatre and Drama. London: Methuen, 1980.

Elam, Keir and Fernando Cioni, eds. *Una civile conversazione: lo scambio letterario e culturale anglo-italiano nel Rinascimento*. Bologna: CLUEB, 2003.

Ennis, Daniel J., and Judith B. Slagle, eds. *Prologues, Epilogues, Curtain-Raisers, and Afterpieces: The Rest of the Eighteenth-Century London Stage*. Newark: University of Delaware Press, 2007.

Fischlin, Daniel, and Mark Fortier, eds. *Adaptations of Shakespeare: A Critical Anthology of Plays from the Seventeenth Century to the Present*. London: Routledge, 2000.

Garber, Marjorie. *Shakespeare after All*. New York: Pantheon Books, 2004.

Genest, John. *Some Account of the English Stage*. 10 vols. Bath: H.E. Carrington, 1832.

Genette, Gérard. *Paratexts: Thresholds of Interpretation*. Translated by J. E. Lewin. Cambridge: Cambridge University Press, 1997. Originally published as *Seuils* (Paris: Éditions du Seuil, 1987).

Palimpsests: Literature in the Second Degree. Translated by Channa Newman and Claude Doubinsky. Lincoln: University of Nebraska Press, 1997. Originally published as *Palimpsestes. La littérature au second degré* (Paris: Éditions du Seuil, 1982).

Henke, Robert. *Pastoral Transformations: Italian Tragicomedy and Shakespeare's Late Plays*. Newark: University of Delaware Press, 1997.

Hogan, Charles Beecher. *Shakespeare in the Theatre*. 2 vols. Oxford: Clarendon P, 1952–7.

Holderness, Graham, ed. *The Shakespeare Myth*. Manchester: Manchester University Press, 1988.

Textual Shakespeare: Writing and the Word. Hatfield: University of Hertfordshire Press, 2003.

Hotson, Leslie. *The Commonwealth and Restoration Stage*. New York: Russell & Russell, 1962.

Hutcheon, Linda. *A Theory of Adaptation*. London: Routledge, 2012. First published 2006.

Innocenti, Loretta. *La scena trasformata. Adattamenti neoclassici di Shakespeare*. Pisa: Pacini, 2010. First published: Firenze: Sansoni, 1985.

Javitch, Daniel. *Poetry and Courtliness in Renaissance England*. Princeton: Princeton University Press, 1978.

Kidd, Colin. *British Identities Before Nationalism: Ethnicity and Nationhood in the Atlantic World, 1600–1800*. Cambridge: Cambridge University Press, 1999.

Kidnie, Margaret J. *Shakespeare and the Problem of Adaptation*. New York: Routledge, 2009.

Kilbourne, Frederick W. *Alterations and Adaptations of Shakespeare*. Boston: Poet Lore Company, 1906.

Krammick, Jonathan Brody. "Reading Shakespeare's Novels: Literary History and Cultural Politics in the Lennox-Johnson Debate." In *Eighteenth-century Literary History: An MLQ Reader*. Edited by Marshall Brown. Durham, NC: Duke University Press, 1999.

Lejeune, Philippe. *On Autobiography*. Translated by Katherine Leary. Minneapolis: University of Minnesota Press, 1988. Originally published as *Le pacte autobiographique* (Paris: Seuil, 1975).

Levi-Strauss, Claude. *Structural Anthropology*. Translated by Claire Jacobson and Brooke Grundfest Schoepf. New York: Basic Books, 1963. Originally published as *Anthropologie structurale* (Paris: Plon, 1958).

The London Stage, 1660–1800. 5 vols. Carbondale, Southern Illinois University Press, 1960–8.

Maguire, Nancy K. *Renaissance Tragicomedy*. New York: AMS Press, 1987.

Maley, Willy. *Salvaging Spenser: Colonialism, Culture, and Identity*. New York: St. Martin's Press, 1997.

Marder, Louis. *His Exits and His Entrances*. Philadelphia: Lippincott, 1963.

Marsden, Jean Inger. *Fatal Desire*. Ithaca: Cornell University Press, 2006.

ed. *The Appropriation of Shakespeare*. New York: Harvester Weatsheaf, 1991.

"The Re-Imagined Text." PhD diss. Harvard University, 1986.

The Re-Imagined Text. Shakespeare, Adaptation, and Eighteenth-Century Literary Theory. Lexington: University Press of Kentucky, 1995.

Massai, Sonia. *Shakespeare and the Rise of the Editor*. Cambridge: Cambridge University Press, 2007.

Mauss, Marcel. *The Gift. The Form and Reason for Exchange in Archaic Societies*. Translated by W. D. Halls. London: Routledge Classics, 2002. First published 1990. Originally published as *Essai sur le don. Forme et raison de l'échange dans les sociétés archaïques*. In l'Année Sociologique, seconde série, 1923–1924, in Sociologie et anthropologie. Paris: Les Presses universitaires de France, 1968, Quatrième edition.

Monk, Samuel Holt, "Dryden and the Beginnings of Shakespeare Criticism in the Augustan Age." In *The Persistence of Shakespeare Idolatry: Essays in Honor of Robert W. Babcock*, ed. Herbert M. Schueller, pp. 27–75. Detroit: Wayne State Press, 1964.

Mullini, Roberta, and Romana Zacchi. *Introduzione allo studio del teatro inglese*. Napoli: Liguori, 2003.

Murphy, Andrew. *Shakespeare in Print, A History and Chronology of Shakespeare Publishing*. Cambridge: Cambridge University Press, 2003.

Munro, John, ed. *The Shakespeare Allusion-Book: A Collection of Allusions to Shakespeare from 1591 to 1700*. 2 vols. London: Oxford University Press, 1932. First published 1909.

Murray, Barbara A. *Restoration Shakespeare*. Madison, NJ: Fairleigh Dickinson University Press, 2002.

Nel laboratorio di Shakespeare. Dalle fonti ai drammi. Volume 1. Il quadro teorico. Parma: Pratiche, 1988.

Nicoll, Allardyce. *A History of English Drama, 1600–1900*. 2 vols. Cambridge: Cambridge University Press, 1952–9.

A History of Restoration Drama, 1660–1700. Cambridge: Cambridge University Press, 1923.

Odell, George C. D. *Shakespeare from Betterton to Irving*. 2 vols. New York: Charles Scribner's Sons, 1920.

Orgel, Stephen. *Imagining Shakespeare*. Basingstoke: Palgrave Macmillan, 2003.

Impersonations. Cambridge: Cambridge University Press, 1996.

Pavis, Patrice. *Dictionary of the Theatre. Terms, Concepts, and Analysis*. Translated by Christine Shantz. Toronto: University of Toronto Press, 1998. Originally published as *Dictionnaire du theatre* (Paris: Editions Sociales, 1980).

Ralli, Augustus. *A History of Shakespearean Criticism*. London: Oxford University Press, 1932.

Rawson, Claude, ed. *Great Shakespeareans*. Vol 1. London: Continuum, 2010.

Rowe, Katherine A. "Dismembering and Forgetting in Titus Andronicus." *Shakespeare Quarterly* 45, no. 3 (1994): 279–303.

Saggini, Francesca. *La messinscena dell'identità. Teatro e teatralità nel romanzo inglese del Settecento*. Viterbo: Sette Città, 2003.

Sanders, Julie. *Adaptation and Appropriation*. Routledge: London, 2006.

Sawyer, Robert. *Victorian Appropriations of Shakespeare*. Madison NJ: Farleigh Dickinson University Press, 2003.

Serpieri, Alessandro. *Polifonia shakespeariana*. Rome: Bulzoni, 2002.

Sestito, Marisa. *Storia del teatro inglese. La Restaurazione e il Settecento*. Roma: Carocci, 2002.

Solomon, Diana K. *Prologues and Epilogues of Restoration Theater: Gender and Comedy, Performance and Print*. Newark: University of Delaware Press, 2013.

Spencer, Hazelton. *Shakespeare Improved*. New York: Ungar, 1963. First published 1927.

Sportelli, Annamaria. *Generi letterari. Ibridismo e contaminazione*. Roma, Bari: Laterza, 2001.

Sportelli, Annamaria and Alberto Destro, eds. *Ai confini dei generi. Casi di ibridismo letterario*. Bari: B. A. Graphis, 1999.

Summers, Montague. *The Restoration Theatre*. London: Kegan Paul, 1934.

Taylor, Gary. *Reinventing Shakespeare*. Oxford: Oxford University Press, 1989.

Turner, Victor. *The Ritual Process*. New Brunswick: Transaction, 1969 [2008].

Vickers, Brian, ed. *Shakespeare. The Critical Heritage*. 6 vols. London: Routledge & Kegan Paul, 1974.

Walsh, Jaquelyn W. *The Impact of Restoration Critical Theory on the Adaptation of Four Shakespearean Comedies*. Lewiston, Queenston, Lampeter: The Edwin Mellen Press, 2000.

Wells, S. B. "An Eighteenth Century Attribution." *Journal of English and Germanic Philology* 38 (1939): 239–46.

Wells, Stanley. *Shakespeare: For All Time*. London: Macmillan, 2002.

Werstine, Paul. "Editing after the End of Editing." *Shakespeare Studies*. 24 (1996): 47–54.

Wiley, Autrey Nell. *Rare Prologues and Epilogues, 1642–1700*. London: Allen & Unwin, 1940.

Zacchi, Romana. *La società del teatro nell'Inghilterra della restaurazione*. Bologna: CLUEB, 1984.